THE FATHERS
OF THE CHURCH

A NEW TRANSLATION

VOLUME 34

THE FATHERS OF THE CHURCH

A NEW TRANSLATION

EDITORIAL BOARD

ROY JOSEPH DEFERRARI
The Catholic University of America
Editorial Director

RUDOLPH ARBESMANN, O.S.A.
Fordham University

STEPHAN KUTTNER
The Catholic University of America

MARTIN R. P. McGUIRE
The Catholic University of America

WILFRID PARSONS, S.J.
The Catholic University of America

BERNARD M. PEEBLES
The Catholic University of America

ROBERT P. RUSSELL, O.S.A.
Villanova University

ANSELM STRITTMATTER, O.S.B.
St. Anselm's Priory

JAMES EDWARD TOBIN
Queens College

ST. LEO THE GREAT

LETTERS

Translated by
BROTHER EDMUND HUNT, C.S.C.

New York
FATHERS OF THE CHURCH, INC.
1957

NIHIL OBSTAT:

JOHN A. GOODWINE
Censor Librorum

IMPRIMATUR:

✠ FRANCIS CARDINAL SPELLMAN
Archbishop of New York

November 13, 1956

Copyright 1957 by
FATHERS OF THE CHURCH, INC.
475 Fifth Avenue, New York 17, N. Y.
All rights reserved

First Paperback Reprint 2004
ISBN 0-8132-1403-3 (pbk)
ISBN-13: 978-0-8132-1403-0 (pbk)

INTRODUCTION

POPE ST. LEO THE GREAT was probably Tuscan in origin, but he spoke of himself as a Roman. He was one of the archdeacons of the diocese of Rome under Pope Sixtus III (432-440), possibly earlier. He was chosen Bishop of Rome while on an embassy in Gaul, trying to reconcile two factious generals of the Western emperor. He got back to Rome within forty days and was consecrated on September 29, 440. His rule lasted until late in 461—a period of great trials for the Church, barbarian invasions, social upheavals and religious heresies, all of which served as a background to accentuate the nobility and forcefulness of the Pope.

Leo was the single great light of the period. Several great bishops, like Cyril of Alexandria, had just died. In the East, Theodosius II was easily duped and a principal backer of the farcical Robber Council of Ephesus; Pulcheria with her husband, Marcian, and Emperor Leo were Catholics, but not capable of resisting barbarians or of lifting their vision beyond Eastern problems. In the West, Valentinian III was a perfect model of an imperfect ruler; Ricimer (with his puppet Emperors Avitus and Majorian) took from Rome what little the barbarian pillagers had left. These were the civil authorities with whom Leo the Great had to contend.[1]

Leo held a meeting of Italian bishops each year on the anniversary of his consecration. While Milan, Ravenna, and Aquileia also held meetings, it seems that other metropolitans in Italy did not; they met with the Vicar of Rome each September. It is said, too, that Leo consecrated 185 bishops during his reign as Pope. The number is not impossible since the ten provinces had over 200 sees, but the procedure of local elections with consecrations in Rome was not the usual one. Leo is also said to have repaired St. Peter's and St. Paul's and to have built a church in honor of St. Clement, to have instituted some sort of honor guard of clerics for the tombs of the Apostles, and to have made some changes in liturgy.

At his death he was buried—the first non-martyr Pope—within old St. Peter's. In 688, Pope Sergius I moved the body into a chapel, together with bodies of the three succeeding Leos. In 1607, the body was discovered and moved into the new St. Peter's, and a second transfer was made in 1763. In 1754, Benedict XIV had declared Leo the Great to be a Doctor of the Church. His feast in the Western world is observed on April 11.

Leo the Great is the first Pope whose letters and sermons have been preserved in a fairly complete collection. He kept copies of his letters in papal archives, and some cities preserved copies sent to them. Even so, quite a number of letters must

---

[1] An old life of Leo the Great is given by L. Duchesne, *Liber Pontificum* (Paris 1886) I 238-239; *PL* 54.50-60. Cf., also, Vacant-Mangenet, *DTC* (Paris 1926) IX 218-301; Smith-Wace, *Dictionary of Christian Biography* (London 1882) III 652-672; Pauly-Wissowa-Kroll, *Real-Encyclopädie* (Stuttgart 1925) XII 1962-1973).

have perished.² The style of the letters is periodic, a bit wordy and repetitive. Leo was not ashamed to repeat passages in order to be sure of informing those who were still ignorant.³ Rarely is there any attempt at flowery or epigrammatic expression, though it is obvious that Leo was well trained in rhetoric. He was far more interested in what he said than in clever ways to say it. He did not know Greek.⁴ The letters are practical in content, not speculative; they abound in well-expressed expositions of Catholic doctrine that are easily passed over as unoriginal and not profound. We use the same expositions today.

The letters fall into categories: the doctrinal ones, chiefly concerned with the Incarnation in opposition to the Eutychians;⁵ the rescript type, answers given to inquiries about ecclesiastical custom;⁶ letters of correction against abuses he was informed of;⁷ executive letters of acknowledgment, encouragement, arrangement.⁸ About 140 of the letters are considered genuine. There is some possibility that Leo kept Prosper of Aquitaine in Rome as a secretary, but, if style is evidence, it is more likely that Leo did most of the composition himself.

Some initial observations are in order here. The letters are not sent to Spanish bishops; they are informed by their

---

2 There is a discussion of the letters probably lost in *PL* 54.1217-1233.
3 Cf. Leo the Great, *Sermo* 25.1 (*PL* 54.208).
4 Cf. Letters 113 and 130. On Leo's style cf., also, W. J. Halliwell, *The Style of St. Leo the Great* (Washington 1939); Silva-Tarouca, *Textus et Documenta* (series theol.), (Rome 1934) 15 xxiii-xxxii.
5 Chiefly, Letters 28 and 165; parts of Letters 35, 44, 59, 102, 119, 124, 139, etc.
6 Such as Letters 6, 66, 108, 119, 159, 166, and 167.
7 Most of the Letters up to 19, and 42, 104, 105, 106, 109, 149, and 150.
8 For example, Letters 22, 40, 41, 42, 50, 51, 52, 72, 93, 127, 129, 140, and most of those written to the emperors.

brothers in Gaul.⁹ Most of the letters to Western bishops are to correct some departure from apostolic custom or canon law, while the majority of letters deal with heresies in the Eastern world. There is a surprising lack of historical information in letters written in the midst of catastrophic social upheavals. Leo does not mention his role in turning back Attila and the Huns in 452 nor his meeting with Genseric the Vandal in 455. The various sackings of Rome, deaths or changes of Western rulers all go unannounced. Finally, he at times refrains from putting touchy ecclesiastical problems in writing; he sends an envoy to impart his instructions orally.¹⁰

It is possible to summarize a few points about Leo's attitude and principles. He is determined to adhere to tradition in doctrine and practice; this generally means adhering to the canons of Nicaea.¹¹ Yet he occasionally hedges on the grounds of expediency, mercy or the preservation of harmony.¹² At times it is not clear just what canon he is insisting on, or else he uses a somewhat corrupted version of a given canon.¹³ But, unquestionably, such terms as 'the canons of the Fathers, apostolic and evangelical regulations' are the most repeated ones in the letters. He wants no innovation in teaching or in ecclesiastical procedure. Secondly, he insists on the primacy of the Roman See and the universal responsibility of the Bishop of Rome.¹⁴ The metropolitans and vicars must have their rights, but when there is an appeal or when a problem cannot be settled locally, the whole matter must

---
9 Cf. Letter 102.
10 For example, Letters 67 (end), 80 n. 8, and 85.
11 Cf. Letters 106, 114, and 119 n. 11.
12 Cf. Letters, 10, 16, 19, 104, 117, 119, 131, and 138.
13 Cf. Letter 4 n. 10, Letter 16 n. 28, and Letter 44 n. 8.
14 Cf. Letters 8, 9, 10, 14, 33, 75, 86, 95, 104, 119, 120, 124, and 156.

be referred to Rome.¹⁵ A council may not publish its canons before they are approved of by the Bishop of Rome.¹⁶

Leo the Great was fearless in attacking abuses in the Church, but he was surprisingly tolerant of civil rulers. When they summoned councils or made demands, he always tried to comply, even against his better judgment.¹⁷ He spoke of their priestly, as well as royal, power; he used all the flattering terminology characteristic of the age.¹⁸ He often spoke to them as on his side, attacking an innovator or heretic.¹⁹ Yet he could not have been unaware at times of their complicity, court intrigues, and errors, particularly in the case of Theodosius II and his wife. The most interesting letters in this category are those to Pulcheria, sister of Theodosius II and wife of the Emperor Marcian; she was his staunchest ally in the East in defense of Catholic doctrine.

Leo's relations with bishops can best be studied in the letters to Flavian and Anatolius of Constantinople, to his friend Julian of Cos, and in Letter 10, in which he restricted St. Hilary of Arles. In general, it can be said that he was intrepid and rigidly conservative, yet the letters abound in instances of concession and merciful pardon. Leo wished to show justice to all bishops, justice tempered with mercy. He did not often write to priests; those called presbyters were mostly abbots.

In his youth Leo the Great spent much time combating Pelagians, Manichaeans, and Nestorians; his chief struggles

---

15 As in Letters 5, 6, 12, 14, 23, 44, and 85.
16 Cf. Letters 93, 95 n. 4, 100, and 116.
17 Cf. Letters 37, 44, 89, 90, 94, 162, and 164.
18 As in the opening paragraphs of letters to rulers; cf., also, Letters 149 and 162.
19 Cf. Letters 44, 50 n. 3, and 104.

as Pope were against Eutyches and his followers. They caused him to define the Incarnation with a precision not attained by anyone before him. The chief doctrinal letters are the major and minor *Tomes* (Letters 28 and 165). At one time or another most of the bishops, at his request, signed Letter 28 as the official teaching of the Church.[20] At times, Leo had to protest that Eastern heretics made erroneous Greek versions of the letter.[21] Both *Tomes* are important documents, and their subsequent history has been a glorious one.[22] There has been considerable discussion of Leo's sources. His explanations are not novel or speculative; there are no definitions of nature, person, substance, and consubstantiality. He does not teach a new doctrine, but only what he has learned from the Fathers. It is true he does considerable reasoning of his own, but this is based on the Scriptures or on the Apostolic or Nicene Creeds. The result is not new; he even made a collection of excerpts from the Fathers to prove it.[23] However, aside from two major borrowings and passages repeated from his sermons, the explanations in the *Tomes* are original in the sense that they were not copied verbally from previous writers.[24] There are, of course, doctrinal passages in other letters.

The letters sent to correct abuses do not cover too wide a field:[25] ordinations and consecrations must be held only on Sundays (with ministers and recipients both fasting); baptism is ordinarily to be administered only on Easter or Pentecost;

---

20 Cf. Letters 67, 68, 80 n. 3, 97, 99, 100, and 102.
21 For example, Letters 124, 130, 131, and 152.
22 Cf. Silva-Tarouca, *op. cit.* 9 VI-XII; C. Hefele, *Histoire des Conciles* (Paris 1908) II 567-580.
23 Translated below, after Letter 165.
24 Cf. Silva-Taruca, *op. cit.* 9 XII-XV and, below, Letter 28 n. 1.
25 Cf. above, note 7.

there is no license to take interest on loans, to move from one diocese to another, to consecrate outside one's jurisdiction; bishops must be chosen by the people and clergy of a city from among the deacons or priests; provincial councils are to meet twice a year; there are numerous reminders of regulations on marriage for the clergy, on observing Easter on the same day throughout the world. He attacks other individual abuses, and in some instances he sends along a bishop or priest to see that his instructions are carried out.[26]

This edition of Leo the Great gives a translation of the principal letters. Where available, the text of Silva-Tarouca (given in various numbers of the Gregorian Studies) was used. Schwartz's text in Acta Conciliorum Oecumenicorum was used for Letters 21, 49, 156; the CSEL text for Letters 169-173; and the *Patrologia Latina* for the others.[27] The numbering of the letters as in Migne has been retained in order to achieve uniformity. Where available, the texts of Silva-Tarouca and Schwartz are cited in the notes, but only the first cited is used for the translation. Both Silva-Tarouca and Schwartz were primarily interested in letters dealing with heresy and with the councils; hence, they did not edit the early letters and others dealing with discipline or answering inquiries from Western bishops.

26 Cf. Letters 12, 16, and 19.
27 Introductions in Silva-Tarouca, *op. cit.*, and in Sister M. Magdeleine Mueller, *The Vocabulary of Pope St. Leo the Great* (Washington 1943), give charts of the numbering of letters in different texts.

SELECT BIBLIOGRAPHY

Texts:

Sancti Leonis Magni Opera Omnia, ed. Ballerini, *PL* 54 (Paris 1881).
Epistolae Imperatorum Pontificum, ed. O. Guenther, CSEL (Vienna 1895).
Acta Conciliorum Oecumenicorum I-IV, ed Schwartz (Berlin 1927-1932).
S. Leonis Magni Epistulae (Textus et Documenta [Gregorian University], series theologica, fasc. 9, 15, 20, 23, ed. C. Silva-Tarouca (Rome 1932-1935).

Other Sourcees:

L. Duchesne, *Liber Pontificum* I (Paris 1886).
C. Feltoe, *The Letters and Sermons of Leo the Great* (NPWF XII, ser. 2, New York 1895).
R. Galli, 'S. Leone Magno e i suoi scritti,' *Didaskaleion* 3 (1930) 51-235.
C. Gore, *Leo the Great* (New York 1932).
C. J. Hefele, *Histoire des Conciles* I-II (Paris 1907-1908).
T. Jalland, *The Life and Times of St. Leo the Great* (New York 1941).
W. Kissling, *Das Verhaltiniss zwishen Sacerdotium und Imperium nach den Anschauungen der Päpste von Leo d. G. bis Gelasius I* (Paderborn 1921).
J. Mansi, *Sacrorum Conciliorum Nova et Antiquissima Collectio* I-VI (Florence 1759-1761).
T. Sickel, *Liber Diurnus Romanorum Pontificum* (Vienna 1889).
C. Silva-Tarouca, *Nuovi Studi sulle antiche lettere dei Papi* (Rome 1932).
Sister M. Magdaleine Mueller, *The Vocabulary of Pope St. Leo the Great* (Washington 1943).
Sister M. Bridget O'Brien, *Titles of Address in Christian Latin Epistolography to 543 A. D.* (Washington 1930).
C. H. Turner, *Ecclesiae Occidentalis Monumenta Iuris Antiquissima I* (Oxford 1899).

CONTENTS

Letter   *Page*

1	To the Bishop of Aquileia [Januarius?]	19
4	To the bishops presiding in Campania, Piceno, Etruria, and all provinces	23
6	To Anastasius, Bishop of Thessalonica	27
9	To Dioscorus, Bishop of Alexandria	33
10	To the bishops in the province of Vienne	37
12	To the bishops in the sees of Caesarea Mauritania	48
14	To the Bishop Anastasius	58
16	To the bishops in Sicily	68
19	To Dorus, Bishop of Beneventum	77
20	To Eutyches, abbot at Constantinople	81
21	Eutyches to Pope Leo	82
23	To Flavian, Bishop of Constantinople	87
24	To Emperor Theodosius II	89
28	To Bishop Flavian	92
29	To Emperor Theodosius	106
33	To the bishops assembled at Ephesus	108
35	To Julian, Bishop of Cos	111
37	To Emperor Theodosius	116

Letter		Page
38	To Bishop Flavian	118
40	To the bishops in the province of Arles	120
42	To Ravennius, Bishop of Arles	121
44	To Emperor Theodosius	122
49	To Bishop Flavian	128
50	To the church at Constantinople	129
60	To Pulcheria, sister of Theodosius II	132
66	To the bishops presiding in Gaul	134
67	To Bishop Ravennius	136
69	To Emperor Theodosius	137
75	To Faustus and Martin, priests and abbots at Constantinople	142
79	To Pulcheria	144
80	To Anatolius, Bishop of Constantinople	147
81	To Bishop Julian	151
83	To Emperor Marcian	153
85	To Bishop Anatolius	156
88	To Paschasinus, papal legate	159
89	To Emperor Marcian	162
93	To the Synod of Nicaea	165
95	To Pulcheria	168
102	To the bishops presiding in Gaul	172
104	To Emperor Marcian	177
106	To Bishop Anatolius	182
107	To Bishop Julian	189
108	To Theodore, Bishop of Forum Julii	190
109	To Bishop Julian	194
117	To the same	199
119	To Maximus, Bishop of Antioch	203

Letter		Page
126	To Emperor Marcian	210
127	To Bishop Julian	211
129	To Proterius, Bishop of Alexandria	214
130	To Emperor Marcian	218
131	To Bishop Julian	220
136	To Emperor Marcian	223
138	To the bishops presiding in Gaul and Spain	226
139	To Juvenal, Bishop of Jerusalem	227
143	To Bishop Anatolius	232
144	To Bishop Julian	232
145	To Emperor Leo I	234
149-150	To Bishops Basil, Juvenal, Euxitheus, Peter, and Luke	236
152	To Bishop Julian	239
153	To Aetius, priest	240
156	To Emperor Leo	242
159	To Nicetas, Bishop of Aquileia	249
162	To Emperor Leo	252
164	To the same	257
165	To the same [*The Tome*]	262
	[Testimonia]	275
167	To Rusticus, Bishop of Narbonne	289
169	To Emperor Leo	297
173	To the bishops in Egypt	300

ST. LEO THE GREAT

LETTERS

Translated by
BROTHER EDMUND HUNT, C.S.C., Ph.D.
St. Edward's University
Austin, Texas

1. *[To the Bishop of Aquileia, 442 (?).]*

WE HAVE RECEIVED a report (it is appended to this letter) from our holy brother and fellow bishop Septimus.[1] From it we have learned that in your province certain priests, deacons, and clerics of different ranks, previously involved in the Pelagian (or Coelestian) heresy, have been admitted into Catholic society without having been required to make any condemnation of their particular error. While the shepherds set to watch were sound asleep, wolves clothed in the skins of sheep, but still retaining their bestial instincts, invaded the Lord's sheepfold.[2] These men have presumed to do what is not permitted even to the guiltless on the authority of the canons and our decrees: that is, they have abandoned the churches in which they received the clerical state or into which they were taken back, thus spreading their instability from place to place, bent always on wandering about and not remaining fixed on the foundation set by the Apostles. For men who have not been tested by any examination or bound by any previous judgment as to what they profess are especially effective in gaining this result: they enter quite a number of homes, under cover of belonging to the Church, and corrupt the hearts of many who are unaware of their false name. They could not do this, of course, if the heads of the churches

---

1 Septimus, Bishop of Altino, wrote to the Pope to complain of two faults in the whole province of Aquileia, or at least in his own section. Leo's reply is here directed to the Metropolitan of Aquileia. His name is not known, but in Letter 18 Leo addresses a Januarius, Bishop of Aquileia—quite likely the same man. Letter 2 in Migne is the Pope's reply to Septimus himself, with much the same content as in Letter 1.
2 Cf. Matt. 7.15.

had exercised the necessary precaution in taking back such men and if they had not allowed any of them to wander from place to place.

Hence, in order that this rash conduct may not be attempted in future and lest a pestilence introduced by certain men's carelessness tend to the destrucion of many souls, we charge your Fraternity's zeal with the following task. With our command as authorization for it, call a meeting of all the clerics in your province (whether priests or deacons or clerics of every rank) who, after associating with Pelagians (or Coelestians), were taken back into Catholic communion, imprudently, without first having been forced to condemn their error. In that way, at any rate, they may be compelled to genuine amendment after their hypocrisy is in some measure laid bare. This can be of profit to them and cannot harm others. In their frank professions let them condemn the authors of this arrogant heresy and let them repudiate whatever the universal Church has disapproved of in their teaching. And embracing all those synodal decrees which the authority of the Apostolic See has ratified for the stamping out of this heresy, let them announce in complete and frank statements, signed by their own hands, that they also completely agree with those decrees. Let nothing obscure be found in their language, nothing ambiguous. For we know that they are clever in this way: they think that none of their views is in jeopardy when they have kept distinct from the main body of the heresy some particular point of teaching that should be condemned.

And while they put on an act of disapproving and of giving up all their definitions in order to facilitate their entering by stealth, they use every art of trickery to maintain this exception (unless they are caught) : they hold that the grace of God is given only according to the merits of the recipients. But, of course, if it is not a free gift, it is not grace at all, but, rather, a reward and a merited compensation. As the Apostle says: 'For by grace you have been saved through faith; and that not by yourselves, but it is a gift of God; not as the outcome of works, lest anyone may boast. For his workmanship we are, created in Christ Jesus in good works, which God has made ready beforehand that we may walk in them.'[3] Hence, every bestowal of good works is of God's preparing, for no one is justified by his own excellence before he is by grace, which is the principle of justice for everyone, as well as the source of his good works and the starting point of his merits. But those heretics say that grace comes as a result of our natural efforts. In that way it would appear that [man's nature][4] was not afflicted by any wound of original sin, since it possesses excellence through its own efforts before receiving grace. And what Truth says would thus be false: 'For the Son of Man came to seek and to save what was lost.'[5]

Consequently, your Charity must be careful and must with great diligence prevent such men from reviving scandals that have already been eliminated. You must see to it that no sprout of this same evil may rise anew in your province from a teaching already cut down. Not only would it grow where it has its roots, but it would infect even future generations in the holy Church with poison from its mouth. Let those who wish to appear reformed purge themselves of all suspicion and, by obeying us, prove themselves to be on our side. If any of those clerics or laymen refuses to comply

---
3 Eph. 2.8-10.
4 If the text is otherwise correct, some feminine noun is needed.
5 Luke 19.10.

with our salutary orders, let him be expelled from the society of the Church, lest, having destroyed his own soul, he plot against the salvation of others.

There is, too, that provision of ecclesiastical discipline by which the holy Fathers in the past and we also have frequently decreed that no one in the priesthood or in the diaconate or in the next lower clerical order is at liberty to transfer from church to church.[6] We admonish you to renew the original force of this regulation, so that everyone may persevere in the place where he was ordained, not drawn away by ambition, not seduced by greed, not corrupted by the influence of men. If anyone, seeking what is his own and not the things of Jesus Christ,[7] thus neglects to return to his people and his church, consider him as removed from his privileged office and from the bond of communion. Now, your Charity may be sure that we are going to be more distressed if (we do not think this will happen) what we decide for the safeguarding of the canons and the integrity of the faith is neglected, for no one is to be blamed more for the faults of the lower orders than sluggish and negligent superiors, who often nourish a great plague while delaying to administer a rather harsh medicine.

[2. Leo I to Septimus, Bishop of Altino.]

---

6 The canons constantly prohibit priests (and also bishops) moving from one diocese to another under pain of excommunication if the party fails to return. Cf. apost. canons 13-14; Nicaea, c. 15-16; Arles, c. 2, 21; Carthage IV, c. 27 (Mansi, I 31; II 471, 473, 681, 682; III 953). Cf., below, Letter 14, at note 11.

7 A common paraphrase of St. Leo's; cf. Phil. 2.21.

LETTERS 23

[*3. Paschasinus, Bishop of Lilybaeum, to Leo I, concerning the date of Easter for the year 444. (The Pope, in turn, consults him on the date for 455; cf. Letters 88, 133, 134, 138.)*]

4. Leo, Bishop of the city of Rome, to all bishops presiding in Campania, Piceno, Etruria, and all provinces, greetings in the Lord (October 10, 443).

Just as the well-being of the churches causes us gratification, so we are deeply saddened whenever we learn of any liberties taken with, or acts committed against, canon law and ecclesiastical discipline. We cannot excuse ourself to Him who wished us to be on the watch[1] if we do not repress such practices with the vigilance we should. We cannot excuse ourself if we permit the unsullied body of the Church (which we are bound to keep clean of all spot) to be defiled by contact with those who pursue evil ends. For the very union of the members gets unharmonious elements in it through carelessness.[2]

Here and there men are admitted to sacred Orders without being supported by any excellence of birth or character; slaves who were quite unable to gain freedom from their masters are elevated to the high rank of the priesthood, as if the lowly character of the slave were the one to receive this honor; and it is believed that a slave who has not yet

---
1 Cf. Ezech. 3.17
2 Migne pointlessly changes the manuscript reading *dissimulationem* to *dissimilationem*.

been able to prove himself to his master can be approved of by God. In this matter, of course, the guilt is twofold: the sacred ministry is contaminated by taking in such partners of low rank, and the rights of slave owners are infringed on in so far as their possessions are taken from them illegally. Therefore, dearest brothers, we want all the bishops of your province to avoid such men; and not only them, but others, also, who, because they are serfs[3] or for some other reason, are not free—unless, by chance, the masters who claim some power over them are willing or ask for it. He who is enrolled in God's army must not be bound to others,[4] lest any obligatory ties call him away from the Lord's camp, where his name is inscribed.

Now, once any individual's nobility of birth and character has been agreed on, what sort of man should be associated with the ministry of the holy altar? We have learned this from Apostle's instruction, from divine precept,[5] and from canon law,[6] which a great many of our brothers, we find, have departed from and completely disregarded. For it is well known that men who married widows have been admitted to the priesthood. Certain others, also, men several times married, given over to all sorts of licentious living, were here and there allowed sacred Orders, even having all the paths of access smoothed before them. This is contrary to the words of the blessed Apostle in which he cries out to

---

3 *originali conditioni*: in feudalism, the serf was bound to the land by birth; the more common terms are *originarius* and *colonaria conditio*. This impediment to the priesthood is listed in addition to slavery. For slavery, cf. apost. canon 81 (Mansi, I 46).
4 Cf. 2 Tim. 2.3,4.
5 Cf. below, notes 7-8.
6 Cf. apost. canons 16-17; Carthage IV, c. 69 (Mansi, I 31; III 956); Pope Siricius, *Ad Himerium* 8,11 (Mansi, III 659). Leo repeats this injunction in Letters 6, 10, 12, 14.

such men, saying, 'A man of one wife';[7] and contrary to that precept of the Old Law, where the warning statement is made: 'A priest is not to marry a widow or a rejected wife, but a virgin.'[8] Through the authority of the Apostolic See, then, we demand that such men as have been admitted be removed from ecclesiastical offices and from title to the priesthood. They cannot claim that for which they were not eligible because of the impediment which blocked them. We particularly claim for ourself the responsibility of this investigation so that, if some faults have, perhaps, been committed in these matters, they may be corrected and not be allowed to happen again, and no claim of ignorance may arise as an excuse—although no priest has ever been allowed to claim ignorance of what has been set forth in canon law. And so, we are sending this letter to your provinces through Innocent, Legitimus, and Segetius, our brothers and fellow bishops, so that the evil sprouts that are known to have come up may be plucked out, roots and all, and no weeds may spoil the Lord's harvest.[9] For, if the things which customarily kill the budding crop are quite carefully cut out, what is left uncontaminated will thus yield a bountiful harvest.

And this matter, also, in our opinion, ought not to be passed over. Certain people, ensnared by greed for base gain, are letting out money at interest and seeking to grow rich from the returns. We grieve that this occurs not only among those holding office among the clergy but also among the laity who wish to go by the name of Christians.[10] We order

---
7 1 Tim. 3.2; cf. Titus 1.6.
8 Cf. Lev. 21.14; Ezech. 44.22.
9 Cf. Matt. 13.29,30.
10 The canons usually mention only clerics: Nicaea, c. 17; Arles, c. 12; Neo-Caesarea, c. 5; Carthage IV, c. 67 (Mansi, II 472, 585, 682; III 956). But in 362 the Council of Eliberrae (Elne), c. 20 (Mansi, II 9) excommunicated laymen who did not stop taking interest when reprimanded.

that those convicted of this be severely punished, so as to remove every occasion of sin.

We also thought that some pre-warning should be given about the following point: Just as no cleric may try to let out money at interest in his own name, he may likewise not do so in another's name. It is improper to make gains for another at the expense of sinning oneself. The only interest we should look to and work for is that what we bestow here out of mercy we may be able to recover from that Lord whose return will be many times multiplied and will abide forever.

Consequently, we denounce this with warning: If any of our brothers tries to contravene these decrees and dares to do what is here forbidden, let him realize that he will be removed from office and that a man who has been unwilling to be one with us in discipline is not going to be a sharer in our society. Lest, perhaps, it be thought that we have omitted something, we order that your Charities must observe all the decretals decided on so that, if anyone acts against those regulations, he will know that subsequent pardon is denied him. These include those promulgated concerning the ranks of the clergy and the regulations in the canons by Innocent of blessed memory[11] as well as by all our deceased predecessors.

Issued on the tenth of October in the consulship of the most illustrious Maximus (second time) and Paterius.

---

11 Pope Innocent I (401-417) was preceded by Siricius (384-399) and Anastasius (399-401); he was followed by Zozimus (417-418), Boniface I (418-422), Celestine (422-432), Sixtus III (432-440), and Leo I (440-461).

[5 (Silva-Tarouca, 23, XXIV). Leo I to the bishops of Illyricum (January 12, 444), placing them under Anastasius, Bishop of Thessalonica; insisting on the hierarchy of provincial bishops under metropolitans, metropolitans under the vicar, Anastasius; the type of marriage permitted to priests; serious disputes must be referred to Rome.]

6 (Silva-Tarouca 23, XXIII). *Bishop Leo, to his dearly beloved brother, Bishop Anastasius (January 12, 444).*

Love of our associated colleagues causes us to read over the letters of all bishops with real pleasure of mind, for, through a spiritual gift from God we embrace, as if present, those with whom we share ideas by exchanging letters. But there appears to be a more important motive for us in these letters through which we are informed of the status of the churches and are thus, by considering the nature of our office, forced to vigilance in the exercise of our responsibility. That is, being put in a watchtower, as the Lord willed, we may give our assent to matters that proceed as we wish and, by applying a restraining remedy, correct whatever we see going amiss because of any unlawful encroachment. We hope that abundant harvest will be returned to us from having sown the seed, so long as we do not permit the growth of elements harmful to the Lord's harvest which have begun to sprout.

Consequently, now that we have learned from our son, Nicholas the priest, of your Charity's request that we also grant you the authority over Illyricum in our place for the preservation of discipline, such as was granted to your predecessors, we give consent. And we urge you by our admonition to allow no carelessness, no negligence, to occur in the governing of the churches situated throughout Illyricum, which we are entrusting to your Charity in our stead, following the example of Siricius of blessed memory.[1] He made this concession for the first time according to a fixed plan to Anysius of holy memory, who preceded your immediate predecessor[2] and who at that time merited well of the Apostolic See and was praised for his subsequent actions. This was to enable him to assist the churches situated in that area, which he wanted kept under discipline. Noble examples must be zealously followed so that in every way we may show ourselves like those whose privileges we wish to enjoy. We want you to be an imitator of your predecessor and his predecessor (the latter is known to have exercised and deserved this privilege in like manner) in order that we may rejoice over the progress of the churches which we assign to you in our stead. Just as an assigned task brings glory to one who acts properly and performs skillfully what is in harmony with priestly authority, so also it is considered a source of trouble

---

1 Cf. Letter 4 n. 10; also, Silva-Tarouca, 23 II (Damasus to Acholius), III (Siricius to Anysius), IV (Innocent to Anysius), V (Innocent to Rufus), VI (Boniface to the Thessalonican bishops) : all of which speak of the Bishop of Thessalonica's powers as a vicar. Innocent, writing to Rufus (*ibid.* 23 V, pp. 21-22), fixes the names of the provinces in the jurisdiction and praises Rufus' predecessors, Acholius and Anysius. A possible explanation of why Pope Leo speaks of Anysius as the first, ignoring Acholius, may lie in the words 'according to a fixed plan'—Pope Damasus' arrangement with Acholius may have been personal or temporary.

2 That is, Rufus, who succeeded Anysius in 412. Boniface I praised him highly (Silva-Tarouca, 23 VI-X, pp. 23-36). At Rufus' death, sometime in 435, Anastasius became vicar (*ibid.* 23 XI-XIV, pp. 36-43) under Pope Sixtus III. Having served five years under that Pope, he now (in 444) asks for vicar powers from Leo I. He must not have exercised these powers for the previous four years.

to one who does not use the power entrusted to him with the moderation he should.

Consequently, dearest brother, vigilantly hold the helm entrusted to you and cast the eyes of your mind over all that you see put in your charge, adhering to what will redound to your reward and resisting whatever strives to upset the discipline of the canons. The ordinances of the divine Law must be respected and canon law must be particularly observed. Throughout the provinces committed to you let only those be consecrated bishops of the Lord who have in their favor meritorious lives and the approval of the clerical order. Do not grant any license to personal favor, to canvassing for votes, to votes that are bought. Let those who are to be consecrated be examined with great care and imbued with ecclesiastical discipline over a long period of their life. Even so, let them be consecrated only if they are in harmony with all that has been preserved from the Fathers and if they have met the requirements set forth for such men (as we read) by the blessed Apostle Paul; that is, a bishop is to have but one wife; and she a virgin when he married her, as the authority of the divine Law warns.[3] We want this observed so carefully as to remove occasion for all excuses. Otherwise, someone who took a wife before he received Christ's grace and then at her death married another after being baptized may believe it is possible for him to become a bishop.[4] That first wife cannot be denied, nor can the first

---

[3] Cf. Letter 4 nn. 7-8.
[4] That is, *ad sacerdotium*. While the prohibition was also applied to deacons and priests, the context of this letter indicates 'bishops.' Occasionally, *sacerdos* has an overtone including priests, but Leo I uses it almost always for 'bishop' (more than the handbooks indicate). When he means priests without bishops (as in Letter 19) he uses *presbyter*. *Episcopus* is not very common; *consecrare* and *ordinare* are interchangeable.

marriage be left out of the count; and he is the father of those children born of the first wife before his baptism as well as of those whom he is known to have had by the second wife after his baptism. [For, just as only]⁵ sins and acts that are recognized as unlawful are blotted out by the waters of baptism, so also what is allowed or licit by the ordinance of the Law is not blotted out.

No one is to be consecrated bishop in those churches without consulting you. In that way there will be mature judgment in the selections, so long as there is fear of your Charity's scrutiny. But, if anyone of the metropolitan bishops is consecrated without your knowledge, contrary to our order, let him realize that he has no sure status with us, and those who presume in this matter are going to render an account to us for their unlawful procedure. Just as that authority of having the right to consecrate in their own province is given to individual metropolitans, so also we want those metropolitans to be consecrated by you, though only after mature and well-considered judgment. Although it is proper that all those who are consecrated bishops be approved of and pleasing to God, we desire even superior excellence in those who we know are going to be in charge of fellow bishops under their jurisdiction. We forewarn your Charity to act with great concern and caution in this matter so as to prove that you observe what was written by the Apostle: 'Do not lay hands hastily upon anyone.'⁶

When any brother is summoned to a council, let him hasten and not refuse to be present at the holy meeting, where he knows that plans should especially be presented that can

---

5 Bracketed additions in this letter are suggestions by Silva-Tarouca for gaps in the text.
6 1 Tim. 5.22.

affect ecclesiastical discipline. All faults will be better avoided if more frequent association takes place among the Lord's bishops. Intimate association is a most potent means to reform as well as to charity. If any problems arise, they can with the Lord's direction be settled there, so that no dissension may remain, but charity only among the brothers may bind them together. But, if some major problem arises which cannot be settled there under your Fraternity's direction, consult us by sending your report. Thus, with the enlightenment of the Lord (through whose mercy we admit we are what we are), we can send back an answer which He himself has inspired in us. In that way, through our inquiry, we may justify our claim to decide [cases] in line with long established tradition and reverence due to the Apostolic See. We want you to exercise authority in our stead, but we reserve to ourself those problems that cannot be decided locally or whenever someone sends an appeal to us.

See to it, then, that this information reaches all the brothers, so that in the observance of these orders of ours no one may hereafter find an opportunity to excuse himself through ignorance. We are also sending our letter to the metropolitans themselves in the individual provinces in order to warn them.[7] This is to let them know that apostolic decisions must be complied with, and that they obey us when they begin to obey your Fraternity as our representative according to our written directives. We have, in fact, found out (and we could not pass this over in silence) that certain of our brothers do consecrate only on Sundays but limit this to bishops, whereas in various places they confer the dignity of the priestly order on priests and deacons (in whose case a like [time] for ordi-

---

7 Cf. Letter 5.

nation ought [to be observed]) on any day at all. It is a reprehensible and illegal practice perpetrated in opposition to the canons and traditions received from the Fathers.[8] For that custom handed down to us must be observed in all details with regard to all the sacred Orders. In that way, for long periods of time, he who is to be ordained priest or deacon may advance through all the ranks of the clerical order and may learn over a long period of time what he himself is later going to teach.

Issued on the twelfth of January in the consulship of Theodosius (eighteenth time) and Albinus.

[7. Leo I, to the bishops of Italy, January 30, 444, asking for vigilance against new outbreaks of Manichaeanism, seen even in Rome.]

[8. The decree of the Western Emperor Valentinian III (and Theodosius II), June 19, 445, against Manichaeanism.]

---

8 As stated in T. Sickel, *Liber Diurnus Romanorum Pontificum* (Vienna 1889), p. 6, lines 16-19 (for priests and deacons). Cf., below, Letters 9, at note 4; 10, at note 20. There appears to be no canon prior to Leo I with this insistence on Sunday.

9. Bishop Leo, to Dioscorus, Bishop of Alexandria, greetings (June 21, 445).

How great a feeling of the Lord's charity we bestow on your Charity you can confirm from the fact that we desire to get you more firmly established at the beginning, even though we have had evidence that the benefits of spiritual grace assist you. For we want nothing to seem lacking to your charity to make it perfect. Hence, paternal and fraternal correspondence should be most pleasing to your Holiness and should be accepted by you in the same spirit with which it comes from us, as you know.[1] It is fitting that we should think and act as one so that, as we read, one heart also and one soul may be revealed in us.[2] For, since the most blessed Apostle Peter received the apostolic primacy from the Lord and the Roman Church continues the traditions he established, it is wrong to believe that his holy disciple Mark, who first ruled the Church at Alexandria,[3] formulated decrees with other provisions than those handed down to him. For the single spirit of the disciple and the master was unquestionably from the same source of grace, nor could the one consecrated hand down something different from what he received from his consecrator. Hence, we cannot have it that, while admitting our membership in one body and

---

1 Four years later this bishop engineered the Robber Council of Ephesus (cf. Letters 28 and 44). When Emperor Marcian and the Council of Chalcedon finally excommunicated Eutyches and Dioscorus, the latter was expelled from the see of Alexandria in 451. Cf. Smith-Wace, *Dictionary of Christian Biography* I 854-861.
2 Cf. Acts 4.32.
3 As related by Eusebius, *Hist. Eccl.* 2.16 and 24. Dioscorus would be to Leo I as St. Mark was to St. Peter.

faith, we are at variance in other matters, with some practices seemingly from the master, different ones from the disciple.

Hence we want you also to retain that which we know has been preserved by our Fathers with assiduous care. For instance, the priesthood and diaconate ought not to be conferred on all days at random. Let the ceremonies begin after the Sabbath day, late in that night as it begins to dawn towards the first day of the week.[4] Then let the ministers, fasting, perform the sacred imposition of hands on those to be ordained, also fasting. It will remain part of the same rite if it is celebrated on Sunday morning itself, so long as the Saturday's fast is continued. That [Sunday] period is not separated from the beginnings of the preceding night, which is undoubtedly connected with the day of Resurrection, as is stated also in the Lord's Passover.[5] Aside from the authority of custom, which we know comes from apostolic teaching, even sacred Scripture makes clear that, when the Apostles were sending Paul and Barnabas to preach the Gospel to the Gentiles, as ordered by the Holy Spirit, fasting and praying they laid hands on them.[6] From this we are to understand how devotedly the ministers and recipients should exercise caution that the mystery of so important a blessing may not appear to be administered negligently. Therefore your action will be dutiful and praiseworthy and in line with apostolic institutions if you likewise hold to this observance for the ordaining

---

4 Cf. Letter 6 n. 8.
5 Cf. Matt. 26.20.
6 Cf. Acts 13.3. The Pope means that Paul and Barnabas were thus made priests or bishops, and on a Sunday. There is certainly no basis for the Sunday, and it is possible that the story in Acts may refer simply to a special blessing for a new mission, not a conferring of orders.

of priests⁷ in the churches over which the Lord wished you to preside. That is, those to be ordained are never to receive the blessing except on the day of the Lord's Resurrection, to which the evening of the Sabbath is added as a beginning, as is well known. It is a day which has been hallowed by such great mysteries in the divine plan of events that whatever of major importance the Lord decided on was carried out on this honored day. On this day the world had its origin. On this day, through Christ's Resurrection, death came to an end and life had its beginning. On this day the Apostles received from the Lord the trumpet of the Gospel to be preached to all nations and also received the sacrament of regeneration to be carried to the entire world.⁸ On this day, as blessed John the Evangelist testifies, the Apostles being assembled in one place and the doors being shut, when the Lord entered into their midst, He said: 'Receive the Holy Spirit; whose sins you shall forgive, they are forgiven them; and whose sins you shall retain, they are retained.'⁹ Finally, on this day came the Holy Spirit promised by the Lord to the Apostles.¹⁰ Thus we know through some divine plan the custom was introduced and became traditional whereby the rites for the laying of hands on priests are to be celebrated on that day on which all the gifts of grace were conferred.

Now, in order that all our practices may be in harmony, we want this observance kept, also: Whenever any more solemn festival indicates a larger concourse of people and such crowds

---

7 As indicated in the first paragraph, *sacerdos* in this letter refers to 'deacons and priests'; but the rule of Sunday consecrations refers also to 'bishops'; cf. Letter 6 n. 4, and Letter 10.
8 There is no basis in Matt. 28.16-17 or Mark 16.14-16 for putting this meeting on a Sunday.
9 John 20.23: 'when it was late that same day' would be Easter; hence, Sunday.
10 That is, Pentecost, fifty days after Easter and on Sunday; cf. Acts 2.1.

of the faithful come together that a basilica cannot hold all of them at once, the offering of the sacrifice should unquestionably be repeated. Otherwise, with only those who came first admitted to this sacrifice, the others who came later may seem rejected. Yet it is quite in keeping with devotion and reason to have a later repetition of the sacrifice as often as a new group of people is present to fill the basilica being used. On the contrary, if the custom of having but one Mass is kept and only those who came early in the day can offer the sacrifice, then, of necessity, some part of the people will be deprived of their religious devotion. Zealously, therefore, and affectionately we admonish your Charity also to be solicitously careful about what has become a part of our customs, in the pattern of traditions received from the Fathers, so that in all matters of belief and practice we may be in harmony. That is why we are giving this letter for delivery to your Fraternity to our son, Possidonius the priest, who is making the trip back to you. He has frequently been present at our convocations and consecrations. And because he has been sent so often,[11] he knows what of apostolic authority we hold to in all matters.

Issued on the twenty-first of June.

---

11 Possidonius may have brought the letter from Cyril of Alexandria (*PL* 53.602), but once or twice is hardly 'so often.' Either some letters to Leo from Alexandria are lost or 'to us' is not editorial but means 'to the Popes.' Possidonius had brought letters to Pope Celestine.

10. Leo, Bishop of Rome, to our dearly beloved brothers, all the bishops presiding in the province of Vienne (c. July 1, 445).

Our Lord Jesus Christ, Saviour of the human race, desired to have the observance of divine religion shine out through God's grace unto all nations and races. He established it in such a way that truth, previously contained only in proclamations of the Law and the Prophets, might proceed from the Apostles' trumpet for the salvation of all, as it is written: 'Their sound has gone forth unto all the earth: and their words unto the ends of the world.'[1] Now, the Lord desired that the dispensing of this gift should be shared as a task by all the Apostles, but in such a way that He put the principal charge on the most blessed Peter, the highest of all the Apostles. He wanted His gifts to flow into the entire body from Peter himself, as it were from the head. Thus, a man who had dared to separate himself from the solidity of Peter would realize that he no longer shared in the divine mystery. The Lord wanted Peter, taken into a companionship of inseparable unity, to be named from what he really was [the rock], saying: 'Thou art Peter and upon this rock I will build my church';[2] so that the building of the eternal temple, by a marvelous gift of God's grace, might stand on the solidity of Peter. Christ strengthened His Church with this solidity so that the rashness of men might not attack it and the gates of hell might not prevail against it.[3] But the man who attempts to infringe on its power by furthering his own

---
1 Ps. 18.5.
2 Matt. 16.18. For the etymology of 'Peter' see Letter 28 n. 40.
3 Cf. Matt. 16.18.

desires and not following practices received from antiquity is trying, with absolutely blasphemous presumption, to destroy this most sacred solidity of that rock, established with God as the builder, as we mentioned. For he believes that he is subject to no law, that he is not restrained by any regulations that the Lord ordained. Being intent on novel assumption of power, he departs from what you and we are accustomed to; he presumes to do what is illegal and neglects traditions that he ought to have maintained.

But with God's inspiration, as we believe, and retaining toward you the grace of our charity, which, as you recall, the Apostolic See has ever shown to your Holinesses, we are striving to correct these abuses with more mature deliberation. We are striving to set your churches in order while sharing the labor with you, not starting something new but renewing the old, so that we may continue in those customary practices given us by our Fathers and may be pleasing to our God by doing a good work in removing the stumbling blocks of disorder. Your Fraternities should, of course, realize with us that the Apostolic See (out of reverence for it) has countless times been reported to in consultation by bishops even in your province. And through the appeal of various cases to it, decisions already made have been either rescinded or confirmed, as dictated by long-standing custom. As a result, with 'unity of spirit in the bond of peace'[4] being preserved, with letters being sent and received, what was done in a holy manner has been conducive to abiding charity. For our solicitude, which seeks not its own interests but those of Christ,[5] does not detract from the dignity given by God to the churches and the bishops of the churches. This was the pro-

---
4 Eph. 4.3.
5 Cf. Phil. 2.21.

cedure always well observed and profitably maintained by our predecessors. But Hilary[6] has departed from it, aiming to disturb the status of the churches and harmony among the bishops by his novel usurpations of power. He seeks to subject you to his authority while not allowing himself to be under the jurisdiction of the blessed Apostle Peter. He claims for himself the right to consecrate in all the churches of Gaul and takes as his own the dignity which belongs to the metropolitan bishops. He even lessens the reverence due to the most blessed Peter himself by his quite arrogant statements. And although the power to bind and loose was given to

---

6 Bishop of Arles in France (429-449) and on the calendar of saints. The city claimed to be the first see of France. About 417 a Bishop Patroclus seized the bishopric, with the favor of the Western Emperor; and Pope Zosimus made him vicar over his own province of Vienne as well as of Narbonne I and II. Boniface I at once began to interfere with this unworthy vicar and officially rescinded such a privilege. At the death of his prince protector, Patroclus was assassinated (426). In spite of Boniface's revocation, Arles always claimed some sort of primacy in Gaul. The views of the next bishop, Honoratus, are not known, but Hilary thereafter began to act as a vicar. His mistakes seem to have been due to haste and Gallicanism; in other matters he was on the side of the canons and rigid discipline, against intrigues and worldliness. When accused, Hilary went to Rome in winter and on foot. He spoke his mind to the assembly of Roman bishops, then departed. The obvious Gallicanism and frankness displeased the Roman court, and in the two issues discussed Hilary seems to have been wrong or hasty. Leo restricted him to the see of Arles and made Vienne temporarily the metropolitan city (Cf. Mansi, VI 431; and Leo's letter in *MGH,* Epist. III. 15, p. 91). The Western Emperor, Valentinian III, also backed up the order (his rescript is among Leo's letters in Migne (*PL* 54.636). It must be said that Hilary obeyed at once. Numerous appeals were made to the Pope to restore Hilary to favor, but to no avail. It is another case of two saints being at odds. At Hilary's death in 449 he was succeeded by a priest of his, Ravennius (cf. Letters 40 and 41), whom Leo I and Pope Hilary used as a kind of intermediary between the Holy See and the Gallic bishops, and who received back some of the sees of the province from the Bishop of Vienne.

Peter before the others,[7] still, in an even more special way, the pasturing of the sheep was entrusted to him.[8] Anyone who thinks that the primacy should be denied to Peter cannot in any way lessen the Apostle's dignity; inflated with the wind of his own pride, he buries himself in hell.

The written record of events, then, shows what has been done here in the case of Bishop Celidonius[9] and also what Hilary said, even while this same bishop mentioned was present and listening to him. After Hilary had nothing reasonable which he could answer at the council of holy bishops, the 'secrets of his heart'[10] switched over to such utterances as no layman could express and no priest listen to. I admit, brothers, that we were grieved and we tried to use our patience as a remedy to cure this pride of his mind. We did not want to aggravate those wounds which he continued to inflict on his soul by his insolent retorts. We sought to mollify him, whom we had taken to ourselves as a brother, rather than irritate him with our remarks, although he on his side got more entangled in his own answers. We acquitted Bishop Celidonius because, through the clear answers of witnesses, given even in his presence, he proved that he was unjustly deprived of his bishopric. In fact, Hilary, who was present with us, had nothing he could say in contradiction of this. His settlement of the case was brought forward and read. The opinion given was that Celidonius, as a man who

---

7 Cf. Matt. 16.18. The real issue was Gallicanism, against the primacy of the Roman bishop. Hilary presided over many Gallic councils and usually acted in consort with some other bishops.
8 Cf. John 21.15ff.
9 Bishop of Besançon, evidently not guilty of the marriage charge on which the Gallic council (Mansi, VI 461-462) deposed him. But the second accusation is equally important: Hilary had no right to decide in the first place; he was not a vicar and not metropolitan over Besançon.
10 1 Cor. 14.25.

had married a widow, could not retain his bishopric; the decision, therefore, was rescinded. Actually, adhering to the provisions of the law, we were quite anxious to have this regulation observed, not only for bishops but also for clerics of lower ranks. That is, those may not join the holy army[11] who have so married or who, contrary to apostolic discipline, are shown to have married more than once.[12] On the contrary, we have decreed that those who cannot find an excuse for their action must not be admitted or, if they have already been accepted, they are to be removed. So also, when men have been falsely accused of this, we must, after holding an inquiry, acquit them and not allow them to lose their office. In fact, the decision made against Celidonius would have been retained had the truth of the charges been proved. Our fellow bishop, Celidonius, therefore, has been restored to his church and to that dignity which he should not have lost, as is proved by the record of events and the pronouncement we made after holding a trial.

After this business was thus finished, the next complaint to come up was that of our brother and fellow bishop Projectus.[13] He sent us a letter, such as to cause sorrow and tears, about the consecration of a bishop in his place. A letter was also sent by his subjects, one which was backed up by many individual signatures. It was filled with most bitter complaints against Hilary: their Bishop Projectus had not been permitted to be sick, his bishopric had been transferred to another without his knowledge, and Hilary, the invader, had brought in a successor to a man still alive, as if filling an unoccupied see. We should like to know what your Fraternities' opinions

---

11 Cf. 1 Tim. 1.18.
12 Cf. Letter 4 nn. 6-8.
13 Probably Bishop of Narbonne; here Hilary seems to have been really hasty.

are about this. Yet, there should be no doubt in our mind as to what you think, for you see that a brother, stretched out on his bed, is not so much distressed by his infirmity of body as he is tortured by grief of another sort. What hope of life is left him when he is beset with despair over his bishopric while another is substituted in his place? Just how gentle of heart Hilary is becomes obvious from the fact that he considered his brother's tardiness in dying as an impediment to his presumptious plans.[14] As much as he could, Hilary extinguished the light for Projectus and took away his life, since he added this affliction to prevent his return to health: he put another bishop in his place. Let us suppose that death comes to a brother, which is customary in our short-lived human status, what is Hilary seeking in another's province? Why does he usurp a right which none of his predecessors before Patroclus possessed? For the concession which was apparently granted to Patroclus by the Apostolic See for a time was afterwards by better judgment canceled.[15] The wishes of the congregation and the testimony of the populace should certainly be waited for; the opinions of the nobles and the choice of the clerics should be asked for—these are the procedures ordinarily observed in the consecrating of bishops by those who know the decrees of the Fathers.[16] That

---

14 Several of Leo's remarks are extremely bitter (see points indicated as notes 22-24).
15 Cf. above, note 6.
16 Bishops were not placed, as is the case today. The Bishop of Rome was the Pope, but picked from deacons or priests in Rome. Leo's list of the people who select the new bishop is not always the same, but in general it is the people of the diocese (plebeians, nobles, and clergy) with the approval of the metropolitan; the metropolitan is chosen with the approval of the bishops of the province (and the vicar, if there is one). See the wording in paragraph six; in Letters 14 and 40; and also the wording of previous canons and papal letters (Mansi, III 32, 466, 953).

would be to preserve in every way the requirement made by apostolic authority which demands that a bishop who is to be in charge of a church must be supported not only by the testimony of his congregation but by a good reputation among outsiders as well,[17] and that no opportunity for such a scandal be left, when he who is going to be the teacher of peace is himself consecrated in peace and in harmony pleasing to God, through the common efforts of all.

But, as we have learned, he, not being expected, came to the people unawares, and departed without warning, making many trips with great speed, rushing through distant provinces in such a hurry that he seems to have aimed at a reputation for giddy speed rather than for the moderation of a bishop. For this is the way it is worded in the letter sent to us by the citizens: 'He left before we knew he had come.' This is not to return but to flee, not to dispense the salutary effects of pastoral care but to attack as a robber and a thief, as the Lord says: 'He who enters not by the door into the sheepfold, but climbs up another way, is a thief and a robber.'[18] Hilary, then, was not so much bent on consecrating a bishop as on killing him who was ill and on deceiving, by an illegal consecration, the man whom he set up as a substitute. But, having taken counsel of all our brothers, we have decided what we believe will please you, as God is our judge: we have ordered that he who was wrongfully consecrated must be removed and that Bishop Projectus is to remain in his bishopric. We have decided that if any of our brothers dies in any province at all, the one who by agreement is the metropolitan of that province shall claim for himself the right to consecrate the successor. The two problems have been

---
17 Cf. 1 Tim. 3.7.
18 John 10.1.

settled, as we see; it appears, however, that in them many acts have been committed against ecclesiastical order, acts which ought yet to be visited with the censure of a just judgment. But we can no longer delay here, since we are called to other matters which need to be discussed quite carefully with your Holinesses.

As we have learned, a group of soldiers follows Bishop Hilary through the provinces and assists him, relying on the assurance of this armed guard, in the turbulent invasion of the churches that have lost their own bishops. The men to be consecrated are hauled before this tribunal, men unknown to those localities over which they are to preside. Now, just as a well-known and tested man is sought for when there is peace, so when an unknown man is brought in, he must be imposed on the people by force. I beg and entreat you and call upon you with prayers to God, brothers, to prevent such happenings and to remove all cause for dissension from your provinces. We have surely justified ourself before God in that we have entreated you not to allow this to happen again. Those who are to become bishops are to be selected in the midst of peace and quiet. The approval of the clergy, the testimony of those of noble rank, and the agreement of the common people should be had. He who is to be in charge of all should be chosen by all. As we have already said above, individual metropolitans, acting in concert with those other bishops who have been in office the longest, should insist on consecrating in their own provinces, according to their right —now restored to them by us. Let no one dare to claim a right which belongs to another. Let each one be content with his own limitations and boundaries, and let him realize that he cannot transfer to another a privilege owed to him.[19] But

---

19 Cf. Antioch, c. 23 (Mansi, II 1318).

if someone, disregarding apostolic orders and putting stock rather in personal favor, wishes to resign from his office with the idea that he can transfer his privilege to another, it is not the one resigning but the one ranking above the other bishops of the province in seniority who is to claim for himself the power of consecrating. Let the consecration take place on the proper day, not just at any time. And when a bishop has not been consecrated on the Sabbath night which precedes the dawn of the first day of the week, or on the Lord's day itself, let him realize that his status is insecure. For our predecessors judged that only the day of the Lord's Resurrection was worthy of this honor; that is, those selected are to be made bishops particularly on this day.[20]

Let individual provinces be content with their own councils, and let Hilary no longer dare to summon synodal meetings and disrupt the decisions of the Lord's bishops by his interference. Let him know that he has been expelled not only from other people's jurisdiction but also from power over the province of Vienne, which he illegally assumed. It is indeed fitting, brothers, that the ancient regulations be restored. For he who claimed the right to consecrate in a province not his own has also at the present time proved himself to be such that, although he frequently sought a sentence of condemnation by his rash and insolent words, he is by our order to retain the bishopric merely in his own diocese. This is granted out of the fatherly concern of the Apostolic See. He is, then, not to be present at any consecration; he is not to consecrate.[21] Realizing what he deserved when he was being questioned about the matter, he was of the opinion that he should with-

---

20 See Letter 6 n. 8.
21 The ordinary punishment for bishops exceeding their jurisdiction; cf. below, Letter 12 n. 14.

draw by a disgraceful flight, as one not sharing in the bishops' society, of which he did not deserve to be a member.[22] God, in our opinion, brought this about, leading him to our court when we did not expect it and inducing him to withdraw stealthily, while the inquiry was being held, to prevent his sharing in our society.

No Christian should be lightly excommunicated, nor should this be done at the whim of an angry bishop. It is a penalty which a thoughtful judge should inflict unwillingly and, as it were, with sorrow, and in order to punish a serious offense. Now, we have discovered that some have been cut off from the grace of membership in the Church for purely trivial acts and statements; and the soul which Christ shed His blood to save, being wounded by the inflicting of so severe a penalty, unarmed, as it were, and stripped of all defense, has been subjected to the attacks of the Devil so as to be easily overcome. Naturally, if at times a case arises in which, because of the nature of the crime, someone receives excommunication as a just penalty, then only the one involved in the crime must be punished; no one should share in a penalty unless his complicity in the deed is proved. But would it be anything unusual for a man who customarily rejoices over the condemnation of clerics to show himself of like sentiments against laymen?[23]

Our intention appears to be far different, since we desire to maintain a settled state in all the churches and harmony among the bishops. Therefore, urging you to unity in the

---

22 Hardly his motive for leaving; cf. above, note 14.
23 It is not clear what this paragraph on excommunicating laymen has to do with Hilary. The last sentence is another bitter comment and seems almost like a marginal interpolation.

bond of charity, we entreat and, with proper dispositions, warn you to preserve, in the cause of peace and dignity among you, the decisions which we have made through the inspiration of God and the most blessed Apostle Peter, now that all the cases have been investigated and discussed. We know for certain that such decisions as we have made are of profit not so much to our honor as to yours. We have not reserved to ourself consecrations in your provinces—a false claim which Hilary, as is his custom, can perhaps make in order to mislead your Holinesses' minds.[24] But in our solicitude we justify your right in order that no innovation may be allowed in the future and no further opportunity may exist for the usurper to infringe on your privileges. If the diligence of the Apostolic See is maintained among you undiminished and if, through a watch over priestly discipline, we do not permit any loss to your honor (from unlawful usurpations) of what belongs to it, we admit that this can only redound to our credit also. And since respect must always be paid to seniority, we desire that our brother and fellow bishop, the worthy Bishop Leontius,[25] be honored with the following dignity, if this pleases you. Your Holinesses ought not to convoke a council in another province without his consent; and all of you should honor him as his age and merit demand, though the metropolitans are to retain their honored position of privilege. It is but just and seems to cause no injury to any of our brothers if those who rank first because of their years in the priesthood have deference paid to them, as their age merits, by the other bishops in their own provinces. May God keep you safe, dearest brothers.

---

24 Cf. above, note 14.
25 Not otherwise known.

[*11*. The Constitution of Valentinian III, the Western Emperor at Ravenna, sent to the patrician Aetius to execute; it supports Pope Leo's decision against Hilary of Arles and specifically forbids the bishops of Gaul to act against the Bishop of Rome.]

12. Leo, Bishop of Rome, to all the bishops presiding in the sees of Caesarea Mauritania, greetings in the Lord (August 10, 446).[1]

Since we learned from rather frequent statements of visitors to us that certain irregularities in the consecration of bishops have arisen among you, the dictates of fatherly care demanded that, because of the solicitude which through God's ordaining we dispense for the universal Church, we strive to find out the reliability of the reports. We delegated our brother and fellow bishop Potentius,[2] who was setting out from Rome, to represent us in this concern of ours. According to the letter which we sent you through him, he was to inquire about the bishops whose selection was said to be at fault, to find out what truth there was in the report and he was to give a faithful account of all this to us. This same bishop has now fully explained the entire situation to us and by his frank

---
1 The year 446 is not certain. There is an alternate version of this letter in Migne; it varies only slightly, but breaks off in paragraph nine with the word 'leniency.' In the version above, paragraphs eight and eleven are similar, and most of the final chapters seem 'tacked on.' Perhaps there were two original letters. However, there seems no reason to suspect Leo's authorship.
2 Not otherwise known.

report has shown what bishops and what sort of bishops rule over certain of Christ's people in parts of the province of Caesarea. Therefore, we could not help expressing also in this present letter to your Charities the sorrow of our heart, for we are anxious in our heart over dangers to the Lord's flocks. We are astonished that the presumption of intriguers or the rioting of the populace had so much weight with you in a time of disorder that unworthy persons and those far from deserving the episcopal dignity were given the chief pastorate and rule over the Church. This is not to deliberate for the interests of the people but to harm them; this is not to furnish discipline but to increase dissension. The welfare of the subjects lies in the integrity of their rulers; and where obedience is unimpaired, there the character of the doctrine is sound. But when ruling power is established by civil strife or acquired by campaigning, even though there is no scandal of conduct and action, its very origin sets a pernicious precedent. And it is difficult to bring to a good conclusion affairs that began with a false start.

But if wise and prudent care must be exerted so that nothing may be amiss or out of order in the Lord's house in any of the Church's ranks, with how much greater effort must mistakes be avoided in choosing him who is set up over all ranks? The welfare and order of the Lord's entire family will falter if what is required of the body is not likewise found in the head. In that passage where the blessed Apostle Paul, inspired by the Spirit of God, gave instruction to all Christ's bishops in the person of Timothy, the statement is also made for each of us: 'Do not lay hands hastily upon anyone, and do not be a partner in other men's sins.'[3] What does 'lay hands hastily' mean except to give the episcopal honor to the untried, to

---
[3] 1 Tim. 5.22.

those who have not reached the age of maturity,[4] before the time of examination, before their obedience has been tried, before they have experienced discipline? And what is to 'be a partner in other men's sins' except for the one consecrating to become like the non-deserving person whom he consecrates? Just as he reaps for himself the fruit of a good work who uses right reason in choosing a bishop, so he inflicts serious loss on himself who receives among his colleagues an unworthy person. Consequently, whatever is contained in general regulations must not be passed over in any individual's case. Nor is that dignity to be considered legitimate which has been bestowed contrary to the precepts of divine Law.

The Apostle says, among his other requirements for choosing a bishop, that a man should be consecrated who, by common knowledge, was or is the husband of but one wife.[5] And that precept has been considered so sacred that the condition was thought binding even on the wife of the bishop-elect; otherwise, while possibly marrying a man without a previous wife, she herself might have been married to a previous husband. Who, then, would dare tolerate anything done to injure so great a sacrament when regulations concerning this great and venerated mystery were not lacking even in the divine Law? In them it is clearly set down that a priest is to marry only a virgin, and that she who is to become a priest's wife is not to have been married to another man.[6] Even in those times the spiritual marriage of Christ and the Church was prefigured in priests, so that 'because a husband is head of the wife,'[7] the bride of the Word might learn to

---
4 The age usually set for deacons was twenty-five; for priests it was thirty (when Christ began His active life); cf. Neo-Caesarea, c. 11; Carthage III, c. 4 (Mansi, II 546, 541).
5 Cf. Letter 4 n. 7.
6 Cf. Letter 4 n. 8.
7 Eph. 5.23; cf. 1 Cor. 11.3.

know no other husband than Christ, who rightly chooses her alone, loves her alone, and marries no other but her. If, therefore, even in the Old Testament this stipulation for the marriages of priests is observed, how much more should we, existing under the grace of the Gospel, obey the apostolic precepts? That is, a man may be found to have a good character or may be adorned with holy works to any degree, but he is still not to rise to the rank of the diaconate or to the priestly dignity or to the height of the bishopric if it is certain that he has married more than once or that his wife was previously married.

Now, where the Apostle warns, saying: 'And let them first be tried, and if found without reproach, let them be allowed to serve,'[8] what else do we think this must mean than that we should consider in these promotions not only the sanctity of the marriages but also the merit of works performed, lest the pastoral office be entrusted to men recently baptized or to those recently converted from the affairs of the world?[9] For consideration must be given to advancements in rank throughout all the grades of the Christian army as to whether the more important ones can be entrusted to any given person. When the blessed Fathers in their venerable regulations spoke of the selection of bishops, they rightly thought those same men suited for the sacred offices who, having advanced through the individual grades of office over a long period, had given plausible proof of themselves, so that in all men the correctness of their acts might bear witness to their lives. If it is improper to attain the dignities of the world without

---
8 1 Tim. 3.10.
9 The emphasis is on 'going through the lower orders,' but there were many notable exceptions in which qualified converts or even laymen were ordained in a short time. Cf. apost. canon 79; Nicaea, c. 2; Sardica, c. 13; Laodicaea, c. 3 (Mansi, I 46; II 578, 678; III 27). Cf. Pope Zosimus, *Ad Hesychium* 1-3 (Mansi, IV 347-348).

the support of time, without the merit of labor, and if office-seeking that is not supported by evidences of uprightness is commonly frowned on, then how careful and how wise a dispensing must be made of divine offices and heavenly dignities? Otherwise, apostolic and canonical decrees may somehow be violated, and the rule of the Lord's Church may be entrusted to men who, being ignorant of lawful institutions and devoid of all humility, desire to have leadership starting at the top and not to make progress from the bottom. Yet, it is quite unjust and absurd to have the uninstructed preferred to the instructors, the new to the old, the unpractised to the experienced. Now, in a great house, as the Apostle explains, it is necessary to have different sorts of vessels, some of gold and some of silver; but others also of wood and of clay.[10] The purpose of these, however, varies with the quality of the material; the precious ones and the cheap ones are not put to the same use. Everything will be out of order if the clay ones are preferred to the gold, and the wooden ones to the silver. But, just as the nature of men who as yet are not outstanding for excellence is figuratively like that of the wooden and clay vessels, so in the silver and gold ones we have unquestionably a representation of those who have deserved to be tried gold and unalloyed silver, having been purified by the fire of long instruction and the furnace of long labor. If reward is not given to these for their devoted service, then all ecclesiastical discipline is destroyed, all order disturbed; so long as those who have not served in the lower offices of the Church undeservedly attain the highest, through the false judgment of those doing the selecting.

Since the pressure of the populace, then, and the office-seeking of the proud are of so much importance with you

---

10 Cf. 2 Tim. 2.20.

that, as we know, not only laymen but even men who have married a second time or have married widows have been advanced to the pastoral office, are there not the clearest reasons for requiring that churches where such things have been done be corrected by a rather severe sentence? Should not adequate punishment be meted out not only to such prelates but to those who consecrated them? Yet, while on one side of us stands the rigor of justice, on the other is the mildness of mercy. And because 'all the ways of the Lord are mercy and truth,'[11] in fulfilling the fatherly care of the Apostolic See, we are required to temper our decision, so that by weighing the gravity of the misdeeds (for, of course, they are not all of equal importance) we consider some to an extent pardonable, but others absolutely to be repressed. Neither apostolic nor canonical sanctions allow men who have entered into second marriages or who have married widows to become bishops. And this applies even more to the man who, as reported to us, has two wives at the same time (that is, provided in your judgment he is guilty as reported) or the man who, being divorced from one wife, is said to have married another. Those others, however, whose advancement is culpable only because they were chosen while laymen to hold the office of bishop and cannot be blamed for having wives—these we allow to keep the bishopric they received, but without prejudice to the decrees of the Apostolic See and not rescinding regulations made by the blessed Fathers. By these regulations every layman is wisely forbidden advancement to the first or second or third rank in the Church,[12] no matter what support he has to back him up,

---

11 Ps. 24.10.
12 That is, the prohibition (note 9) applied to deacons as well as to priests and bishops.

until he arrives at this deserved height by advancing through the required stages. What we permit in this instance as to an extent venial cannot be left unpunished hereafter if anyone presumes to do what we absolutely forbid, for forgiveness of sin does not give permission to commit sin; nor will it be all right to commit with impunity in the future a fault which for some reason we were able to overlook.

Now, as for Donatus of Salasia,[13] we want him to preside over the Lord's flock; we have found out that he and his people have been converted from the Novatian heresy. But he must not forget to send us a profession of his faith, in which he is to condemn the heretical Novatian teaching and subscribe to Catholic truth in its entirety. As for Maximus, although he was illicitly consecrated while still a layman, we do not expel him from the episcopal dignity, which he somehow acquired, so long as he is no longer a Donatist and has completely abandoned the spirit of schismatic depravity. But he, also, must demonstrate in a written report sent to us that he is Catholic.

But, as to Aggaeus and Tyberianus, whose cases are different from those of others who were consecrated while laymen in that, according to report, their consecrations were accompanied by fierce riots and wild strife: we entrust the entire matter to your judgment. By putting confidence in an inquiry held by you we can find out what ought to be decided about the two mentioned above.

Now, those handmaids of the Lord who lost their perfect virginity because they were violated by barbarians will be more praiseworthy in their humility and their feeling of shame if they do not dare to compare themselves with undefiled virgins. For, although all sin has its source in the will,

---

13 None of the following African bishops is otherwise known.

and a mind which did not yield could remain uncorrupted by the pollution of the flesh, it will hinder them less if they grieve over having lost even in their bodies what they could not lose in their minds.

And so, you see that your Charities have been instructed quite fully about nearly all the matters contained in the report of our brother Potentius; the instruction is sent through our brother and fellow bishop David, who has our esteem both for his merits as a bishop and for his character. Therefore, brothers, it remains for you to accept unanimously our salutary exhortations and, doing nothing out of rivalry but being of one mind in acting devotedly, to obey divine and apostolic decrees, and not to allow the very wise provisions of canon law to be violated in any way. Indeed, what we have overlooked for the present, after a consideration of definite reasons, must in future be observed in accord with ancient regulations, so that we may not hereafter punish with justice what we have let go by on this occasion with fatherly leniency. We will have to proceed with more special and earnest zeal against those who pay scant attention to the regulations of the holy Fathers in the consecrating of bishops and who consecrate men whom they should have rejected. Hence, if any bishops consecrate as bishop such a man as should not be, even though somehow they escape suffering any loss of their own honor, nevertheless, they will have no further right to consecrate; and they will never be present at that sacrament which they conferred on an undeserving person without regard for God's judgment.[14]

We are truly desirous that among all the regulations of the canons the following one pertaining to the episcopal dignity be observed: bishops are not to be consecrated for

---
14 Cf. Letter 10 n. 21; apost. canon 34 (Mansi, I 35).

any sort of place, for any sort of hamlet, and for places where they did not exist previously. For where there are fewer people and smaller congregations, the care of the priests will suffice.[15] But the rule of bishops ought to be restricted to larger groups of people and more populated cities. Otherwise, contrary to the divinely inspired decrees of the holy Fathers, the highest priestly office will be assigned to villages and rural estates or to obscure and out of the way towns; and the honored office, to which more important matters should be entrusted, will be cheapened by the very commonness of it. Bishop Restitutus is now rumored to have taken care of this matter in his diocese.[16] And he has rightly insisted that, when bishops die a natural death in sees where no bishop should have been consecrated, those places are to be returned to the jurisdiction of the same bishop who formerly held them or to whose see they are adjacent. It is pointless to cheapen the episcopal dignity by superfluous multiplications on the part of a consecrator who yields easily without consideration.

Concerning those who were living in the holy state of virginity, as we said above, but were violated by barbarians and lost the perfection of their chastity, not in their minds but in their bodies, it seems best to us that the following middle course should be observed. Let them not be lowered to the rank of widows, and yet let them not be considered among the number of holy virgins still undefiled. But if they persevere in the character of virginity and if they retain in their minds the resoluteness of chastity, then they are not to be denied participation in the sacraments. For it is unfair that they should be branded or accused for losing what hostile

---

15 Cf. Laodicaea, c. 57; Sardica, c. 6 (Mansi, II 590; III 24).
16 That is, province.

force took away, not something they lost of their own free will.

The case of Bishop Lupicinus we also order to be tried there. But at his frequent and insistent request we have restored him to communion for the reason that, since he had appealed to us for a decision, we saw that it was unjust for him to have been excommunicated while his case was being tried. There is, too, an added reason: It is known that another was rashly consecrated in his place, one who should not have been consecrated until Lupicinus had been convicted by a trial conducted in his presence or, at any rate, had confessed and could submit to a just sentence. In that way, as ecclesiastical discipline demands, the other one who was consecrated might occupy the vacant see.

Now, if any other cases arise concerning ecclesiastical welfare and harmony among the bishops, we want you to thresh them out there, in the fear of the Lord. And then a full account of all matters settled and still needing settlement should be sent to us so that whatever has been rightly and reasonably determined according to ecclesiastical custom may be strengthened by having our decision added thereto.

Issued on the tenth of August.

[*13*. (Silva-Tarouca, 23 xxv, with fragment xxvi). To the metropolitan bishops of Illyricum, January 6, 466: congratulations that they accept the overlordship of Anastasius of Thessalonica; they should go to councils summoned by him; no consecrations without the consent of the people, none in another's jurisdiction.]

14. Leo, Bishop of Rome, to Anastasius, Bishop of Thessalonica (after January 6, 446).

Were you to examine with right reason and weigh with just evaluation the importance of matters entrusted to your Fraternity by the authority of the most blessed Apostle Peter, and also the nature of the business turned over to you as a favor from us, we could then greatly rejoice over your devotion to the responsibility entrusted to you.

For, as my predecessors did to yours, so I, also, following them as models, delegated to your Charity the task of governing which is mine, so that, while imitating our clemency, you might share in the concern which, by divine ordinance, we above all are bound to show for all the churches,[1] and might in some way take our place in visiting provinces far from us. For it would really be easy for you by regular and timely inspection to find out in all instances what you might settle on your initiative and what you might reserve for our judgment. Now, since you were free to postpone more serious business and more difficult case-solutions until we could pass on them, there was no reason or need for you to err in a matter exceeding the limits set for you. You have at hand plenty of admonitions in writing in which we often instructed you to be moderate in all your actions so as to attract to salutary obedience, through charitable exhortation, the churches of Christ entrusted to you. For, although among our negligent and sluggish brothers there is generally something requiring correction by a sterner show of authority, the correction should be applied so as not to destroy charity. Hence, also,

---

1 Cf. Letters 5 and 6; Anastasius was made vicar over certain Eastern metropolitans two years previously.

the blessed Apostle Paul, instructing Timothy in the governance of the Church, says: 'Do not rebuke an elderly man, but exhort him as you would a father, and young men as brothers, elderly women as mothers, younger women as sisters in all chastity.'[2] If, by the Apostle's direction, this moderation is to be shown to any members of inferior rank, how much more should it be displayed without offense toward our brothers and fellow bishops? That is, although men of priestly rank sometimes do things that are reprehensible, kindness toward those to be corrected is more effective than severity, admonition more than anger, charity more than power. But those who 'seek their own interests, not those of Jesus Christ,'[3] easily depart from this rule. And while they exult more in dominating than in taking counsel for their subjects, honor puffs up pride, and what was counted on to effect harmony tends to do harm. It is from no small anguish of mind that we have to speak thus. I feel that I myself am somehow involved in blame when I realize that you have unduly departed from the instructions given you. If you had small concern for your own reputation, you should at any rate have spared mine, so that what you did only according to your own lights might not seem done through a decision of ours. Your Fraternity should read again what we wrote to you and all the writings which bishops in the Apostolic See sent to your predecessors, and find out whether either I or my predecessors ordained what, we are certain, was merely presumed on your part.

The metropolitan bishop of Old Epirus, our brother Atticus, has come to us, together with bishops of his own province, and with tears complained of the undeserved affliction he

---
2 1 Tim. 5.1,2.
3 Phil. 2.21.

has endured. This was done in the presence of your deacons, who by saying nothing to contradict these tearful complaints showed that the report being given us was reliable. We also read in your letter (which these same deacons of yours brought along) that our brother Atticus had come to Thessalonica and had even sealed his agreement with a written profession. Consequently, the only possible opinion we could have of him was that he had come of his own free will and spontaneous sense of duty and had signed the paper containing his promise of obedience. Yet, in the mere mention of this paper, a mark of injustice was displayed. He should not have been obliged to write it, since he already proved his obedience by the very act of deference in coming of his own accord. And so, these words in your letter were so much evidence added to the complaints of the bishop mentioned above. And there was uncovered by what you wrote that other circumstance which up to then was cloaked in silence, namely, that recourse was had to the prefect of Illyricum, and the most exalted power among secular potentates was incited to take action against an innocent bishop. As a result, in the executing of a terrible sentence, one which involved all the public officials in carrying out the order, the bishop was dragged from the entrance of the church, even though he was accused of no crime or, at any rate, of a false one. No consideration was given him because of his ill health or the severity of the winter, but he was forced to proceed through pathless snows over a road beset with dangers and rough. It was so arduous that, according to report, some of those who accompanied the bishop faltered.

 I am much amazed, dearest brother—nay, I am very much grieved—that you could have been so violently and cruelly angry at a man against whom you made no greater charge than that he had delayed coming when summoned and offered his infirmity as an excuse. I am especially grieved since, even if he merited some such treatment, you ought to have waited to see what answer I would make to the inquiries you sent me. But, as I see it, you correctly estimated my usual dispositions and you quite accurately saw beforehand how gently I would answer in order to preserve harmony among the bishops. Hence, you hastened to pursue without dallying your own inclinations. You knew that, once you had received our moderate answer outlining a different course, you would not be at liberty to do what you did. Was it, perhaps, that you had discovered some illicit act and the burden of the new misdeed was a serious charge against a metropolitan bishop in your area? Even you admit that this supposition does not fit his case at all, since you made no charge against him. But, even if he had committed some serious and insupportable sin, you ought to have waited for our decision; that is, you yourself should not have decided anything until you found out what our pleasure was. We entrusted our office to your Charity, but only in that you were asked to share in our responsibility, not in the fullness of our power. Hence, just as we are quite happy over what you have dutifully taken care of, so also we are grievously saddened by the wrong you have done. And now that we have experienced many of these instances, we must look into matters more carefully and take better precautions so that, by a spirit of charity and peace, every source of scandal may be removed from the churches of the Lord which we entrusted to you. You will, of course, retain your exalted position over those provinces within your jurisdiction, but every excessive assumption of power will be cut off.

Therefore, according to the canons of the holy Fathers established through the Holy Spirit and hallowed by the respect of the entire world, we decree that the right of dignity handed down to them inviolate from antiquity belongs to metropolitan bishops of individual provinces,[4] and your Fraternity's care is exerted over them by delegation from us. But they are not to depart from established ordinances by any neglect or presumption.

The procedure to be followed for selecting new bishops in those cities where the bishops have died is this. Even if the people testify to a man's virtuous life, he is not to be chosen if he is a layman, a neophyte,[5] a man married to a second wife, or a man who has or had but one wife, but she a widow when he married her.[6] This choosing of bishops is so pre-eminent a matter that what is not called a fault for other members of the Church is, nevertheless, to be considered illicit for them.

Although persons outside the clerical state are free to seek after marital union and the procreation of children, still, in order to exemplify the purity of perfect chastity, carnal marriage is not permitted even to subdeacons, so that those who have wives may be as if they had none,[7] and those who have none may remain single. But if it is proper for this clerical state (the fourth from the top) to observe this practice, how much more should it be kept in the first or second or third order? Otherwise, someone who has not yet shown any curb on his desire for marital pleasures may be

---
[4] Cf. Antioch, c. 9; Nicaea, c. 4; Arles, c. 6 (Mansi, II 464, 539, 1323).
[5] Cf. Letter 12 n. 8.
[6] Cf. Letter 4 nn. 6-8; Letter 6 n. 3; and Letter 12 n. 5.
[7] Cf. 1 Cor. 7.29.

thought suitable for the office of deacon or the priesthood or the excellence of the bishopric.

When, then, the selection of the highest priest is being taken care of, let him be preferred above all whom the clerics and people have harmoniously agreed to ask for.[8] But if, perhaps, some voters come out in favor of another person, then let that one be preferred who, in the judgment of the metropolitan, has greater efforts and merits in his favor. No one, of course, is to be consecrated against the wishes of the people and without their requesting it. Otherwise, the citizens will despise or hate the bishop they do not want and thus become less religious than they should, on the grounds that they were not permitted to have the man of their choice.

The metropolitan bishop is to inform your Fraternity about the person of the bishop-elect and about the agreement of the clerics and people. And he is to let you know what is wanted in the province, so that, for a consecration to be duly carried out, it may also have the support of your authority. If everything is in order, you must not be the occasion of delay or hindrance; otherwise, the Lord's flocks may for a long time lack pastoral care. But, when a metropolitan dies and another must be chosen in his place, the bishops of the province will have to meet in the metropolitan city, so that, after the wishes of all clerics and citizens have been discussed, they may choose the best man from among the priests or deacons of the same church.[9] The provincial bishops are to inform you of his name, with the idea of carrying out the wishes of the petitioners once they know that what has pleased them has also pleased you. While we do not want valid

---
8 Cf. Letter 10 n. 16.
9 Cf. *ibid.*

selections dragged out by any delays, we also do not permit anything to be presumed without your knowledge.

Now, concerning episcopal councils, we do not order anything different from what the holy Fathers have profitably ordained: that is, meetings are to be held twice each year.[10] Decisions may be made at these councils on all the complaints which commonly arise among the various orders of the Church. And if, by chance, a problem arises among the very ones who are in charge, involving greater sins (may there be none!), one that cannot be solved by provincial investigation, the metropolitan will see to it that your Fraternity is instructed as to what the whole affair is about. Then, if it is not settled by your decision, with both parties present before you, the affair (whatever it is) is to be transferred to us for trial.

If any bishop, objecting to the small size of his diocese, seeks to administer one with greater reputation and transfers himself to a larger congregation for any reason at all, he will indeed be expelled from the see which is not his and will likewise lose his own.[11] As a consequence, he will not preside over those whom he coveted out of avarice or over those whom he spurned out of pride. Let each one, therefore, be content with the boundaries that are his and not try to exceed the limits of his jurisdiction.

Let no one receive or invite a cleric not his own against the will of the man's bishop unless it be agreed to as an arrangement of charity between the giver and the receiver.[12] He is guilty of grave injustice who dares to entice or retain

---

10 Cf. apost. canon 36; Nicaea, c. 5; Antioch I, c. 20 (Mansi, I 35; II 679, 1326).
11 Cf. Letter 1 n. 6.
12 Cf. Sardica III, c. 18; Carthage IV, c. 27 (Mansi, III 29, 953).

from the church of a fellow bishop something of considerable use and value. Hence, the metropolitan will compel the cleric to return to his own church, in case this happens inside a province. But if the man has gone further afield, he will be recalled as ordered by your authority. In that way, no occasion will be left for greed or ambition.

We want you to use the greatest moderation in summoning bishops to you, lest, under the guise of greater diligence, you appear to gloat over injuries done to your brothers. Hence, if some major cause comes up, making it necessary and reasonable to call a meeting of your brothers, it will suffice to have two bishops come to your Fraternity from each province—those whom the metropolitans think should be sent. But those who have assembled are not to be delayed more than fifteen days beyond the time set for the meeting.

But if you feel that, on the matter to be handled and decided in conjunction with your brothers, their opinion was different from what you wanted, then let the entire matter, in the form of minutes of the proceedings, be referred to us. Thus, when doubts have been removed, a decision may be made which is pleasing to God. It is to this end that we direct all our zeal and concern: that whatever pertains to harmonious unity and the maintenance of discipline may not be disturbed by any dissension, may not be neglected through any sloth. Therefore, dearest brother, I exhort and admonish you, as well as those brothers of ours who are offended by your excesses (even though all of them do not have the same matter for complaint), that ordinances duly made and salutary arrangements are not to be disrupted by any strife. Let no one seek his own gain, but his neighbor's, as the Apostle says: 'Let everyone of you please his neighbor by doing good, for his edification.'¹³ Indeed, the bond of our unity cannot be firm unless the bond of charity has tied us together in indivisible solidarity. For, 'just as in one body we have many members, yet all the members have not the same function, so we, the many, are one body in Christ, but severally members one of another.'¹⁴ It is the connection of the entire body that makes for one health, one beauty. And this connection requires indeed the unanimity of the entire body, but it particularly demands concord among the bishops. Although dignity is common to them, they do not all have the same rank. For even among the most blessed Apostles, alike in honor, there was a certain distinction in power. Although they were all equal in being chosen, one was allowed to stand out above the others. From this arrangement there arose, also, distinctions among the bishops. And through a vast hierarchy it was provided that everyone might not arrogate everything to himself, but particular bishops were to be set up in each province, whose opinion among the brothers was to be considered first.¹⁵ Certain others, again, were to assume a greater pastoral responsibility in the larger cities.¹⁶ And through them the care of the universal Church was to converge in the one see of Peter, and nothing was ever to be at odds with his leadership. He, therefore, who knows that he has been set above certain others should not take it amiss that another is set over him. But he should also display the same obedience which he demands. And as he

---
13 Rom. 15.2; cf. Phil. 2.4.
14 Rom. 12.4,5.
15 That is, metropolitans.
16 That is, vicars.

himself does not wish to bear the burden of a heavy load, so, too, he should not dare to pile an insupportable load on another.[17] We are disciples of the meek and humble Master, who said: 'Learn from me, for I am meek and humble of heart; and you will find rest for your souls. For my yoke is easy, and my burden light.'[18] Shall we ever experience this unless still another saying of the Lord finds a place in our observance: 'Whoever wishes to become great among you shall be your servant[19] . . . for everyone who exalts himself shall be humbled, and he who humbles himself shall be exalted'?[20]

[*15*. An interesting letter to Bishop Turribius of Astorga in Spain, July 21, 447, on how to deal with remnants of the Priscilliantists there. The letter is considered spurious by K. Künstle, *Antepriscilliana* (Freiburg 1905) 117-126.]

---

17 Cf. Matt. 23.4.
18 Matt. 11.29,30.
19 Matt. 20.26.
20 Luke 14.11.

16. Bishop Leo, to all the bishops presiding throughout Sicily, greetings in the Lord (October 21, 447).

We are aroused by divine orders and apostolic admonitions to a vigorous zeal for the welfare of the churches. And when anything blamable is discovered anywhere, we are aroused to recall men, by a speedy show of concern, from faults due to ignorance or practices illicitly taken for granted. We are warned by the Lord's command, in the passage where the most blessed Apostle Peter is deeply impressed with the mystical order, three times repeated, that he who loves Christ is to feed Christ's sheep.[1] Hence, out of reverence for the See itself over which we preside through the abundance of God's grace, we are bound to avoid as much as possible the danger of sloth. Otherwise, there would be found wanting in us that profession of the greatest Apostle in which he claimed that he loved the Lord. For he who negligently feeds the flock so often commended to him is convicted of not loving the chief Shepherd.

Solicitous as I am because of fraternal affection, I have received well-founded information concerning your Charities' actions. You are departing from custom as set by the Apostles for the chief sacrament of the Church; that is, you perform the sacrament of baptism more often on the Epiphany than during the Paschal season. I am, therefore, amazed that you or your predecessors could have introduced such an unreasonable innovation; that is, by confusing the mysteries of the two seasons, you believed there was no difference between the day on which Christ was adored by the Magi and the day on which Christ arose from the dead. You could not have fallen

---
1 Cf. John 21.15-17.

into this error at all if you used as a basis for all your observances the same source from which your consecrated office is derived and if the See of the blessed Apostle Peter, which is the mother of your priestly dignity, were also your teacher in ecclesiastical procedure. That you departed from its regulations could be endured with even less calmness had you received any previous rebuke from us as a warning. Now, however, since we do not despair of amendment, we must preserve clemency. And although it is scarcely supportable for bishops to offer ignorance as an excuse, we prefer to moderate the necessary censure and instruct you with the reasoning of most obvious truth.

It is true that the redemption of the human race ever remained immutably predetermined in the eternal plan of God, but the order of events to take place in time through Jesus Christ our Lord began with the Incarnation of the Word. Hence, there is a time when, at the angel's announcing, the blessed Virgin Mary believed that she was to be with child by the Holy Spirit, and she conceived.[2] It is a different time when, preserving her virginal integrity, she bears a Son, and this is declared to the shepherds by the exultant joy of the heavenly ministers.[3] It is still another time when the Infant is circumcized;[4] another, when the victim required by the Law is offered for Him;[5] another, when the three Magi, led by the brightness of a new star, arrive in Bethlehem from the East and worship the adorable Child, presenting gifts of mystical import.[6] And the days on which He was snatched from the blasphemous Herod, being by divine

---
2 Cf. Luke 1.26.
3 Cf. Luke 2.7.
4 Cf. Luke 2.21.
5 Cf. Luke 2.24.
6 Cf. Matt. 2.1-12.

direction transferred to Egypt, are not the same as the days on which He was recalled to Galilee on the death of that persecutor.[7] Also included among these events varying in time is the growth of His body: the Lord grows, as the Evangelist testifies, by advancing in age and grace.[8] During the Paschal season He comes with His parents to the Temple of Jerusalem; on His being absent from the returning party, He is found sitting with the elders and discoursing in the midst of admiring teachers. In giving a reason for His remaining behind, He says: 'How is it that you sought me? Did you not know that I must be about my Father's business?'[9] By this He meant that He was the Son of the One whose temple He was in. Then, in His later years, when He was to be announced more openly and sought the baptism of His forerunner, John, what doubt was left about the divinity of the Lord Jesus Christ when, at His baptism, the Holy Spirit in the form of a dove came down upon Him and remained, as the voice of the Father from heaven was heard saying: 'Thou art my beloved Son, in thee I am well pleased.'[10] As briefly as possible, then, we have put together all these events so that your Charities may know that all Christ's days were consecrated by countless excellences and that mysteries shone forth in all His actions, but that one time applies to the announcing of each event by signs; another, to its fulfillment in fact. And all that is listed in the works of the Saviour cannot promiscuously pertain to the time for baptism. For, if we also celebrate without distinction of honor those deeds which we know the Lord performed after His baptism by the blessed

---

7 Cf. Matt. 2.13-19.
8 Cf. Luke 2.52.
* 9 Luke 2.49.
10 Luke 3.22; cf. Matt. 3.17.

John, the entire time of His life would have to be considered a continuous series of festivals, because the entire time was filled with the miraculous. But, since the Spirit of wisdom and knowledge instructed the Apostles and the teachers of the whole Church so as to allow nothing unregulated, nothing confused in Christian observance, the reasons behind the solemnities must be kept separate, and well-ordered distinction must be preserved in all customs begun by the Fathers and our predecessors. For in no other way are we one flock and one shepherd unless, as the Apostle teaches, we all say the same thing and are also perfectly united in one mind and in one judgment.[11]

Although, then, what pertains to Christ's lowliness and what pertains to His glory come together in one and the same person, and although whatever divine power and human weakness exist in Him all tend to effect our redemption, it is especially in the death of the Crucified and in His resurrection from the dead that the power of baptism establishes a new creature out of the old. That is, both the death and the life of Christ operate in those being reborn, as the Apostle says: 'Do you not know that all we who have been baptized in Christ have been baptized into his death? For we were buried with him by means of baptism into death, in order that, just as Christ has risen from the dead through the glory of the Father, so we also may walk in newness of life. For if we have been united with him in the likeness of death, we shall be so in the likeness of his resurrection also.'[12] And there are other things which the Teacher of the Gentiles treated more fully in recommending the sacrament of baptism. Hence it is apparent from the spirit of this teaching that, for baptizing

---
11 Cf. 1 Cor. 1.10.
12 Rom. 6.3-5.

the sons of men and adopting them as sons of God, that day and that season were chosen on which the actions performed on the members might be, through symbolism and mystical rite, in harmony with what was done in the Head itself. For, in the rite of baptism death comes from the slaying of sin, and the triple immersion imitates the three days of burial, and the rising out of the water is like His rising from the tomb. Hence, the very nature of the rite shows that ordinarily the right day for the reception of this grace is the one on which both the power of the gift and the form of the rite had their origin. What follows helps very much to confirm this point. The Lord Jesus Christ Himself, after He arose from the dead, gave to His disciples (and in them He instructed all those who are in charge of churches) the rite and the power of baptizing, saying: 'Go, therefore, and make disciples of all nations, baptizing them in the name of the Father, and of the Son, and of the Holy Spirit.'[13] Of course, He could have instructed them about this even before His passion, except that he especially wanted it understood that the grace of rebirth began with His resurrection. Actually, the Feast of Pentecost, which is hallowed by the coming of the Holy Spirit and is attached to the Feast of Easter as an appendage, is also used for this rite of baptism. Although other feasts are celebrated on different days, this Feast of Pentecost always occurs on that day of the week made famous by the Lord's Resurrection.[14] It somehow extends the hand of helping grace and invites those who were excluded from the Easter day by a troublesome sickness or a long journey or difficulties in sailing, so that those hindered by any necessities whatever may gain the effect they desire as a gift of the Holy Spirit.

---

13 Matt. 28.19.
14 Cf. Letter 9 n. 10.

The very Son of God, the Only-begotten, wished that there be no distinction between Himself and the Holy Spirit, either in what the faithful believed about them or in the power of their works, since there is no difference in their nature. He says: 'I will ask the Father and he will give you another Advocate, to dwell with you forever, the Spirit of truth'; and again: 'But the Advocate, the Holy Spirit, whom the Father will send in my name, he will teach you all things, and bring to your mind whatever I have said to you'; and again: 'When he, the Spirit of truth, has come, he will teach you all the truth.'[15] And so, since Christ is truth and the Holy Spirit is the Spirit of truth and the title 'Advocate' is proper to both, there is no difference in the feast where there is but one mystery.

Now we give a sufficiently apt example as proof that we are not defending this idea on our own authority but are holding to it on apostolic authority. We are following the example of the blessed Apostle Peter, who, on that very day when the promised coming of the Holy Spirit filled the entire group of believers, consecrated in the waters of baptism 3,000 persons whom his preaching had converted. This is taught by the reliable account of holy Scripture, of which the Acts of the Apostles are a part, where it says: 'Now on hearing this they were pierced to the heart and said to Peter and the rest of the Apostles, "Brethren, what shall we do?" But Peter said to them, "Repent and be baptized every one of you in the name of Jesus Christ for the forgiveness of your sins; and you will receive the gift of the Holy Spirit. For to you is the promise and to your children and to all who are far off, even to all whom the Lord our God calls." And with very many other words he bore witness, and exhorted them, saying,

---

15 John 16.16,26,13.

"Save yourselves from this perverse generation." Now they who received his word were baptized, and there were added that day about three thousand souls.[16]

Therefore, since it is obviously quite clear that these two times about which we spoke are the right ones for baptizing the elect in the Church, we warn your Charities not to add any other days for this observance. For, although there are also other feast days on which great reverence is due to the honor of God, for the principal and greatest sacrament we must hold to an exception, for which there are reasons and mystical significance. We are, however, at liberty to assist those in danger by administering baptism at any time. Thus we put off the free vows of those who are well and live in peaceful security to those two connected and related feasts, but not so as to deny at any time to anyone this single source of salvation when there is danger of death, critical times of siege, trials from persecution or fear of shipwreck.

Someone, however, may possibly feel that the Feast of the Epiphany, which must be celebrated with the honor due to its rank, also possesses the privilege of baptism, since certain men think that on that same day the Lord approached St. John to be baptized. The man who thinks this should realize that the grace of that baptism by John and the reason for it were of a different order and did not share in that same power whereby regeneration is brought, through the Holy Spirit, to those about whom it is said: 'Who were born not of the blood, nor of the will of the flesh, nor of the will of man, but of God.'[17] The Lord did not need to have any sin forgiven, nor was He seeking a way of rebirth. He simply wished to be baptized (as He wanted to be circumcized and to have a

---
16 Acts 2.37-41.
17 John 1.13.

victim offered as a purification for Himself)[18] in order that He who had been born of a woman, as the Apostle says, might also be under the Law, which He had not come to destroy but to fulfill and, by fulfilling, to consummate it.[19] As the blessed Apostle proclaims, saying: 'For Christ is the consummation of the Law unto justice for everyone who believes.'[20] Christ devised the sacrament of His own baptism in Himself because, 'in all things having the first place,'[21] He showed that He was Himself the source of it. And He ratified the power of regeneration at the time when there flowed forth from His side the blood of redemption and the water of baptism.[22] Hence, just as the Old Testament was a witness to the New and the 'Law was given through Moses, grace and truth came through Jesus Christ,'[23] just as diverse sacrifices prefigured the one victim and the killing of many lambs ended with the immolation of Him about whom it is said, 'Behold the Lamb of God, who takes away the sins of the world'[24]—so also John, not Christ but His forerunner, not the Bridegroom but the friend of the Bridegroom, was so faithful and a man who sought not his own but the things of Christ[25] that he professed himself unworthy to loose the sandals on Christ's feet.[26] For He indeed baptized with water unto penitence, but Christ would baptize 'with the Holy Spirit and with fire,'[27] Christ who with His twofold power would restore life and destroy sins. Consequently, dearest

---

18 Cf. Luke 2.21-24.
19 Cf. Matt. 3.13-16; Gal. 4.5.
20 Rom. 10.4; cf. Matt. 5.17.
21 Col. 1.8.
22 Cf. John 19.34.
23 John 1.17.
24 John 1.29.
25 Cf. Letter 1 n. 7.
26 Cf. Matt. 3.11; Luke 3.16.
27 Matt. 3.11.

brothers, because of these real proofs, so many and so weighty, which remove all doubt, you see clearly that only two periods, namely Easter and Pentecost, are to be used for baptizing the elect.[28] And according to apostolic regulation, they are to be investigated with exorcism, made holy by fasting, and instructed by frequent discourses. We lay it to your Charities' charge not to deviate at all in future from customs initiated by the Apostles. For hereafter, no one can be excused if he believes that apostolic regulations can be neglected in any way.

Our first demand, therefore, for the preservation of the most harmonious unity is this: Since it has been most profitably ordained by the holy Fathers that there be a meeting of bishops twice each year,[29] three of you are always to meet without delay in a council of our brothers at Rome on the twenty-ninth of September. For with the help of God's grace provision can more easily be made to prevent any scandals, any heresies, from starting in Christ's churches, since this deliberation must always take place in common in the presence of the most blessed Apostle Peter, so that all its decisions and canonical decrees may be kept without violation by all the Lord's bishops. These are the matters on which, by the Lord's inspiration, we thought it necessary to inform you. We want them brought to your attention by our brothers and fellow bishops Bacillus and Paschasinus.[30] May we learn from their

---

28 Baptizing only on Easter and Pentecost was probably a custom fairly well observed, but there appears to be no basis for it in canons prior to Leo I. Previous to him, however, is a letter from Pope Siricius, *Ad Himerium* 2 (Mansi, III 656), and, after Leo, canon 4 of the Council of Gerunda (Mansi, VIII 549). Cf., also, T. Sickel, *Liber Diurnus Romanorum Pontificum*, p. 6, lines 20-25.
29 Cf. Letter 14 n. 10.
30 Bacillus is not otherwise known. Paschasinus was Bishop of Lilybaeum (Marsala) in Sicily; he was later the Pope's delegate to the Council of Chalcedon. Cf. Letters 3 (*PL* 54.606, note e), 88, 89, and 93.

report how reverently the decisions of the Apostolic See are adhered to by you.

Issued on the twenty-first of October in the consulship of the most illustrious Calepius and Ardaburis.

[17. Leo I to all bishops in Sicily, October 21, 447, forbidding the sale of Church property when there would be no advantage to the Church.]

[18. Leo I to Januarius, Bishop of Aquileia, December 30, 447: any cleric who goes over to a heresy and then returns to the Church must receive the same rank he had at leaving and never advance further.]

19. *Bishop Leo, to his dearly beloved brother, Dorus (March 8, 448).*

We are grieved that the hopes we entertained for you have come to nothing. We notice that you have committed acts which, as reprehensible innovations, have contaminated the entire system of ecclesiastical ordinances. For you know very well with what solicitude we desire that the canonical regulations of the Fathers be observed in all the Lord's churches; and that we particularly want the bishops of all peoples to share in this responsibility, so that the provisions of the holy canons may not be corrupted by any deviations. Hence we are amazed that you, who had the best opportunity of observing most closely the official pronouncements of the Apostolic See,[1] have acted so carelessly, or, rather, so insolently, as to show yourself a transgressor rather than a guardian of the laws handed down to you. We have found out, in fact, from the written report (attached to this letter) of Paul, a priest of yours, that the priestly order has been disturbed by novel intrigues and foul trickery. That is, from the hasty and ill-considered promotion of one, something of dispiritedness took hold of those whose age recommended them for the honor,[2] and in whom no fault lessened their right to it. Suppose the endeavors of an intriguer and the ignorant zeal of his supporters demanded what custom has never allowed, namely, that a beginner be preferred to experienced persons, a tyro to men of years. It would have been for your zeal and teaching to restrain by a reasonable show of authority the unjust desires of these petitioners. Thus, he whom you hastily promoted to the priestly dignity would not enter upon a course injurious to his associates and would not become an inferior person as the vice of pride, rather than the virtue of humility, grew strong in him. You were not unaware of the Lord's saying that 'He who humbles himself shall be exalted, and he who exalts himself shall be humbled',[3] and of the same Lord's statement: 'But you seek to grow big from something small, and from what

---

1 Dorus was Bishop of Beneventum and seems to have been consecrated at Rome by Leo himself; hence the Pope's high hopes for him and his expected knowledge of papal pronouncements and desires.
2 That is, the priesthood; either a more important assignment in it, or the ordination of some deacon ahead of time.
3 Cf. Luke 14.11; 18.14.

is greater to become smaller.'⁴ Now, both of these are out of order, out of place. And every reward for labor is done away with, every measure of merit is nullified if the acquiring of dignity is in proportion to the amount of flattery dispensed. Thus, the urge to be illustrious discredits not only the ambitious person but also the one who connives with him. But if, as is reported, those priests holding the first and second places were so much in agreement in having Epicarpus put above them that they asked to have him honored at the expense of their own dignity, then this request should certainly not have been granted to men who by their own judgment were degrading themselves. For it would have been worthier of you to refuse rather than yield to so wretched a wish. Even so, their base and cowardly submission could not be prejudicial to those whose consciences were good and who were doing nothing to nullify the grace of God. That is, they could not eliminate the rank of those immediately below them by transferring their precedence to another through any sort of arrangement, nor might a man in last place stand out above the others just because these men had put him above themselves.

Although, then, the priests mentioned (who admitted that they were unworthy of their dignity in rank) have deserved even to be deprived of their priesthood, they are, however, just to be considered last in rank among all the priests of the church, that mercy thus may be shown to them through the fatherly concern of the Apostolic See. And in order that

---
4 These words (evidently in Leo's manuscript) occur in some Greek and Latin texts between Matt. 20.28 and 20.29. As interpreted by what follows here: the ambitious man is wrong for stepping from insignificance to the top; and the priests who preferred to have others put above them (*de majores esse minores*) are also wrong.

they may suffer the sentence which they passed on themselves, they will be even lower than the man whom by their own judgment they preferred to themselves. The other priests are to remain in that precedence marked out for each according to the time of his ordination. Nor is anyone to suffer the injury of having his rank lowered, except the two mentioned above; let this degradation fall only on the rank of those who chose to become inferior to a man ordained recently and without consideration. Thus they will realize that they are included in that statement of the Gospel which reads: 'With what judgment you judge, you shall be judged; and with what measure you measure, it shall be measured to you.'[5] Now, Paul the priest is to have the rank which, with laudable firmness, he did not give up, and nothing may be presumed in the future to the detriment of anyone. In that way your Charity, against whom beats all the ill will from this action, and not undeservedly, may hasten to make amends by using at least this remedy: You are to put into effect without delay these decisions which we are making. Otherwise, if another just complaint comes to us, we will of necessity be moved to greater severity; whereas, rather than increase punishment, we prefer to restore discipline by having those who have done wrong make amends. Know, then, that we have entrusted to our brother and fellow bishop Julius[6] the carrying out of our orders, so that all matters may at once be established as we have decided.

Issued on the eighth of March in the consulship of the most illustrious Posthumianus.

---

5 Matt. 7.2.
6 Very likely Julius, Bishop of Puteoli, who became the Pope's representative at the Robber Council of Ephesus; cf. Letter 28, at note 55.

LETTERS 81

20. Bishop Leo, to his dearly beloved son, Eutyches the priest (June 1, 448).[1]

Your Charity's letter has brought to our attention the fact that, through the efforts of certain persons, there has been a revival of the Nestorian heresy. We reply that your concern in this matter has pleased us, for the letter we received is an indication of your attitude: it shows that there is no doubt in your mind that the Lord, the Author of true faith, will be with you in everything. When we have been able to learn more fully through whose perversity this is happening, we must with God's help see to it that the heinous poison, and one condemned long ago, is completely eliminated. May God keep you safe, dearly beloved son.

Issued on the first of June in the consulship of the most illustrious Posthumianus and Zeno.

---
[1] Eutyches was an abbot at Constantinople; those who did not accept his views of the Incarnation were Nestorians. He himself was the heretic. The Greek text is that of Schwartz, *Acta* II.1 (2), p. 45.

21. Eutyches the priest, to Leo, venerable Lord and Archbishop of glorious Rome (December, 448).[1]

God is indeed my witness before all others of my faith and hope concerning the Lord Jesus Christ, who in judging decides what is true in the souls and minds of men. Yet I also implore your Holiness [to attest to the correctness of my views][2] and statements. For the Devil, the prince of all evil, being hostile to our efforts and purpose, has stirred up all his forces against us, using as tools those by whom his strength should have been destroyed. The holy man Eusebius, then, Bishop of Dorylaeum, presented a document of complaint to the devout Flavian, Bishop of Constantinople, and to certain others who at that time happened to be in the same city, occupied with their own business.[3] In it he accused me of being a heretic, not being induced to accuse me by any real evidence, but still devising ruin for me and disturbing the holy Churches of God. On that account I was called to answer and refute the charges. And although detained by a serious illness and worn out with age, I made haste to answer, even though I was not unaware that a trap had already been set against my welfare. I then wrote out a document setting forth my profession of faith and presented

---

1 This letter is included as an exception. It is valuable toward understanding the whole series of letters on the Eutychian controversy which follow. The text used (Schwartz, II.2, pp. 33-35) varies considerably from the alternate version in Migne, and no Greek text has survived.
2 A lacuna, supplied from the version in Migne.
3 Flavian, Bishop of Constantinople, presided over a council which in November, 448, condemned Eutyches as a heretic. The proceedings are in Schwartz, II.2, pp. 14-21 (Greek: II.1, pp. 139-145). Eusebius did not name the heresy (cf. *ibid.* II.2, p.3, and, below, Letter 24 n. 2). For the two points of Eutyches' heresy, cf. Letter 26, below.

it to these same men. The devout Bishop Flavian did not accept this written document or cause it to be read, but he listened while I answered questions and orally explained what I believed about matters decided by the Council of Nicaea and also confirmed by the Council of Ephesus.[4] I was then required to admit the 'two natures' and to condemn those who did not agree with that teaching. But in the light of your decrees[5] I was afraid to add to or detract any word from the faith as set forth by the most holy Council of Nicaea, for I knew that our holy and most blessed Fathers, Julius and Felix and Athanasius and Gregory, holy men and bishops, steered clear of the label 'two natures.' And I did not dare to discourse on the nature of the divine Word, who came into the flesh in the last days in the womb of the Virgin Mary, in the way in which He willed, not lessening Himself nor suffering change, but putting on the real nature of man, not just an apparition; nor did I dare to condemn our Fathers mentioned above. Since, then, these matters were thus being dealt with, I asked that they be brought to your attention so that you might decide what course I ought to follow and I agreed to follow in every detail what you approved of.[6]

---

4 The unaccepted document and Flavian's attitude are given in Schwartz, II.2, pp. 34-35; translated below, at note 10. Flavian's attitude at the trial was: 'Read it yourself'; and later: 'Why read a paper? Since you are here, we can discuss it.' Cf. *ibid*. II.2, p. 16, notes 124-129.

5 The Migne version is probably the correct one: 'as enjoined by the Council [of Ephesus],' which removed from office all clerics and excommunicated all laymen who did not accept the Council of Nicaea's explanation of the Incarnation. But Leo also constantly 'decreed' no changes in the canons of Nicaea.

6 Flavian, Letter 26 (*PL* 54.747), says this is a lie, and the proceedings of the trial do not mention it. Theodosius II held an inquiry in April, 449, as to whether the proceedings were falsified. One bishop admitted that Eutyches told him privately that he would accept the 'two natures' if the bishops of Rome and Alexandria said so. Another said that *after* the condemnation Eutyches said in a low voice that he

When they had spurned what I was saying and had broken off the meeting in haste, they published a sentence of excommunication against me, one which they had prepared before holding the trial. And relying on their faction, they spread around so much slander against me that my safety would even have been endangered had not a group of soldiers snatched me from the trap through God's assistance and your prayers. They insisted, nevertheless, on forcing the abbots of other monasteries to subscribe to my degradation. Never was such a practice carried out against those who openly confessed to being heretics—not even in the case of Nestorius himself. And when in order to justify myself before the Christian people, I published statements in self-defense,[7] they did not allow these to be circulated or come to the knowledge of the public. In short, those who through faction and deliberate calumny wanted everyone to judge me a heretic by removing my statements in self-defense seized them at once.

Hence, I take refuge in you, who preside over mercy and religion and whose habit it is to oppose and reject such factions. From my youth to the present time my belief has not been contrary to the faith professed by Catholics. But I condemn Apollinaris, Manes, Valentinus, Nestorius, and those who say that the flesh of Jesus Christ, our Lord and God, came down from heaven and was not produced by the Holy Spirit and the Virgin Mary, and all heretics back to the time of Simon Magus. Although I make such a profession,

---

appealed to the bishops of Rome, Jerusalem, and Alexandria. (Either appeal would have left him safe, since Dioscorus of Alexandria was on his side.) Others claimed to know nothing of such an appeal to the Pope. Cf. Hefele, *Histoire des Conciles* II 552.

7 A sample given in Schwartz, II.2, p. 35; Flavian refers to them in his Letter 26.

because of trickery and faction and enmity I stand in jeopardy like a heretic. And I ask that, acting without prejudice toward me in regard to what has been done through trickery and faction, you decide with all frankness whatever seems best to your Holiness in the matter. I beg you not to allow me to suffer any danger at the hands of those who are laying traps for me and not to allow me to be separated from the number of the faithful, a man who has spent more or less seventy years in the service of Christ, devotedly and chastely. Do not allow me to be shipwrecked by rivals now that I am at the very end of my life. I have attached to this letter of mine the written complaint that was presented against me and the written appeal which I presented but which was not accepted;[8] also a statement in self-defense which I gave out to the people, as well as those pronoucements made by our Fathers concerning the 'two natures.'[9] And the signature —I, Abbot Eutyches, have with my own hand subscribed my name to this written appeal:[10]

I call you to witness through God who gives life to all and in Jesus Christ, the Saviour, our God, who under Pontius Pilate spoke that excellent profession of faith—I call upon you to do nothing out of bias. My beliefs are those of the Fathers and those in which I was baptized at the start of my

---

8 Eusebius' written complaint (Schwartz II.2, p. 3); Eutyches' appeal (*ibid.*, pp. 34-35).
9 Not translated here are the excerpts from the Fathers that Eutyches sent to the Pope (Schwartz, II.2, pp. 35-42). There are twelve fragments (not the same ones as given in Migne). Eutyches picks an eminent galaxy. All Eutychians claimed to follow Cyril and the Council of Nicaea; they simply interpreted vague passages to fit their ideas. The only excerpts substantiating Eutyches are taken from a letter of Pope Julius. But this is a spurious affair already circulated by the heretic Apollinaris, whom Eutyches in part followed.
10 His profession of faith, not allowed to be read at the Council of Constantinople, follows; cf. above, note 4.

life, the same faith which the Council of the 318 bishops set forth at Nicaea and which the holy Council of Ephesus confirmed and decreed to be the only tenable doctrine. Nor have I ever believed anything other than the one, true and correct faith, and rightly so. I agree to and follow whatever was considered right by the holy Council of Ephesus, over which Cyril of holy memory, one-time bishop of the Alexandrian church, presided. And I am in harmony with the beliefs of the holy and elect of God: Gregory the Great, Gregory and Gregory,[11] Basil and Athanasius, Atticus and Proclus.[12] All these I have considered Catholic and trustworthy, and I have venerated them as my holy teachers. On the contrary, I condemn Nestorius and Apollinaris[13] and all heretics back to Simon [Magus] and those who say that the flesh of the Lord came down from heaven rather than that the divine Word Himself, coming down from heaven without a body,[14] was made flesh in the womb of the holy Virgin Mary from her flesh, without suffering change and without alteration; so that He who was perfect as God, before time began, the same might also become perfect man during the last days, for us and for our salvation. May your Holinesses,[15] then, consider this as my belief and profession. And the signature: I, Eutyches the priest, have signed my name.

---

11 That is, Nazianzen and of Nyssa.
12 Atticus, an opponent of Chrysostom, was Bishop of Constantinople (406-426). Proclus served the same see until 434; a firm opponent of Nestorius, he also wrote a *Tome* explaining the Incarnation.
13 Yet Flavian claims Eutyches took his heresy from Apollinaris and Valentinus.
14 Cf. Letter 28 n. 50.
15 That is, his judges at the Council of Constantinople, in 448.

LETTERS   87

[22. From Flavian, Bishop of Constantinople, to Leo I: the abbot Eutyches has been convicted of heretical elements taken from Valentinus and Apollinaris (same details as in Letter 26) and excommunicated by a synod held at Constantinople (cf. Letter 38 n. 2).]

23. *Bishop Leo, to his dearly beloved brother, Flavian (February 18, 449).*[1]

The most Christian and clement emperor, concerned for the peace of the Catholic Church because of his holy and laudable faith, has sent us a letter about what happened in your area to cause a noisy disturbance. Hence, we are amazed that your Fraternity could have kept secret from us what that scandal was about and did not, instead, first take care to instruct us by your informative report, so that we could have no doubt about the actual happenings.[2] We did, indeed, receive a document from Eutyches the priest, who complains that, on the accusation of Bishop Eusebius, he was excommunicated unjustly, especially since (as he says) he came when summoned and did not refuse to be present. Moreover, he claims that at the trial itself he presented a written appeal which, however, was not accepted.[3] And for this reason he

---
1 The texts here are Silva-Tarouca, 15 II; Schwartz, II.4, p. 3 (Greek: II.1, p. 46).
2 Flavian seems to have written and sent the proceedings at the end of 448. The Letter (No. 22) for some reason did not arrive until May of the next year. Concerning the dates of letters exchanged between the Pope and Flavian, cf. Letter 38 n. 2.
3 Cf. Letter 21 n. 4.

was forced to put out in the city of Constantinople tracts written in self-defense.[4] With all these matters in suspense, we still do not know with what justification he was expelled from the society of the Church. But, considering the importance of the case, we want to know the reason for your action and to have complete information sent to us. For we who desire that the judgments of the Lord's bishops be well considered cannot in ignorance of the facts make a decision to the prejudice of either side; we must first hear a true account of all that occurred.

Therefore, your Fraternity should explain in a complete report, brought by a suitable and particularly qualified person, just what innovation has arisen against the ancient faith that merited condemnation by a rather strict sentence. For ecclesiastical restraint and the religious faith of our most devoted emperor require us to show great concern for Christian peace so that, with dissensions eliminated, the Catholic faith may be preserved inviolate and, once those who advocate heresy have been recalled from their error, those whose faith has been approved may be strengthened by our authoritative pronouncement. No difficulty can arise in this matter since the priest mentioned claimed in his own written appeal that he is prepared to take correction if anything in him is found deserving of blame. In instances of this sort we ought, indeed, to take special care to preserve charity and to defend truth without the noise of dissensions. Therefore, since your Charity sees that we cannot but be worried over so important a problem, hasten to explain everything to us clearly and as fully as possible, as you should have done previously. Otherwise, caught between factional claims, we may make a mistake because something is not clear, and in this way foster a dis-

---
4 Cf. Letter 21 n. 7.

agreement which should be avoided at its start. For this is the course which, by God's inspiration, we hold to in our heart: What the venerable Fathers have decided, divinely sanctioned and part of the solid foundation of the faith, is not to be changed by anyone's unprincipled interpretation. God keep you safe, dearest brother.

Issued on the eighteenth day of February in the consulship of the most illustrious Asturius and Protogenes.

24. Pope Leo, to the most glorious and clement Theodosius, Augustus (February 18, 449).[1]

This letter which you sent me is additional proof of how much protection for His Church the Lord has provided in your Clemency's faith. Hence, we rejoice that you have the mind not only of a king but also of a priest, since, aside from your cares for the realm and the people, you have a most devoted concern for the Christian religion. That is, you are careful to prevent schisms or heresies or any other stumbling blocks from gaining strength among God's people. For your realm is in the best possible condition when men serve the eternal and unchanging Trinity while professing but one divinity. But I have not yet been able to learn for certain what trouble took place in the church at Constantinople which could have so bothered my brother and fellow bishop Flavian that he excommunicated the priest Eutyches. Although the priest mentioned did send to the Apostolic See a written appeal complaining of his misfortune, he merely

[1] The texts here are Silva-Tarouca, 15 I; Schwartz, 11.4, p. 31.

touched on some points. He asserted that he held to the decrees of the Council of Nicaea, but to no avail, since he was blamed for erring from the faith.

Now, his accuser, Bishop Eusebius, did not give clear evidence for his opposition in his written document (of which the priest mentioned sent us a copy.)[2] Although he accused the priest of the crime of heresy, he did not state clearly what heretical idea he was accusing him of. Yet the bishop himself claims to adhere to the decrees of the Council of Nicaea. That is why we have no way of learning anything more fully. Because the importance of the case, regard for the faith, and your Piety's praiseworthy solicitude demand it, no room must now be left open for deception. But we must first be instructed about the charges which they think ought to be made against him, so that a proper decision can be made once the facts are well known. I am sending a letter to the bishop[3] mentioned, to let him know that I am displeased that he still keeps cloaked in silence what has been done in so important a matter, whereas he should have been concerned at the beginning to explain the whole case to us. We believe, too, that after the admonition he will bring all the facts to our attention, so that, with those matters brought to light which apparently are still hidden, a decision may be made in harmony with evangelical and apostolic teaching. May the omnipotent God protect your realm and your welfare unto length of days, most glorious and clement Emperor, Augustus.

Issued on the eighteenth of February in the consulship of the most illustrious Asturius and Protogenes.

---

2 Given in Schwartz, II.2, p. 3; cf. Letter 21 n. 3.
3 Flavian; cf. Letter 23 n. 2.

[25. From Peter Chrysologus to Eutyches: the teaching of the Church on the Incarnation has been decided already and should be believed; Eutyches should get the truth from the Pope's writings.]

[26 Flavian's *second* letter to Leo I concerning the condemnation of Eutyches (cf. Letter 38 n. 2). Eutyches is guilty of renewing parts of the heresies of Apollinaris and Valentinus. A double error: (1) before the Incarnation there were two natures in Christ, afterwards but one; (2) though Christ took His body from the Virgin, it was not exactly of the same nature as ours. There are lies in Euthyches' appeal to the Pope, in that Eutyches had not actually presented a written appeal to the Council of Constantinople or to the Pope, as he claimed (cf. Letter 21, especially notes 6 and 13).]

[27 (Schwartz, II.4, p. 9). Leo I to Flavian, May 21, 449: he has received Flavian's report on Eutyches (Letter 22); he praises Flavian and promises a full reply. Silva-Tarouca considers this suspect; cf. Letter 38 n. 2.]

28. Bishop Leo, to his dearly beloved brother, Flavian, Bishop of Constantinople (June 13, 449).[1]

We have read your Charity's letter (we are amazed that it came so late) and have reviewed the proceedings of the council of bishops.[2] At last we have found out about the obstacle to the integrity of the faith which arose in your area; what before seemed obscure has now been disclosed and clarified for us. Eutyches, who appeared to be honorable because of his priestly title, is revealed by your letter to be quite rash and ignorant. Hence, the saying of the Prophet also fits him: 'He would not understand that he might do well. He hath devised iniquity on his bed.'[3] What is more iniquitous than to hold blasphemous opinions and not yield to those who are more learned and informed? Those men fall into this foolishness who, when they are impeded by some lack of intelligence from learning the truth, have recourse, not to the voice of prophecy, not to the epistles of the Apostles, not to the authority of the Scriptures, but to themselves. Hence, they are teachers of error because they were not pupils of the truth. For, what knowledge of the Old

---
1 Leo I's most famous letter, called the *Tome*. Together with Letter 165 (at times better exegesis, though not so famous), it is the best explanation of the mystery of the Incarnation. It is idle to speculate on his sources. Except for a short borrowing from St. Augustine and a possible adaptation of Gaudentius, the ideas seem to be interpretations of his own, based on the Creed and Scripture; several passages he had written earlier in his Sermons. Cf. Hefele, *op. cit.* 567-580; Vacant-Mangenot, *DTC* VII 478-482; Silva-Tarouca, 9, pp. 6-15. The texts here are Silva-Tarouca, 9, pp. 20-33; Schwartz, II.2, pp. 24-33 (Greek: II.1, pp. 10-11); Syrian version, *Mélanges de l'Université St. Joseph, Beyrouth,* 16 (1932) 121-165.
2 Cf. Letter 21 n. 3. On the late arrival of the letters, see Letter 23 n. 2 and Letter 38 n. 2.
3 Ps. 35.4,5.

and New Testaments has he acquired who does not even comprehend the elements of the Christian Creed itself and in his heart, even as an old man, does not understand the words which everywhere in the world are exacted from those about to be baptized?

Not knowing, therefore, what he ought to believe about the Incarnation of the divine Word and not being willing to labor in order to enlighten his mind from the breadth of holy Scripture, he might at least by careful attention have learned the common and uniform profession of faith which all the faithful make: namely that they believe in one God, the Father Almighty, and in Jesus Christ, His only Son, our Lord, who was born of the Holy Spirit and the Virgin Mary. It is by these three ideas that the machinations of almost all heretics are destroyed. For, when there is belief in God and the omnipotent Father, then the Son is shown to be co-eternal with Him, in no way differing from the Father, because He was born God from God, the Omnipotent from the Omnipotent, the Co-eternal from the Eternal, not coming later in time or inferior in power, not of unequal glory, not separate in essence. This same only-begotten Son of the eternal Father was truly born eternal of the Holy Spirit and the Virgin Mary. This birth in time in no way minimized His divine and eternal birth, nor did it add thereto. He sacrificed His entire self in order to redeem man (who had been deceived), to overcome death, and by His power to destroy the Devil, who held sway over death.[4] We could not overcome the author of sin and death had not Christ taken on our nature and made it His; sin could not defile Him nor death hold Him in bondage. He was truly conceived of the Holy Spirit within the womb of His Virgin Mother, who bore Him

---
4 Cf. Heb. 2.14.

while preserving her virginity just as, preserving her virginity, she conceived Him.

But, if Eutyches was unable to draw from this most pure fount of Christian faith a clear understanding, because he had darkened the light of clear truth by his blindness, he might have betaken himself to the teaching of the Scriptures, where Matthew says: 'The book of the origin of Jesus Christ, the son of David, the son of Abraham.'[5] He might also have sought instruction from the Apostle's teaching, reading in the Epistle to the Romans: 'Paul, the servant of Jesus Christ, called to be an apostle, set apart for the gospel of God, which he had promised beforehand through his prophets in the holy Scriptures, concerning his Son who was born to him according to the flesh of the offspring of David.'[6] He might have applied pious study to the writings of the Prophets, and coming upon the promise of God to Abraham, where He says: 'In thy offspring shall all nations be blessed,'[7] in order not to have doubts about the proper significance of this 'offspring,' he might have followed the Apostle saying: 'The promises were made to Abraham and to his offspring. He does not say, "And to his offsprings," as of many; but as of one, "And to thy offspring," who is Christ.'[8] He might also have understood by deeper attention the teaching of Isaias saying: ' "Behold, the virgin shall be with child, and shall bring forth a son; and they shall call his name Emmanuel"; which is, interpreted, "God with us." '[9] He might have read the words of the same Prophet: 'A child is born to us, and a son is given to us, and the government is upon his shoulders:

---

5 Matt. 1.1
6 Rom. 1.1-3.
7 Gen. 22.18; cf. 12.3.
8 Gal. 3.16
9 Matt. 1.23; cf. Isa. 7.14.

and they shall call his name, Angel of the Great Counsel, God the Mighty, the Prince of Peace, Father of the world to come.'[10] And he would not speak nonsense, saying that the Word was made flesh in such a way that Christ, born from the Virgin's womb, had a man's form, yet did not have the reality of His Mother's body. Or did Eutyches by chance think that our Lord Jesus Christ was not of our nature because the angel sent to the blessed Mary said: 'The Holy Spirit shall come upon thee and the power of the Most High shall overshadow thee; and therefore the Holy One to be born shall be called the Son of God";[11] that is, because the Virgin's conceiving was a divine work, the flesh of Him who was conceived was not taken from the nature of her who conceived Him? But that birth, singularly wonderful and wonderfully singular, must not be understood as meaning that, because of the new type of procreation, the intrinsic quality of the birth was changed. Fecundity was given to the Virgin by the Holy Spirit, but the reality of the body was taken from her body; and with Wisdom building a dwelling for Himself,[12] 'The Word was made flesh, and dwelt among us";[13] that is, in that flesh which He took from a human being and which He animated with the breath of rational life.

In this preservation, then, of the real quality of both natures, both being united in one person, lowliness was taken on by majesty, weakness by strength, mortality by the immortal. And in order to pay the debt of our fallen state, inviolable nature was united to one capable of suffering so that (and

---
10 Cf. Isa. 9.6.
11 Luke 1.35.
12 Cf. Prov. 9.1.
13 John 1.14.

this is the sort of reparation we needed) one and the same mediator between God and men, the man Jesus Christ,[14] could die in the one nature and not die in the other.[15] In the whole and perfect nature of the true man, then, the true God was born, complete in His own nature, complete in ours. But by ours we mean that which the Creator formed in us at the beginning and which He took upon Himself, to redeem it. That part which the Deceiver added and man, deceived, accepted left no traces in the Saviour. He did not share in our sins just because He undertook to share in our weaknesses. He took on the aspect of servitude without the stain of sin; He added to the humanity but did not lessen the divinity. For that putting off of self whereby He the invisible made Himself visible and as Creator and Lord of all things wished to become one of the mortals was an inclination to mercy, not a failure of power.[16] He who keeping the form of God created man, the same was made man in an aspect of servitude.[17] Both His natures keep their intrinsic quality without defect; and, just as the aspect of God does not remove the aspect of servitude, so also this latter does not lessen the aspect of God. Because[18] the Devil boasted that man, deceived by his trickery, lacked help from God; that man, deprived of the gift of immortality, had undergone the hard sentence of death; and that man had found a sort of solace in his misfortunes by associating with the Deceiver; that God, also, because the course of justice demanded it,

---

14 Cf. Phil. 2.5.
15 These two sentences may be compared with Leo's *Sermo* 21.2 (*PL* 54.192).
16 Compare these sentences with Leo, *Sermo* 23.2 (*PL* 201); also, St. Augustine, *De Trinitate* 1.7 (*PL* 42.829).
17 Cf. Phil. 2.7.
18 For the next four sentences, ending 'laws of death,' cf. his *Sermo* 22.1-2 (*PL* 54.194-195).

had changed His own design in regard to man, whom He had created with so much honor—for these reasons God had to arrange a secret design whereby the unchanging God, whose will cannot be deprived of its clemency, might actually fulfill His original plan of fatherly care towards us by a much hidden mystery; and man, led into sin by the cleverness of the Devil's iniquity, might not perish contrary to the plan of God.

The Son of God, then, enters into this weakness[19] of the world, coming down from His heavenly throne, begotten in a new type of birth, but not departing from His Father's glory in the new order. The 'order was new' in that, being invisible in His own nature, He became visible in ours; incomprehensible, He desired to be comprehended; enduring before time began, He began to exist in time; the Lord of the universe assumed the aspect of servitude with a shadow veiling the immensity of His majesty. A God, incapable of suffering, He deigned to become a man who could suffer, and, being immortal, to become subject to the laws of death. He was born in a 'new type of birth' in that undefiled virginity experienced no concupiscence, yet supplied the material for the flesh. From the Mother the Lord took His nature, but no fault; and the Lord Jesus Christ, born from a virgin's womb, does not have a nature different from ours just because His birth was an unusual one. He who is true God is also true man; there is no falsity in this union, wherein the lowliness of man and the greatness of the divinity are mutually united. Just as God is not changed by His show of mercy, so the man is not changed by being swallowed up in majesty. Each[20] aspect performs its own acts in co-operation with the other;

---

19 That is, *infirma;* other texts read *infima* ('lower regions').
20 Compare the next three sentences with his *Sermo* 54.2 (*PL* 54.319).

that is, the Word doing what is proper to the Word, the flesh pursuing what pertains to the flesh. The first of these is ablaze with the miraculous, the other is overpowered by injuries. And just as the Word does not give up any of His equality in the Father's glory, so also the flesh does not abandon the nature of our species.[21] He is one and the same, truly Son of God and truly Son of man. He is God because of the fact that 'in the beginning was the Word, and the Word was with God, and the Word was God'; and man through the fact that 'the Word was made flesh, and dwelt among us'; God, because 'all things were made through him, and without him nothing was made';[22] a man through the fact that 'He was born of a woman, born under the Law.'[23] The[24] birth of flesh is a manifestation of human nature; that a virgin should give birth is a show of divine power. The infancy of the babe is displayed by the lowliness of the cradle; the greatness of the Almighty is proclaimed by the voices of angels.[25] He has a man's helpless infancy in that Herod impiously tries to kill him; but He is the Lord of all, before whom the Magi rejoice to kneel in supplication.[26] Already when He came to be baptized by John, the precursor, lest it be unknown that divinity was being covered by a veil of flesh, the voice of the Father thundering from heaven said: 'This is my beloved Son, in whom I am well pleased.'[27] And

---

21 The preceding sentences are of the type that could easily be falsified and attacked by the Palestinian monks, who said that Leo 'divided the substance' of Christ as did the Nestorians. Cf. below, Letters 124, 129, 130, 131.
22 John 1.1,14,3.
23 Gal. 4.4.
24 From here to the end of the paragraph the ideas are much the same as those in Gaudentius, *Sermo* 19 (*PL* 20.983-986).
25 Cf. Luke 2.7,13.
26 Cf. Matt. 2.16,11.
27 Matt. 3.17.

so, He whom the cleverness of the Devil tempts, as if He were a man, is accompanied by the ministration of angels, as to God.[28] To hunger, to thirst, to grow tired, and to sleep: these are evidently human.[29] But to satisfy 5,000 men with five loaves of bread[30] and to give the Samaritan woman living water, a drink which frees the one drinking from further thirst,[31] to walk on top of the sea without sinking,[32] and to calm the waves stirred up by a storm[33]—are doubtless the work of God. Hence, to skip over many other items, just as it is not part of the same nature to weep over a dead friend from the emotion of pity and then by the command of His voice to call forth this same man alive, after rolling back the stone from a tomb closed for four days;[34] or to hang on a cross of wood, and yet turn day into night and cause the elements to tremble;[35] or to have been pierced with nails, yet to open the doors of paradise to the faithful thief[36]—so also to say: 'I and the Father are one' and to say: 'The Father is greater than I'[37] are not both pertinent to the same nature. Although in the Lord Jesus Christ there is one person, of God and man, it is only from one of these sources that contempt comes to both in common and from the other source that glory comes to both in common. From us He has a humanity less than the Father; from the Father, a divinity equal to the Father's.

Because, then, of this union of personality (to be under-

---

28 Cf. Matt. 4.1-11.
29 Cf. Matt. 4.2; John 4.8; Luke 8.23.
30 Cf. John 6.12.
31 Cf. John 4.10.
32 Cf. Matt. 14.25.
33 Cf. Luke 8.24.
34 Cf. John 11.35-43.
35 Cf. Matt. 2.51; Luke 23.44.
36 Cf. Luke 23.43.
37 John 10.30; 14.28.

stood of both natures) 'the Son of man', as we read, came down from heaven when the 'Son of God' assumed flesh from that Virgin through whom He was born. And again, the 'Son of God' is said to have been crucified and buried, although this did not pertain to His divinity as such, in which the Only-begotten is co-eternal and consubstantial with the Father; but He endured this in the weakness of His human nature. Hence, too, we all profess in the Creed that the only-begotten 'Son of God' was crucified and buried, according to that statement of the Apostle: 'For had they known it, they never would have crucified the Lord of glory.'[38] When our Lord and Saviour Himself was teaching the faith to His disciples, He questioned them, saying: 'Who do men say that I the Son of man am?'[39] And when they had given Him various opinions of others, He said: 'But who do you say that I am?' That is, I, who am the Son of man and one whom you see in a condition of servitude and the reality of the flesh, whom do you say that I am? When blessed Peter by divine inspiration said (and by his profession he would be of service to all peoples): 'Thou art the Christ, the Son of the living God,' not undeservedly he was called 'blessed' by the Lord and derived from the word *rock* that solidity associated with his virtue and his name.[40] It was Peter who, through the revelation of the Father, professed that Christ and the Son of God were the same. For to have possessed one of these without the other was of no value for salvation; it was equally dangerous to believe that the Lord Jesus Christ

---

38 1 Cor. 2.8. Note the similarity of the first sentences in the paragraph to St. Augustine, *Contra Serm. Arian.* 8 (*PL* 42.688).
39 Cf. Matt. 16.13.
40 Quoted or paraphrased from Matt. 16.15-18; cf. Leo, *Sermo* 4.2; 51.1 (*PL* 54.150,309), and, above, Letter 10 n. 2: *Petrus* associated with *petra*.

was either God only without man, or man only without God. After the Lord's resurrection (which, of course, was the resurrection of His real body, since the one who came to life was the same as He who had been crucified and died), why did He delay on earth for forty days except to clear away every cloud from the fullness of our faith? Speaking with His disciples and living and eating with them, He allowed Himself to be touched by the attentive and curious hand of those who were afflicted by doubt.[41] For the same reason He also entered into a room with His disciples while the doors were shut and by breathing on them He gave them the Holy Spirit.[42] And having bestowed light on their intelligence, He explained the mysteries of holy Scripture. And once more He pointed out the same wound in His side, the holes left by the nails, and all the marks of His quite recent passion, saying: 'See my hands and feet that it is I myself. Feel me and see; for a spirit does not have flesh and bones, as you see I have.'[43] This was to show us that there remained in Him the particular qualities of both the divine and human natures, and that we might thus realize that the Word is not the same as the flesh and might therefore confess that the one Son of God is both the Word and flesh. That man Eutyches must be considered as totally lacking in this mystery of the faith. He did not recognize our nature in the only-begotten Son of God, neither through the lowliness of His mortal state nor through the glory of His Resurrection. And Eutyches did not fear the sentence of the blessed Apostle and Evangelist John, saying: 'Every spirit that confesses that Jesus Christ has come in the flesh, is of God. And every spirit that severs

---

41 Cf. Acts 1.3.
42 Cf. John 20.19-23.
43 Luke 24.39.

Jesus, is not of God, but is of Antichrist.'⁴⁴ What is meant by 'severing' Jesus if not the taking away from Him of His human nature and nullifying by the foulest imaginings the mystery through which alone we have been saved? But, being in the dark about the nature of Christ's body, he is of necessity also ignorant about the passion because of the same blindness. If he does not think the cross of Christ was false and does not doubt that it was endured as a real satisfaction for the salvation of the world, then let him admit the flesh of the one whose death he believes in. Let him not deny that one who, by his admission, was capable of suffering was a man with a body like ours. For a denial of the actual flesh is also a denial of bodily suffering.⁴⁵ If, then, he accepts the Christian faith and does not turn away his ear from the teaching of the Gospel, let him see which nature it was that, pierced with nails, hung on the wood of the cross; let him realize whence the blood and water flowed, when the side of Christ was opened by the soldier's spear, so that God's Church might be wet therewith by washing and drinking.⁴⁶ Let him also listen to the blessed Apostle Peter preaching that sanctification of the spirit is effected by sprinkling with the blood of Christ.⁴⁷ Let him read, not cursorily, the statement of the same Apostle saying: 'You know that you are redeemed from the vain manner of life handed down from your fathers, not with perishable things, with silver or gold, but with the precious blood of Christ, as of a lamb without blemish and without spot.'⁴⁸ Let him likewise not resist the testimony of blessed John the Apostle saying: 'And the blood of Jesus, the

---

44 1 John 4.2,3.
45 Here, as often in the letter, he opposes the view that Christ's human nature was not exactly like ours.
46 Cf. John 19.34,35.
47 Cf. 1 Peter 1.2.
48 1 Peter 1.18,19.

Son of God, cleanses us from all sin'; and again: 'And this is the victory that overcomes the world, our faith'; and: 'Who is there that overcomes the world if not he who believes that Jesus is the Son of God? This is he who came in water and in blood, Jesus Christ; not in the water only, but in the water and in the blood. And it is the Spirit that bears witness that the Spirit is the truth. For there are three that bear witness . . . the Spirit, and the water, and the blood; and these three are one.'[49] This means the Spirit of sanctification and the blood of redemption and the water of baptism, which three are one and remain distinct, and none of them is separated from union with the others. This is the faith by which the Catholic Church lives and progresses, namely, that humanity is believed to exist in Jesus Christ not without real divinity, and divinity, not without real humanity.

But when Eutyches answered the questions put to him at your investigation, saying, 'I confess that our Lord had two natures before they were united, but I confess that after the union He had one nature,'[50] I am amazed that so absurd and so perverse a profession was not corrected by any rebuttal on the part of the judges and that a totally insipid and blasphemous statement was passed over as if nothing to give offense was heard. The fact is that it was as impious to say that the only-begotten Son of God had two natures before the Incarnation as it was blasphemous to assert that He had a single nature after the Word was made flesh. Hence, in order that Eutyches may not think that what he said was right or tolerable on the grounds that it was not refuted by

---
49 Cf. 1 John 1.7; 5.4-8.
50 In the proceedings (Schwartz, II.2, pp. 17-18, notes 145 and 154). It is true that the judges did not ask him to explain his view. Eutyches appears to be more orthodox in writing to the Pope directly; cf. Letter 21, at note 14.

any opinion of yours, we strongly exhort your Charity's zeal so that, dearest brother, if ever this case is satisfactorily concluded through the intervention of God's mercy, the folly of an ignorant man may also be purged of this pernicious item of belief. As the record of the proceedings made clear, Eutyches had indeed made a good start toward giving up his views at the time when, pressed by your ideas, he admitted that he was saying what he had not said previously and that he was yielding to a belief that previously was not his.[51] But when he was unwilling to agree to a condemnation of the impious doctrine, it was your Fraternities' understanding that he was remaining in his perfidious belief and deserved to have a judgment of condemnation passed against him.[52] If he faithfully and profitably repents this action and recognizes, even at this late date, how justly episcopal authority was aroused against him, or if he makes the fullest satisfaction by a condemnation read aloud and signed by him personally against all his heretical opinions, then no fault will be found with any show of mercy toward him who has repented. For our Lord, the true and good Shepherd, who laid down His life for His sheep[53] and who came to save the souls of men, not to destroy them,[54] wishes us to be imitators of His fatherly care. That is, sinners are indeed to be restrained by justice, but through mercy they are not to be driven away when converted. The true faith is then at last most fruitfully defended when a false opinion is condemned even by its supporters.

---

51 Cf. Schwartz, II.2, pp. 16-17, notes 134, 136, 140, 147: a sort of double talk—'I say so if you say so, but this was never my view in the past.'
52 Cf. Schwartz, II.2, p. 18, notes 152 and 160: he refused to anathematize all who did not hold to the 'two natures' because, in his view, that would be to condemn such Fathers as Cyril and Athanasius. On Cyril's real views, cf. Hefele, *Histoire des Conciles* II 503-505.
53 Cf. John 10.11.
54 Cf. Luke 9.56.

We are sending our brothers, Julius the bishop and Renatus the priest, as well as my son Hilary the deacon, to represent us in seeing that the entire problem is settled with piety toward and faith in God. With these we are associating Dulcitius, our notary, whose faith has been proved to us.[55] We are confident that God's assistance will be present so that he who erred may be saved through the condemnation of his heretical ideas. May God keep you safe, dearest brother.

Issued on the thirteenth of June in the consulship of the most illustrious Asturius and Protogenes.

---

55 Other texts read *tituli sancti Clementis* after Renatus' name, likely a marginal comment by someone who knew to which Roman church Renatus was attached. In the *Gesta de nomine Acaci* (CSEL 35, p. 442), three of these men are mentioned as the Pope's delegates at the Robber Council of Ephesus; then it says that Renatus died on the way out, on the island of Adelos (i.e., Delos). The proceedings of the council do not mention Renatus. Bishop Julius was from Puteoli. Hilary succeeded Leo as Pope. Cf. Hefele, *op. cit.* 566, 617-620.

29. Bishop Leo, to the most glorious and clement Theodosius, Augustus (June 13, 449).[1]

How much Divine Providence deigns to care for human affairs is shown by your Clemency's solicitude, enlivened by the Spirit of God; you want nothing unsettled, nothing at odds, in the Catholic Church. For faith (which does not exist unless it is one) can in no way consist of anything dissimilar to itself. So, as the minutes of the episcopal proceedings have made clear,[2] Eutyches was found to be in error through ignorance and imprudence, and he should have given up his belief, which is deservedly condemned. Nevertheless, since your Piety (you love Catholic truth most religiously unto the honor of God) has determined to have a decision made by a council,[3] in order that the truth to which an ignorant old man is quite blind may be pointed out to him, I am sending my brothers, Julius the bishop, Renatus the priest, and my son Hilary the deacon.[4] They are men capable of taking my place, considering the nature of the business, and men who will bring with them such a spirit of justice and kindness that the depravity of the entire heresy may be condemned (since there can be no doubt as to what the integrity of the Christian

---

1 The texts here are Silva-Tarouca, 15 III; Schwartz, II.4, p. 9 (Greek: 11.1, p. 45).
2 The Pope finally received Flavian's letter and the proceedings condemning Eutyches, in May, 449 (cf. Letter 21 n. 3 and Letter 38 n. 2), about the same time he received an invitation to the council proposed by Theodosius II. On June 13 he sent the four envoys, the *Tome* to Flavian, this reply to the emperor, and Letters 30-35 to various people in the East—to insure the condemnation of Eutyches.
3 In March, 449, Theodosius sent invitations to many dignitaries, e.g., the one to the infamous Dioscorus of Alexandria (Schwartz, II.1, p. 68; II.2, pp. 42-43). The Pope's delegates admitted that he, too, received an invitation (*ibid.*, II.2, p. 44, notes 5-6).
4 Cf. Letter 28 n. 55.

profession of faith consists of); if he who has gone astray repents and requests forgiveness, then priestly clemency may assist him. For, in the written appeal which he sent to us, he at least reserved for himself the right to earn pardon by promising that he would correct whatever our thinking disapproved of in those views which he had been erroneous in holding.[5] Now, I am sending a letter to my brother and fellow bishop Flavian, one which gives a rather full treatment of what the Catholic Church everywhere believes and teaches concerning the mystery of the Lord's Incarnation. May the omnipotent God watch over your realm and your welfare unto length of days, O most glorious and clement Emperor, Augustus.

Issued on the thirteenth of June in the consulship of the most illustrious Asturius and Protogenes.

[*30-31* (Silva-Tarouca, 15 IV and IVb; Schwartz, II.4, pp. 10-15; Greek version of IV: II.1, pp. 45-46). Leo I to Pulcheria, sister of Theodosius II and practically co-ruler of the East. The first letter differs little from No. 29. The second (oddly, issued on the same day, June 13, 449) includes more discussion of Eutyches' errors; he also says he cannot accept the emperor's invitation to attend the proposed Council of Ephesus.]

---
5 Letter 21 n. 6.

[*32* (Silva-Tarouca, 15 VIIII; Schwartz, II.4, p. 10; Greek: II.1, p. 42). Leo to Faustus and Martinus and other abbots in the East, June 13, 449. He condemns Eutyches, but asks that he be shown mercy for repentance; he announces that he is sending Letter 28 to Flavian.]

33. To our dearly beloved brothers, greeting in the Lord (June 13, 449).[1]

Our most clement emperor, knowing in his religious faith that it is especially pertinent to his glory should there arise no germ of any heresy within the Catholic Church, has invoked the authority of the Apostolic See in order to effect a holy settlement [of the present dispute]. In this he has shown reverence for divine institutions, desiring, as it were, that the most blessed Apostle Peter proclaim those words in his profession of faith which were praised [by Christ]. It was when[2] the Lord said: 'Whom do men say that I the Son of God am?' and the disciples listed various opinions of others; but when He asked them what they themselves believed, the prince of the Apostles (embracing the fullness of faith in a few words) said to Him: 'Thou art the Christ, the Son of the living God.' This means: 'You are truly the Son of Man and also truly the Son of the living God; you are,' I say, 'real as to divinity, real as to flesh, and while both are one, each nature retains its own special character.' If Eutyches

---

1 To the bishops assembled at Ephesus. It is unlikely that they read it or that they would have been influenced by his defense of papal supremacy. The texts here are Silva-Tarouca, 15 VIII; Schwartz, II.4, p. 15 (Greek: II.1, pp. 43-44).
2 Cf. Matt. 16.13,16-18.

had an intelligent and vigorous belief in this, he would in no way wander from the path of this belief, one which brings to Peter the Lord's answer: 'Blessed art thou, Simon Bar-Jona, for flesh and blood has not revealed this to thee, but my Father in heaven. And I say to thee, thou art Peter, and upon this rock I will build my Church, and the gates of hell shall not prevail against it.' He who does not accept this profession of the blessed Peter and contradicts Christ's Gospel is completely removed from association with this 'building.' He shows that he never had any zeal for understanding the truth and that he appeared to be honorable merely on the surface since he did not adorn the white hairs of his old age with any maturity of thought.

Since we should not neglect the care of even such men and since the most Christian emperor has piously and devotedly willed that a council of bishops be held in order to blot out every error by a fuller trial, I am sending our brothers, Julius the bishop, Renatus the priest, and my son Hilary the deacon, and with them Dulcitius the notary, whose faith has been proved to me.[3] They are to be present at your Fraternities' holy meeting in my place and, in common with you, come to a decision that will please the Lord. The idea is first to condemn the pernicious heresy and then deal with the restoration of that man who has imprudently erred. However, you are to do this only if he embraces the true doctrine and if he himself reads and signs a full and clear condemnation of the heretical views in which his ignorance ensnared him. He even agreed to this in the written appeal which he sent to us, promising that in every way he would follow our views. Now that we have received a letter from our brother and fellow bishop Flavian, we are sending

---
3 Cf. Letter 28 n. 55.

him a fuller answer to these matters which he seems to have referred to us.⁴ We do this in order that, with the elimination of this heresy which apparently has arisen, there may be throughout the entire world but one belief, one and the same profession of faith unto the praise and glory of God, and in order that 'at the name of Jesus every knee should bend of those in heaven, on earth and under the earth, and every tongue should confess that the Lord Jesus Christ is in the glory of God the Father.'⁵ May God keep you safe, dearest brothers.

Issued on the thirteenth of June in the consulship of the most illustrious Asturius and Protogenes.

[*34*. (Silva-Tarouca, 15 vii; Schwartz, II.4, p. 16). Leo I to Juvenal, Bishop of Jerusalem (not to Julian of Cos, as listed in Migne), June 13, 449, about Eutyches' guilt and the envoys to the proposed Council of Ephesus.]

---
4 In Letter 22.
5 Phil. 2.10,11.

35. Bishop Leo, to his dearly beloved brother, Julian (June 13, 449).[1]

In the interests of the faith we are sending quite a complete letter against an absolutely impious heresy to our brother Flavian, through those envoys whom we are dispatching from Rome. Even so, since we received a letter from your Charity through our son Basil the deacon[2] (a letter which pleased us greatly because of the intensity of its Catholic views), we are sending this letter in addition, one which is in agreement with that letter.[3] You may thereby offer a united and constant resistance to those who seek to corrupt Christ's Gospel, since in us and in you there is but one and the same knowledge and doctrine, from the Holy Spirit. Whoever does not accept it is not a member of Christ's body, and he cannot take pride in that Head in which, as he asserts, his own nature has no part.[4] He also wanders from the right path who claims that the only-begotten Son of God was born from the womb of the blessed Virgin in such a way that, while He put on the appearance of a human body, the reality of human flesh was not united to the Word. For He departs from the truth as much as did Nestorius, who kept the divinity of the Word distinct from the human nature which He assumed. Who does not see what monstrous ideas spring from this enormous falsehood? Indeed, he who denies

---
1 The texts here are Silva-Tarouca, 15 VI; Schwartz, 11.4, pp. 6-8 (Greek: II.1, pp. 40-42).
2 Julian's letter is lost. On Julian, cf. Letters 81 n. 2 and 136 n. 4. Basil is also mentioned as a messenger in Letter 38 n. 3.
3 The *Tome* to Flavian (Letter 28).
4 Silva-Tarouca at this point leaves out a sentence as a possible interpolation.

that Jesus Christ is true man is of necessity involved in numerous blasphemies. Either Apollinaris claims him as his own or Valentinus lays hold of him or Mani holds him fast—none of whom believed that the reality of human flesh existed in Christ.[5] If, of course, this humanity is rejected, there is no belief that the same being who retained the form of God was also born in the aspect of servitude with flesh and a rational soul. There also is no belief that He was crucified and died and was buried, and that on the third day He arose, and that He sits at the right hand of the Father and will come in the same body in which He was judged,[6] in order to judge the living and the dead. For these pledges of our redemption are voided if one does not believe that Christ assumed the real and complete nature of a real man.

Will the proofs for His body be called false because the marks of His divinity were outstanding? And will the proofs for both His natures be valid for accepting Him as the Creator, but no good for keeping Him as a creature? The flesh in Him does not lessen His divinity; the divinity does not remove the humanity.[7] The same Christ is eternal from the Father and temporal from the Mother. In His power He is unchangeable; in our weakness He is capable of suffering; of one and the same nature as the Father and the Holy Spirit as part of the triune Godhead, but not of the same nature as the divinity in the taking on of humanity, even though He is of one and the same Person. In that way the same Christ might be rich in poverty, omnipotent in subjection, incapable of suffering while enduring the passion, dying yet immortal. The Word was, in fact, not changed

---

5 Cf. Letters 26 and 165.
6 That is, by Pilate.
7 Cf. Letter 28, at notes 16-18; most of the ideas that follow are also in the *Tome*.

in any aspect of Himself into either flesh or soul, since the nature of God is simple and unchangeable, is always complete in its own essence, not experiencing loss or increase of itself, so exalting the assumed nature that it remains glorified in Him who glorifies it. Now, why should it seem incongruous and impossible for the Word and the flesh and the soul to be one Jesus Christ and at the same time Son of God and of man, if flesh and soul (which are unlike in nature) unite to make one person, even when there is no connection with the Incarnation of the Word? For it is much easier for the power of God to effect this union of Himself with man than for the weakness of man alone to effect the union of [its own two] elements. Hence, the Word was not changed into flesh nor the flesh into the Word, but they both remain in one, and the one exists in both, not separated by their differences nor yet indistinguishable because of their mingling. He is not one Person from the Father and another from the Mother, but He is the same Person derived in one way from the Father before anything began and in another from the Mother at the end of aeons, so that He might be the 'Mediator between God and men, himself man, Christ Jesus,'[8] in whom might dwell the 'fullness of the Godhead bodily.'[9] For there is an elevation of the assumed nature, not of the nature assuming, in that 'God has exalted him and has bestowed upon him the name that is above every name, so that at the name of Jesus every knee should bend of those in heaven, on earth and under the earth, and every tongue should confess that the Lord Jesus Christ is in the glory of God the Father.'[10]

---

8 1 Tim. 2.5; Letter 28 n. 14.
9 Col. 2.9.
10 Phil. 2.9-11.

In that Eutyches dared to say in the bishops' court that there were two natures in Christ before the Incarnation but only one after the Incarnation, he should have been pressed with frequent and solicitous questions from the judges to make him give a reason for his statement.[11] This would have prevented the skipping over as something unimportant what was clearly nothing but the outpouring of one who had imbibed poisonous doctrines. I think that in making such statements he was under the impression that the soul which the Saviour assumed had lived in heaven before it received birth from the Virgin Mary and that the Word joined this soul to Himself in the womb. But Catholic minds and ears do not tolerate this, since the Lord, on coming from heaven, brought with Him nothing belonging to our state. He did not take a soul which had existed beforehand or flesh which was not part of His Mother's body. Indeed, our nature was not assumed in such a way that it was created first and then taken on, but it was created in the very act of being assumed. Hence, that teaching which was rightly condemned in Origen[12] must also be blamed in Eutyches, unless he prefers to give up his view. Origen stated that souls not only had lives but even performed various actions before they were inserted into bodies. Now, it is true that the Lord's birth according to the flesh had certain peculiarities by which it was raised above the births of human beings; for one thing, because He alone was conceived and born without concupiscence from a stainless virgin; for another, because He proceeded from His Mother's womb in such a way that her fecundity gave birth while her virginity remained. In spite

---

11 Cf. Letter 28 n. 50.
12 Cf. Origen, *De princip.* II.6,3 (*PG* 11.210-215). There is no particular reason for saying that Eutyches' teaching also included this idea.

of this, His flesh was not of a nature different from ours; and a soul was breathed into Him as into the rest of men, not from a different source, not superior because of a difference in kind but in the greatness of its excellence. He had no opposition in His flesh, nor did any lack of harmony in desires cause a conflict of wills. His bodily senses were vigorous without the law of sin; His emotions, which were real, were not tempted by allurements and did not give way to harmful influences since they were under the control of His divinity and His mind. True man was united to true God. As for His soul, it was not brought down from a previous existence in heaven; as for His flesh, it was not created out of nothing. He possessed the same person in the divinity of the Word and had a nature in common with us so far as His body and soul were concerned. He would not be the 'Mediator between God and men' unless the same God and the same man were one and real in both aspects. The vast amount of material entices one to discuss the subject at length, but for one of your learning there is no need for copious elaboration. This is especially so since we have already sent our brother Flavian by our envoys a letter which is adequate for strengthening the minds not only of priests but also of the laity. As we believe, God's mercy will see to it that, without the loss of any soul, what is sound can be protected and what is wounded can be cured, even in the face of tricks of the Devil. God keep you safe, dearest brother.

Issued on the thirteenth of June in the consulship of the most illustrious Asturius and Protogenes.

[*36* (Schwartz, II.4, p. 17). A note from Leo to Flavian, June 20, 449, to acknowledge receipt of Letter 26. He sees no need of a council, but will comply with the emperor's request. It is considered suspect by Silva-Tarouca, *Nuovi Studi*, p. 183.]

37. Bishop Leo, to the most glorious and clement Theodosius, Augustus (June 20 449).[1]

From the letter[2] received from your Clemency I have concluded that the universal Church should greatly rejoice over your desire that the Christian faith, in which God is honored and worshiped, should have in it no variation and no discord. What more efficacious support can there be for obtaining God's mercy in human affairs than to have everyone present to His majesty but one act of thanksgiving and the offering of a single profession of faith? In this offering, the devotion of the priests and of all the faithful will thus be finally complete when no one holds any other opinion than the one which Christ ordered to be preached and believed about Him concerning what was done for our redemption through the only-begotten Son of God, Himself true God. No consideration will permit me to be present on the day which your Piety has set for the meeting of the bishops, since in doing this I should not be following any precedents and my present obligations do not allow me to be absent from the city. This is especially so since the point of faith at issue is so obvious

1 The texts here are Silva-Tarouca, 15 x; Schwartz, II.4, p. 17.
2 That is, a letter received on May 13, as stated in Letter 31.

that it would have been more reasonable to have refrained from summoning a council.³ Although I cannot come, I have striven zealously (in so far as the Lord deigns to help me) to comply in large part with your Clemency's orders. I have sent my brothers from here who should be capable, considering the nature of the case, of eliminating the stumbling blocks and of being present as my representatives.⁴ For the question that has arisen is not one about which there can be or ought to be any doubt. Most glorious and clement Emperor, Augustus, may the omnipotent God watch over your realm and your welfare unto length of days.

Issued on the twentieth of June in the consulship of the most illustrious Asturius and Protogenes.

---
3 His strongest statement to Theodosius II; cf., also, Letter 36.
4 Cf. Letter 28 n. 55.

38. Bishop Leo, to his dearly beloved brother, Flavian (July 23, 449).[1]

After our envoys had already set out, those whom we sent you in the interests of the faith, we received your Charity's letter[2] through our son Basil the deacon.[3] You rightly did not put much in it about the business which is our common worry, since the proceedings brought to us earlier had instructed us sufficiently on all points, and Basil, mentioned above, was at hand to answer our inquiries personally. We now send back our reply through him and exhort your Charity through the grace of our Lord, in which we trust, using the words of the Apostle and saying: 'Do not be terrified in any way by the adversaries; for this is to them a reason for destruction, but to you for salvation.'[4] For what is so destruc-

---

1 The texts here are Silva-Tarouca, 15 XI; Schwartz, II.4, p. 18.
2 There is a difficulty about the dates of letters exchanged by Flavian and the Pope. Leo wrote Letter 23 on Feb. 18 to complain about not being informed concerning Eutyches. Actually, Flavian had sent Letter 22 probably at the end of 448, but for some reason it did not reach Leo until the middle of May 449. Leo then acknowledged its receipt (No. 27) and by June 13 had written and sent on the *Tome* (No. 28). Having received Letter 23, Flavian sent Letter 26 with a new set of council proceedings, the receipt of which was acknowledged in Letter 36. Silva-Tarouca (*Nuovi Studi*, p. 183) considers Letters 27 and 36 as at least suspect, but that does not change the essential chronology. He (*ibid.*, p. 108) considers Letter 38 as the Pope's answer to still a third letter of Flavian's, '*Nulla res diaboli*' (Schwartz, II.2, pp. 21-22; *PL* 54.727), a letter ordinarily thought to be an alternate version of Letter 22.
3 Basil is mentioned as the letter bearer here and in Letter 104. He was also in Rome on June 13 (cf. Letter 35 n. 2). That would have allowed him only until July 23 to go East, bring back Flavian's third letter ('*Nulla res diaboli*') and then act as carrier of this Letter 38.
4 Phil. 1.28.

tive as to want to remove all hope of man's salvation by a denial of the reality of Christ's Incarnation, and to contradict the Apostle's statement: 'And obviously great is the mystery of godliness: which was manifested in the flesh'?[5] And what is so glorious as to fight against the enemies of Christ's birth and cross, on behalf of the faith of the Gospels? In the letter which we already sent to your Charity[6] about most pure light and unconquered strength of this faith, we laid bare what was in our heart so that nothing can appear to be uncertain between us on matters we have learned and teach in line with Catholic doctrine. Indeed, proofs for the truth are so clear and so cogent that the man who has not at once projected himself from the darkness of error into the brilliance of light and reason must be considered quite blind and obstinate. Hence, we want you to apply the medicine even of patience to the curing of this madness among the ignorant so that, through paternal admonitions, those who in the old age of their bodies are still mentally children may learn to obey their elders. If they put aside the emptiness of their ignorance and grow wise and if, having condemned every error, they accept the one true faith, the mercy of kindness on the part of the bishops is not to be denied them. But if the impiety, deservedly condemned, persists in its depravity, then the judgment previously rendered will stand. May God keep you safe, dearest brother.

Issued on the twenty-third of July in the consulship of the most illustrious Asturius and Protogenes.

---
5 1 Tim. 3.16.
6 Letter 28.

120   ST. LEO THE GREAT

[*39* (Schwartz, II.4, pp. 18-19). Leo I to Flavian, August 11, 449, asking him why he does not answer letters. Flavian could send no letter at this time, since he was already condemned and possibly already dead. Cf. Letters 44 n. 8 and 49 n. 1. This letter is considered suspect by Silva-Tarouca, *Nuovi Studi*, p. 183.]

40. Pope Leo, to our dearly beloved brothers: Constantine, Audentius, Rusticus, Auspicius, Nicetas, Nectarius, Florus, Asclepius, Justus, Augustalis, Ynantius, and Chrysaphius (August 22, 449).[1]

We have just and reasonable cause to rejoice when we learn that the Lord's bishops have acted in harmony with the canonical regulations of the Fathers and customs instituted by the Apostles. The entire body of the Church cannot but have a healthy growth if the members who are its leaders are outstanding for vigorous authority and peaceful rule. Accordingly, we ratify with our sanction the good action done by your Fraternities in the diocese of Arles. On the death of Hilary of holy memory[2] you unanimously consecrated a man approved also by us, our brother Ravennius, according to the wishes of the clergy, the nobles and the

---

1 Bishops of the province of Arles (split from that of Vienne; cf. Letter 10 n. 6; but see the list given in Letter 66).
2 Just a stereotyped phrase for a dead person; the attitude of Letter 10 had not changed.

people. We believe that the peaceful and harmonious election, in which neither personal merits nor the efforts of the citizens were lacking, was as much the work of divine inspiration as the choice of men. And so, dearest brothers, let the bishop mentioned use this gift of God and let him realize what is expected of his devotedness, according to the harmonious desires of all classes, so that, by being an energetic and moderate administrator of the task entrusted to him, he may measure up to your statements in support of him and may be in every way quite worthy of our favor. May God keep all of you safe, dearest brothers.

Issued on the twenty-second of August in the consulship of Asturius and Protogenes.

[*41*. To Ravennius, Bishop of Arles (*c*. August 22, 449), congratulating him and urging him to be moderate in governing and to consult the Holy See frequently.]

42. Pope Leo, to his dearly beloved brother, Ravennius (August 26, 449).

We want you to be circumspect and careful to prevent blameworthy presumption from being able to justify itself in anything. For, when it gains entrance by creeping in illegally, it stretches out to greater boldness in the name of the dignity it has usurped. We have learned that a certain Petronianus, footloose and always wandering about through Gaul, has boasted that he is a deacon of ours and that, under cover of this dignity, he is making the rounds of the various churches in that province. We learned this from the reliable reports of your clergy. Dearly beloved brother, we want your Charity to check such abominable boldness in this man, so that, after the bishops of the entire province have been warned and the man is detected in his trickery, you may expel him from the society of all the churches and thus prevent his repeating this illegal usurpation. May the Lord keep you safe, dearest brother..

Issued on the twenty-sixth of August in the consulship of the most illustrious Asturius and Protogenes.

[*43*. Silva-Tarouca considers this letter to Emperor Theodosius II as a spurious interpolation of Letter 44, devised by the Eastern eunuch Chrysaphius; cf. *Textus et Documenta* 15, p. 30, and his *Nuovi Studi,* pp. 150, 183]

44. Bishop Leo and the holy council which has met in the city of Rome, to the most glorious and clement Theodosius, Augustus (October 13, 449).[1]

From the letter[2] which, in your love for the Catholic faith,

---

1 The texts here are Silva-Tarouca, 15 XII, Schwartz, II.4, pp. 19-21 (Greek: II.1, p. 25).
2 That is, the letter mentioned in Letter 37 n. 2, received by the Pope on May 13. It announced the coming Council of Ephesus. By this date (October 13) the Pope had learned news of that council from his deacon Hilary. Appalled, he at once sent Letters 44, 45, 47, 48, 49, 50, and 51 to the East in protest.

your Clemency recently sent to the See of the blessed Apostle Peter we derived so much confidence for the defense of truth and peace through you that we did not expect that any harm could lurk in a case so simple and so well supported. We felt this particulary because the men sent to the meeting of bishops, which you ordered held at Ephesus, were so instructed that, if the Bishop of Alexandria[3] had allowed the bishops to hear read the letter which our envoys brought to the holy council and to Bishop Flavian, the noise of all strife would have quieted down through the exposition of the most pure faith, which we have received and hold as divinely inspired. In that way the ignorance would not spread further, nor would rivalry find an opportunity for doing harm. But while private interests are being carried on under the cloak of religion, through the impiety of a few such an act has been committed as to wound the entire Church. Our information has come from no uncertain reporter of what was done, but rather from a most credible one, our deacon Hilary, who escaped with difficulty rather than be forced to subscribe [to the proceedings].[4] We learned that very many bishops had come to the council, whose presence would naturally have been useful for consultation and judgment if the one who claimed the office of president for himself had been willing to preserve priestly moderation; so that, after all had freely expressed their opinions according to custom, a decision might be arrived at by calm and fair inquiry as to what was in harmony with the faith and of assistance to the erring. But we have learned that not all who came together were

---

[3] Dioscorus, friend of Eutyches, with the emperor's permission presided instead of the Pope's legate. He refused to allow Leo's letters to be read (Schwartz, II.2, p. 78, notes 24-25).
[4] Having escaped, Hilary wrote a letter to Pulcheria, telling of his experiences at the council (*PL* 54.838).

present at the trial itself. Indeed, we found out that some were not admitted[5] and others were let in who, at the bidding of the bishop mentioned above, impiously offered their captive hands to subscribe to the proceedings. They were men who knew that he would harm their position unless they did what he ordered and that the opinion he brought forward was such as to vent rage against the whole Church while persecuting one man.[6] The men whom we sent from the Apostolic See saw that this was so impious and contrary to Catholic faith that no pressure could force them to consent to it. And they constantly protested in the same council, as they should have, that what was being decided was not at all acceptable to the Apostolic See.[7] The entire mystery of the Christian faith is, in fact, cut asunder (may this not occur during the period of your Piety's rule) unless this most iniquitous action, which exceeds all sacrileges, is blotted out.

Diabolical iniquity subtly deceives the unwary and, through a semblance of devotion, so tricks the ignorance of

---

5 The principal person excluded was the accuser of Eutyches, Eusebius (Schwartz, II.2, p. 80 n. 16). Dioscorus used troops and by threats cajoled many bishops whom he admitted to sign the proceedings.
6 That is, Flavian, who was favored by Pulcheria. But her brother Theodosius II was at the time influenced by a faction headed by the eunuch Chrysaphius, a violent opponent of Flavian and Pulcheria. The entire matter was largely political. So long as they kept shouting that they followed Cyril and the Council of Nicaea, the emperor was deceived into thinking that he and they were Catholic.
7 The Pope's legates did not speak Greek and answered through Florentius, Bishop of Sardis (Schwartz, II.2, p. 50, notes 51-52). Eutyches did not want them seated because they had stayed with Flavian on the way out and were 'prejudiced' (*ibid.*, p. 59, notes 52-53). Hilary 'objected' to the new interpretation and to the anathematizing (as Nestorians) of Eusebius and Flavian since they had fought Nestorius, Eusebius while still a layman. Hilary escaped. There is no more mention of the legate Bishop Julius. He may have returned to Puteoli, allowing Hilary (who got away earlier) to report to the Pope. Leo I was the one who labeled such a council *latrocinium* (Letter 95). On the high-handed proceedings, cf. Hefele, *op. cit.* 584-606.

some men that it entices them to what is harmful instead of to what is salutary. Remove, therefore, we beg you, this peril to religion and to the faith from your Piety's conscience. And may you in dealing with divine matters display the same qualities as you do in secular affairs by the equity of your laws, in order that human presumption may not do violence to the Gospel of Christ. Behold me, O venerable and most Christian Emperor, together with my fellow bishops, fulfilling my sincere duty of reverence for your Clemency and desiring that you be in every way pleasing to God (to whom the Church prays for you), and in order not to be judged guilty before the Lord's tribunal for keeping silent—we beg you to order the restoration of all matters to that state in which they were before this whole decision was made, until a greater number of bishops assembles from the entire world. We ask this in the presence of Christ's holy angels, in the presence of the indivisible Trinity of the one Godhead, who is wounded by such action, since He is the source and guardian of your ruling power. Do not allow yourself to be burdened by another's sin, for we fear (and we must say this) that God's indignation will be aroused when His religion is being destroyed. Have before your eyes and reverently regard with all the acuteness of your mind the glory of blessed Peter and the crowns which all the Apostles have in common with him and the victory palms of all the martyrs, who had no other reason to suffer than their profession of the true divinity and the true humanity in Christ.

Because a few imprudent men now impiously oppose this mystery of faith, all the churches in our area, all the bishops, entreat your Benevolence with groans and tears to order the holding of a general council in Italy, on the grounds that our envoys loyally contradicted those men and Bishop Flavian gave them a written appeal. This council will be to drive out all obstacles, or else minimize them, so that there may no longer exist any doubt in the faith or any lack of harmony in our charity. That is, when all the bishops of the eastern provinces meet and if any of them, overcome by threats and injuries, have deviated from the path of truth, they may be called back to a healthy state by salutary remedies; and if those whose cases are more involved yield to better counsels, they may not drop out of union with the Church. Now the decrees of the canons established at Nicaea, which were drawn up by the bishops of the whole world, show how necessary it is to ask for this council now that an appeal has been made (these decrees have been added below).[8] Show favor to Catholics, as is your custom and was that of your parents, give liberty for the defense of the faith, which (so long as reverence for your Clemency is preserved) no power, no earthly terror, will be able to do away with. We are acting in the interests of the Church as well as of your realm and welfare so that you may possess your provinces in justice without disturbance. Defend the solid status of the Church against heretics so that your rule also may be protected by the right hand of Christ. May the omnipotent God watch over your realm and welfare unto length of days, O most glorious and clement Emperor, Augustus.

Issued on the thirteenth of October in the consulship of the most illustrious Asturius and Protogenes.

---

8 When a convicted bishop appealed to the Pope, he had a right to a retrial. This right was actually a canon of the Council of Sardica, c. 3 (Mansi, III 23). It had already become assimilated with the Nicene canons before Pope Zosimus (Mansi, IV 366). For the corrupted version, cf. Turner, *Monumenta* I.2, p. 456. Flavian's appeal is given in Schwartz, II.2, p. 76 n. 403. He also wrote a *libellus*, formally appealing to the Pope (*ibid.*, pp. 77-79), although he is reported to have died three days after the council; cf. Letter 49 n. 1.

LETTERS   127

[*45* (Silva-Tarouca, 15 xiii; Schwartz, II.4, pp. 23-25; in Greek: II.1, pp. 47-48). Leo I to Pulcheria, sister of Theodosius II, October 13, 449, asking for a council in Italy; he sends her a copy of a previous letter (No. 30), which failed to arrive, and a copy of Letter 44.]

[*46*. Hilary the deacon to Pulcheria: about Dioscorus and the Robber Council of Ephesus, from which he managed to escape.]

[*47* (Schwartz, II.4, p. 22). Leo I to Anastasius of Thessalonica, October 13, 449, congratulating him for not having been able to attend the Robber Council; he is to keep faith, adhere to Flavian, strengthen other bishops. It is considered suspect by Silva-Tarouca; cf. Letter 49 n. 1.]

[*48* (Schwartz, II.4, p. 23). Leo I to Julian, Bishop of Cos, October 13, 449, to console him and ask him to keep the faith. Also considered suspect; cf. Letter 49 n. 1.]

49. Leo, to Flavian, Bishop of Constantinople (October 13, 449).[1]

What sufferings your Charity has endured for the defense of the Catholic faith, and how great they are, we have learned from the deacon[2] who secretly slipped away from Ephesus. And although we praise God, who comforts you with the power of His grace, we cannot but grieve over the ruin of those who attack the truth and shake the very foundations of the entire Church. But your Fraternity should know (since God's providence always grants necessary aid unto His own) that we are omitting nothing that should be done for the common cause, so that, first of all, we may deserve to accomplish what is useful for the faithful as a whole. It remains for your Charity in the meantime to bear bravely those afflictions which, you do not doubt, will profit you for eternal glory. The bearer of this note will surely be able to give you an accurate report of the goal toward which we are striving, animated with faith and charity, the Lord assisting us.

Issued on the thirteenth of October in the consulship of Asturius and Protogenes.

---

1 Silva-Tarouca (*Nuovi Studi*, p. 183) considers Letters 47-49 as at least suspect because of variations in style. The text here is Schwartz, II.4, p. 23. It is fairly certain that Flavian was already dead when this letter was written. The Robber Council began on August 8, 449; according to tradition, Flavian died on August 11 at Epipa (Hypepe) in Lydia, possibly as a result of physical abuse received after Dioscorus condemned him. Cf. Pope Gelasius, *Gesta de nomini Acacii*, CSEL 35 443; Hefele, *op. cit.* 614-615.
2 That is, Hilary; cf. Letters 44 and 46.

LETTERS   129

50. Bishop Leo and the holy synod which has met in Rome, to our dearly beloved sons: the clergy, nobles, and people living in Constantinople (October 13, 449).[1]

We admit that our mind was afflicted with great sorrow when we received news of the events which took place at Ephesus; they were the opposite of what all expected. And we could not readily have believed that so much license was granted to wickedness if it were not that our son Hilary the deacon, refusing to be a party to the unjust sentence, had returned in flight (he had been sent to the council with others to represent us there). Indeed our delegates expressed their dissent in the council;[2] but the bishop of Alexandria, who claimed that the handling of the entire case was his sole right as president, scorned to listen to it. He induced the bishops against their will to co-operate in what he wanted, so that, although they found no valid reason for the condemnation, they signed their names to it under pressure. But we trust that these bold deeds will not please our pious and Christian emperor.[3] Now, since we have learned that your church is in turmoil over this matter, we thought you ought to be consoled and advised by a letter from us so that, in the defense of the Catholic faith, you may resist the iniquity of treacherous men. We assuredly do not want your Charities

---
1 The texts here are Silva-Tarouca, 15 xv; Schwartz, II.4, pp. 21-22 (Greek: II.1, pp. 50-51).
2 Cf. Letter 44 n. 7.
3 One wonders how much the Pope really believed this. Theodosius II, in spite of appeals from the Pope, from his sister Pulcheria, and his relatives ruling in the West, refused to consider the work of his presiding official at the Robber Council as a mistake. He and the heretics kept repeating that they were interpreting the correct sense of the decisions of the Council of Nicaea. For his attitude, cf. Letters 62-64.

to be overwhelmed by this misfortune, for a greater glory will result from your constancy if no fear and no threats pull you away from your noble bishop. Indeed, whoever dares to take over your Bishop Flavian's see while he himself is still alive and in health will never be considered a sharer in our society nor can he be numbered among the bishops.[4] Just as we have condemned Nestorius for his perversity, so we condemn by a like sentence those who deny that the reality of our flesh exists in the Lord Jesus Christ.[5]

Stand firm, therefore, in the spirit of Catholic truth and receive the exhortation of the Apostle through the medium of our words: 'For you have been given the favor on Christ's behalf—not only to believe in him but also to suffer for him.'[6] Dearly beloved, do not think that divine protection is or is going to be lacking to His holy Church. The purity of the faith really shines forth when the dregs of heresies are removed from it. Hence, we entreat you again and again in the sight of the Lord and likewise warn you not to be moved by anyone's snares or influence to leave the faith in which you are rooted and in which we are sure the most Christian emperor abides.[7] Rather, in the person of your bishop, may you have in the eyes of your heart Him on whose behalf this same bishop did not fear to suffer all the attacks that were made upon him. We want you to imitate him in every way so that with him you can share the common reward of the faith. May God keep you safe, my dearest sons.

Issued on the thirteenth of October in the consulship of the most illustrious Asturius and Protogenes.[8]

---

4 Cf. Letters 49 and 69 n. 3.
5 Just one of the tenets of Eutyches; cf. Letter 26.
6 Phil. 1.29.
7 Cf. note 3, above.
8 Silva-Tarouca reads: 'in the consulship of the men mentioned above.'

LETTERS   131

[*51* (Silva-Tarouca 15 xiv; Schwartz, II.4, p. 25; Greek: II.1, p. 51). From Pope Leo and the Roman synod, October 13, 449, to Faustus, Martinus, Peter, and Emmanuel, priests and abbots in Constantinople, with much the same content as in Letter 50.]

[*52.* To Pope Leo from Theodoret, Bishop of Cyrrhus, deposed in absentia by the Robber Council; he writes for instructions.]

[*53.* A fragment of letter from Anatolius, the new Bishop of Constantinople, explaining how he obtained the see. Cf. Letter 69 n. 3.]

[*54* (Silva-Tarouca, 15 xvi; Schwartz, II.4, p. 11). Pope Leo writes, December 25, 449, to Emperor Theodosius II to ask for a general council in Italy.]

[*55-58.* Letters written to Theodosius II by members of the imperial family in the West (Ravenna), siding with the Pope: two from Placidia (mother of Valentinian III and Theodosius' aunt); one each from Valentinian himself and from his wife Eudoxia (daughter of Theodosius II).]

[59 (Silva-Tarouca, 15 xvb; Schwartz, II.4, pp. 34-37). Pope Leo I to the clergy and people of Constantinople (December 25, 449), congratulating them for adhering to Flavian and resisting heresy. He proves the reality of Christ's body from the mystery of the Eucharist and His bodily life on earth; shows the necessity of the Incarnation to blot out Adam's sin, as the Prophets predicted, and indicates various errors preached about the Incarnation. Silva-Tarouca (p. 40) gives a different date; thinks it was sent along with Letters 54-58; cf., also, his *Nuovi Studi*, p. 98.]

60. Bishop Leo, to his most glorious and clement daughter Pulcheria, Augusta (March 17, 450).[1]

Your Piety's letter has brought me a great deal of joy and exultation in the Lord. In it you clearly show how much you love the Catholic faith and how much you despise the errors of heretics. O most glorious [Augusta], heresy is truly quite blasphemous and hostile to evangelical truth. It does not try to harm just a portion, but to destroy the very foundations of the Christian religion. It denies that the eternal Son of the eternal Father took from the womb of the blessed Virgin Mary the real flesh of our nature, and it attacks with condemnation those who could not be led away from the evangelical and apostolic faith by any error. And it pointlessly pretends to hold to the faith of the Council of Nicaea, in which it evidently has no part. Now, divine protection does not desert His Church, as the Lord says: 'Behold, I am with

---

1 The texts here are Silva-Tarouca, 15 xvii; Schwartz, II.4, p. 29.

you all days, even unto the consummation of the world.'² And that is why the Spirit of God arouses the solicitude of your Clemency and the concern of our heart in the same endeavor and at the same time, in order that we may both have the same aims as to the remedies to be applied. These I have already asked for and now request again with greater earnestness, having more confidence in my request now that I have received the backing of your esteemed encouragement. But I hope that the mercy of God will assist us so that, with your Clemency's co-operation, the disease of this contagious heresy can be eliminated and that whatever can be done profitably may be accomplished with His inspiration and assistance to the praise of your faith. There can be no surety for human affairs unless what we profess concerning God is protected by priestly and imperial authority.

Issued on March seventeenth in the consulship of the most illustrious Valentinian Augustus (seventh time) and Avienus.

[*61* (Silva-Tarouca, 15 xviii; Schwartz, II.4, p. 28). To the abbots Martin and Faustus, March 17, 450, reminding them of what he had written in Letter 51.]

[*62-64*. Answers of Theodosius II to Letters 55-58, sent by his Western relatives in support of the Pope. He assures them of his Catholicity, but promises no new council in or out of Italy. By Catholicity he meant that the Pope and Flavian were wrong, that he was following the decisions of the Council of Nicaea, as all the Eutychians claimed.]

---

2 Matt. 28.20.

[65. From the bishops of the province of Arles, asking the Pope to restore metropolitan rights to the Bishop of Arles; cf. Letters 10 and 66.]

66. *Pope Leo, to his dearly beloved brothers: Constantine, Armentarius, Audentius, Severian, Valerian, Ursus, Stephen, Nectarius, Constantius, Maximus, Asclepius, Theodore, Justus, Ingenuus, Augustalis, Superventor, Ynantius, and Palladius (May 5, 450).*[1]

Our sons Petronius the priest and Regulus the deacon have brought us your Charities' letter. By reading it we have learned clearly what an affectionate regard you feel for our brother and fellow bishop Ravennius, for you request that rights be restored to him which were deservedly taken away from his predecessor for his excessive presumption. But the Bishop of Vienne sent us his views by envoys and a letter, which came in advance of your Fraternities' petition. He complains that the Bishop of Arles unlawfully took upon himself to consecrate the bishop of Vaison. We must, of course, preserve reverence for the ordinances of the Fathers and still keep the good will of all of you, but not in such a way as to allow any loss of or infringement on the rights of the churches. For that reason we have pursued a middle

---

1 Only seven of these bishops appear in the list addressed in Letter 40; twelve do not. Allowing for a few changes in a year, we still cannot say just which bishops were in the previous province of Vienne (Arles). Probably, this list includes bishops from the section (Vienne) cut off when Hilary was disgraced, men who preferred to be under Ravennius of Arles. Cf., also, the list of Gallic bishops in Letter 102, and the list of signers at the end of Letter 99 (*PL* 54.968-970).

course of justice, one which disregarded neither customs begun in antiquity nor your wishes, in order to preserve peace within the province of Vienne.²

On weighing the statements presented by the clerics who were present for both sides, we find that both Vienne and Arles have always been famous cities within your province. In consequence, for this or that particular reason, first one and then the other has been pre-eminent for ecclesiastical privileges. Yet, among the people there is a tradition that at one time both were under a common jurisdiction. Hence, we do not permit the city of Vienne to go completely without honor, as far as ecclesiastical jurisdiction is concerned, especially since in the acquiring of its privilege it is backed by the fact that it was we who previously made this arrangement. It was our opinion that this power which we took away from Bishop Hilary should be transferred to the Bishop of Vienne. ³ We do not want it to appear to him that he has been suddenly demoted. Therefore, he will preside over four neighboring cities, that is, Valence, Tarentaise, Geneva, and Grenoble; with these, Vienne itself will make five. The responsibility for all the churches named belongs to the Bishop of Vienne. But the remaining cities of the same province will come under the authority and government of the Bishop of Arles. We trust that because of the modesty of his unassuming character he will be so zealous for brotherly love and peace that he will by no means consider himself deprived of what he sees conceded to his brother.

Issued on the fifth of May in the consulship of the most illustrious Valentinian (seventh time) and Avienus.

---

2 Even when Arles was a metropolitan see, the province was called Vienne.
3 Cf. Letter 10 n. 6. Leo's order is in *MGH, Epist.* III.15, p. 9.
4 Two manuscripts give a later addition: 'This order of Pope Leo was confirmed by the Apostolic See when Symmachus was Pope in the consulship of the most illustrious Probus.

67. Bishop Leo, to his dearly beloved brother, Ravennius (May 5, 450).[1]

We have kept our sons Petronius[2] the priest and Regulus the deacon in Rome for a long time. For they have merited this favor from us, and the cause of the faith, now attacked by the heresy of certain men, demanded it. We wanted, in fact, to have them present at our discussions and to pick up all the information which we wished brought to all our brothers and fellow bishops through you, dearly beloved. We particularly delegate your Charity to bring to the notice of all our brothers the letter which we sent to the East to defend the faith, as well as the letter of Cyril of holy memory, which is in complete agreement with our views.[3] Being thus informed against those who think that the Lord's Incarnation can be contaminated by depraved interpretations, they may fortify themselves beforehand with spiritual strength. Dearly beloved brother, you have an excellent opportunity to recommend the start of your episcopacy to all the churches and to our God by carrying out this task in the way which we have entrusted it to you and enjoined it upon you. There are, however, matters which were not to be put down in a letter. When you have learned of these from the report of our sons (already named), you will carry them out efficiently and laudably, as we mentioned, with the Lord's assistance. May God keep you safe, dearest brother.

Issued on the fifth of May in the consulship of the most illustrious Valentinian (seventh time) and Avenius.

---
1 The text here is Silva-Tarouca, 15, p. 89; cf., also, his *Nuovi Studi*, pp. 101-102.
2 Petronius is listed as a bishop at the end of Letter 99.
3 This is the first time the letter of Cyril (*II ad Nestorium*) is mentioned as on a par with his *Tome;* cf. Letter 69 n. 4.

LETTERS   137

[*68.* A letter from Bishops Ceretius, Salonius, and Veranus in Gaul, thanking the Pope for the *Tome.* They send copies to be corrected or added to. Oddly, their names do not appear in the list of Gallic signers at the end of Letter 99.]

69. Bishop Leo, to the most glorious and clement Theodosius, Augustus (July 16, 450).[1]

In the midst of the anxieties which we suffer for the faith all your Piety's letters have indeed given us the greatest hope of security through your support of the Council of Nicaea[2] to the extent that you do not permit the priests of the Lord to deviate from it, as you have often said in letters. But to prevent my seeming to have done anything prejudicial to the defense of Catholic doctrine, it was my idea that there should meanwhile be no rash exchange of letters between the two sides concerning the consecration of the man who has begun to preside over the church of Constantinople.[3] I was not refusing my affection, but, rather, awaiting an expression of Catholic truth on his part. I beg your Clemency to bear calmly with this so that, once he has proved himself to be toward the Catholic faith what we want him to be, we

---
1 The texts here are Silva-Tarouca, 15 xviiii; Schwartz, II.4, pp. 30-31).
2 All Eutychians claimed this; cf. Letter 50 n. 3.
3 This was Anatolius, really a deacon of Alexandria, but serving Dioscorus at the court of Constantinople. Was he regularly elected there by the clergy and people in a city not his own? He must certainly have been of the party of Dioscorus, who consecrated him. Naturally, the Pope was slow to accept such a successor to Flavian. Anatolius had written the Pope (Letter 53); cf., also, the Greek in Schwartz, II.4, p. xxxv. For more on Anatolius, cf. Letter 104.

may rejoice more fully and securely over his not being contaminated. To keep any sinister suspicion from worrying him, I remove all occasion of difficulty and ask for nothing that may appear difficult or questionable, but I invite him to do what no Catholic person may refuse to do. Now, there have been well known and famous men throughout all the world who have shone forth before our times by their preaching of Catholic truth, both in Greek and in Latin. Certain men of our generation also have recourse to their knowledge and teaching and from their writings produce instruction of equal value and in great quantity to cut down the heresy which is now springing up, just as it once destroyed the heresy of Nestorius. Let him, then, read over carefully what has been preserved from the holy Fathers, and likewise constantly preached by them, concerning the Lord's Incarnation. There is, too, a letter from Cyril of holy memory, Bishop of Alexandria, in which he attempts to correct and reform Nestorius, criticizing his false teachings and clearly setting forth the faith as defined at Nicaea, a letter sent by him and preserved in the archives of the Apostolic See.[4] When [the new bishop] notes that this letter agrees with the views of previous writers, let him also review the proceedings of the Council of Ephesus. The testimony of Catholic priests concerning the Lord's Incarnation against the infidelity of Nestorius was brought forward and inserted in those proceedings by Cyril of holy memory. Let him also not scorn to read my letter, which he will find to concur on all points with the piety of the Fathers.[5] When he realizes that what would have been useful to Nestorius is the

---

4 In Schwartz, I.5, pp. 337-340 (Greek: I.1, pp. 25-28). Cf. Letter 67 n. 3.
5 That is, Letter 28 (the *Tome*). For the supporting passages from the Fathers, cf. Letter 88 n. 5, and at the end of Letter 165.

very thing being asked and expected of him, he should agree with all his heart with the views of Catholics, so as to express without the slightest reservation before the clergy and all the people an untainted profession of the common faith. This should be sent to the Apostolic See, to all the Lord's bishops and churches, so that, with the world made peaceful by one faith, we can all say what the angels sang as the Saviour of the world was born of the Virgin Mary: 'Glory to God in the highest, and peace on earth among men of good will.'[6]

Now, we and our blessed predecessors, whose teachings we venerate and follow, abide in the harmony of one faith, as the heads of all provinces attest. May the most devoted faith, therefore, of your Clemency act to have a document reach us as soon as possible, such as is our due from the Bishop of Constantinople, as from an approved and Catholic priest. It should, of course, clearly and frankly protest that, if someone believes or asserts anything about the Incarnation of the Word of God other than what is set forth in my profession of faith and that of all Catholics, he will expel such a one from his church. Then we can display toward him, as he deserves, our fraternal charity in Christ. In order that a speedier and fuller result may come from our salutary remedies, God lending His assistance through your Clemency's faith, I am sending to your Piety my brothers and fellow bishops Abundius and Aetherius, as well as the priests Basil and Senator,[7] whose loyalty has been proved to me. Through them and the clear

---

[6] Luke 2.14.
[7] Theodosius II died before this letter arrived. Tho four envoys, sent to test Anatolius' Catholicity, were just in time to attend the provincial Council of Constantinople noted in Letter 80 n. 3. For an account of the two bishops and two priests and their dioceses in Italy, cf. P. Mouterde, 'St. Abundius de Côme et ses trois compagnons à un synode de Constantinople en 450,' *Analecta Bolland.* 48 (1930) 124-129.

instruction we are sending with them you can deign to learn what it is we believe. Thus, if the Bishop of Constantinople agrees to the same profession with all his heart, we may in security rejoice over peace in the Church, as is fitting, and no semblance of doubt may appear to be left to trouble us with suspicions that are possibly without foundation. But if some men are at variance with the purity of our faith and the authority of the Fathers, then may your Clemency allow the holding of a universal council inside Italy, as the synod which met here in Rome to deal with this matter has joined me in requesting. Thus, when all come together, corrective measures may be planned for those who have fallen through ignorance or error; and in future no one may be at liberty to speak of the Council of Nicaea in a way that proves him to be at variance with its beliefs. For it will benefit the universal Church as well as your government if, in a single profession of faith by the whole world, there is adherence to belief in one God, one faith, one pledge of man's salvation. May the omnipotent God watch over your realm and welfare unto length, of days, O most glorious and clement Emperor, Augustus.

Issued on the sixteenth of July in the consulship of the most illustrious Valentinian Augustus (seventh time) and Avenius.

[*70* (Silva-Tarouca, 15 xx; Schwartz, II.4, p. 29). A letter, July 16, 450, from Leo I to Pulcheria, sister of the emperor, a stronger and more faithful character than he. The Pope usually wrote to her at the same time. The content is about the same as in Letter 69.]

LETTERS 141

[*71* (Schwartz, II.4, pp. 31-32). A letter from Leo I, July 16, 450, to the abbots of Constantinople, complaining of Anatolius' delay in sending to Rome a profession of his faith. A mention of the four papal envoys, as in Letter 69.]

[*72*. Leo I to a priest named Faustus (before November, 450), praising his faith and exhorting him to be alert.]

[*73*. Letter from Valentinian III and the now Eastern emperor, Marcian (*c.* September 1, 450), accepting the primacy of the Pope and promising to root out heresy by holding another council.]

[*74* Schwartz, II.4, p. 32). A letter of encouragement for a priest, Martin, September 13, 450. It is considered spurious by Silva-Tarouca, *Nuovi Studi,* p. 183; if genuine, it must have been written before Leo knew of the death of Theodosius II.]

75. Bishop Leo, to his dearly beloved sons Faustus and Martin, priest and abbots (November 9, 450).[1]

I gladly take every occasion of writing and do not cease to address your Charities with priestly affection, so that you can learn from the very frequency of the letters how much concern we have for the entire Church. It is proper that your Pieties should share in our labors for the zealous defense of the most pure faith of this Church. We have sent our brothers, bishops and priests, in the interest of the Christian religion, and we trust that they have been with you for some time.[2] From all the instructions we gave through them you could have found out in a most complete way how intolerable it is to all the priests in our area that certain men in their irreligious folly have tried to attack the pledge of man's redemption. And now through our son, Count Maximus, we constantly urge you by our words to hold fast to spiritual stability against the precursors of Antichrist, now that the liberty of those who are Catholic has been increased through the mercy of God.[3] As blessed John says: 'Every spirit that confesses that Jesus Christ has come in the flesh is of God. And every spirit that severs Jesus is not of God, but is of Antichrist.[4]

---
1 The texts here are Silva-Tarouca, 15 xxi; Schwartz, II.4, p. 33.
2 Theodosius II died of a fall from a horse in July, 450. His sister Pulcheria married a tribune, Marcian, who was at once accepted as emperor. They immediately began to undo the work of the Robber Council of Ephesus. For these envoys, cf. Letter 69 n. 7.
3 The count had been sent by Pulcheria to announce the death of Theodosius II; that death, the Pope hoped and was probably told by the Count, would restore Catholic teaching. Pulcheria had previously been unable to oppose her brother's views.
4 1 John 4.2,3.

Nestorius and Eutyches (involved in different errors, it is true, but having the same spirit of falsehood) were intent on attacking Christ, whereas Catholic faith, imbued with apostolic and evangelical doctrine, detests and condemns both men. This faith confesses that, from the time when the Word co-eternal with the Father was made flesh, the same one whom it believes to be the Son of God is also Son of Man. It professes that in the one true God and true man, our Lord Jesus Christ, it adores not one nature but one person. Take a constant stand and act vigorously, united with us in this faith, inseparably and without deviation. And if there are some delays in carrying out these demands of ours, your Charities should nevertheless instruct us with letters whenever God favors you with reliable opportunities. For it is a great solace to worried minds when they hear that things they wanted done have been carried out. This letter which we are sending to your Charities we want also brought to the attention of other Catholics. In that way they may know that these same exhortations of ours also urge them on to the defense of the faith. May God keep you safe, dearest sons.

Issued on the ninth of November in the consulship of the most illustrious Valentinian (seventh time) and Avenius.

[*76-77.* Letters from Marcian and his wife Pulcheria to inform the Pope of the arrival of four envoys. The emperor agrees to a council, but wants it held in the East. Pulcheria says that Anatolius, Bishop of Constantinople, has signed the *Tome* and is Catholic. She has had the body of Bishop Flavian brought back and buried with honor in the Church of the Apostles. She wants a council in the East to decide on the Catholicity and status of all bishops involved in the Council of Ephesus.]

[*78* (Silva-Tarouca, 15 xxII; Schwartz, II.4, p. 38. Letter from the Pope, April 13, 451, in answer to Letter 76; content about the same as in Letter 79.]

79. Bishop Leo, to his most glorious and clement daughter Pulcheria, Augusta (April 13, 451).[1]

Through experience we now have a complete understanding of what we always took for granted concerning your Piety's attitude. That is, although the Christian faith may be attacked by various tricks of depraved men, it cannot be disturbed so long as you are present and prepared by the Lord to defend it. God neither fails in His pledge to show mercy nor ignores the merits of your labor, through which you have long since driven away from the very vitals of the Church the crafty foe of our holy religion. That was the time

---
1 The texts here are Silva-Tarouca, 15 xxIII; Schwartz, II.4, pp. 37-38.

when the Nestorian impiety was unable to stand guard over its heresy because you, the handmaid and pupil of truth, were not deceived as to the amount of poison being instilled into simple souls by the embellished falsehoods of a talkative man.[2] This contest of powers continued in that, through your solicitude, those matters which the Devil devised through Eutyches did not go undetected, and those men who chose either part of the two-headed heresy[3] fell before the single power of the Catholic faith. This, then, is your second victory over the condemned heresy of Eutyches,[4] most glorious [Augusta]. Since he was long since beaten down and already defeated in the persons who were his sources, if he had any soundness of mind, it could easily have restrained him from attempting to stir up the already buried ashes into a fresh fire and thus passing over into the society of those whose example he followed. We are disposed, therefore, to exult with joy and to offer suitable prayers to God for your Clemency's prosperity —to God, who in all sections of the world in which the Lord's Gospel is preached has already bestowed on you a double victory and a double crown.

Your Clemency, therefore, should be aware that the entire Roman Church is most grateful to you for all the works of your faith, whether for having assisted our envoys in every way with devoted affection and for having brought back the Catholic bishops who were ejected from their churches by an unjust sentence, or for having brought back with fitting honor to the church he governed so well the remains of Flavian of holy memory, an innocent and Catholic bishop.[5]

---

2 Nestorius.
3 Cf. Letter 26.
4 Her present work to undo the effects of the Robber Council would be her second victory; the first was her support of Flavian when Eutyches was excommunicated. Cf. above, Letter 21 n. 3.
5 Her actions as reported in Letter 77; in Greek, Schwartz, II.1, p. 9.

The increase of your glory, of course, is multiplied by all these works, in which you venerate holy men for their merits and desire to have the thorns and weeds removed from the Lord's fields. From the report of our envoys as well as of my brother and fellow bishop Anatolius (whom you deign to recommend to us) we have learned that there are indeed certain bishops of those who apparently gave consent to the impious proceedings that are now asking for a reconciliation and are desirous of Catholic society. We agree to the granting of their wishes; but the favor of peace is to be bestowed only on those who have reformed and who have condemned, in a statement signed by themselves, whatever they did that was wrong, under the supervision of the envoys we sent and the bishop mentioned above. For, that just truth should coerce the obstinate and that charity should not repel those who have reformed are both characteristic of Christian zeal. Since we know to what extent your Clemency deigns to show pious concern for Catholic bishops, we have taken care to inform you that our brother and fellow bishop Eusebius is living with us and is a sharer in our society.[6] We commend to you his church, which, according to report, is being ruined by the man who is said to have succeeded him unjustly. We also ask of your Piety what we are sure you are doing of your own accord: we ask you to treat with the favor you should my brother and fellow bishop Julian,[7] as well as the clergy of Constantinople who by their faithful services adhered

---

6 The position of Eusebius is not quite clear. Theodosius II had not allowed him to attend the Robber Council's sessions. At that time he escaped to the West and lived with the Pope. But why, by April, 451, he had not already left Rome to recover his see from the person who had taken his place is uncertain.

7 Julian, Bishop of Cos, whom he trusted most in the East; cf. Letter 81 n. 2.

to Flavian of holy memory. On all matters we are sending instructions to your Piety through our envoys as to what ought to be done or arranged.[8]

Issued on the thirteenth of April in the consulship of the most illustrious Adelfius.

80. Bishop Leo, to his dearly beloved brother, Anatolius (April 13, 451).[1]

We rejoice in the Lord and glory in the gift of His grace. As we have learned from your Charity's letter and from the report of our brothers whom we sent to Constantinople, He has shown that you are a follower of evangelical teaching. We may thus rightly assume that through the approved faith of its bishop the entire church entrusted to him will have in it no stain, no blemish of any heresy. As the Apostle says: 'For I betrothed you to one spouse, that I might present you a chaste virgin to Christ.'[2] Now, that virgin is the Church, the spouse of one husband, Christ, she who does not allow herself to be violated by any error, so that throughout the whole world we may have a single uncorrupted body of one chaste society. We accept your Charity's fellowship in this society and we approve the record of the proceedings which we received, validated (as is proper) by the necessary

---
8 Cf. Letter 80 n. 8.
---
1 The texts here are Silva-Tarouca, 15 XXIV; Schwartz, II.4, pp. 38-40.
2 2 Cor. 11.2.

signatures.[3] In order, then, that your Charity's mind may in turn be strengthened by words of ours, we are now after the hallowed Feast of Easter sending you, together with our letter, our sons Carterius the priest and the deacons Patricius and Asclepiades, who were the bearers of your letter to us. As we said above, they will show how happy we are over peace in the church of Constantinople. It is a church for which we always show the concern of not wanting it to be corrupted by any deceit of heretics.

From your letter and from the report of our envoys we have learned that there are brothers who desire to share in our society because they are sorry that they did not hold firm against pressure and intimidation and gave consent to another man's crime. For they were so confused by fear that with trembling compliance they co-operated in the condemnation of a Catholic and guiltless bishop and in the acceptance of a despicable heresy. In their regard, we approve what was decided in the presence and with the co-operation of our envoys. That is, for the present they are to be content with being allowed membership in their own churches. But we want an arrangement made, with you and the envoys we sent sharing the responsibility, in which those who condemn their erroneous deeds, making full satisfaction, and who choose to accuse rather than defend themselves may rejoice in being united with us in peace and fellowship. But this is only to be if they previously condemn by a suitable anathema the doctrines which they accepted against the Catholic faith. If the

---

[3] When Theodosius II died, some sort of synod must have been held under Anatolius, Bishop of Constantinople. The envoys of the Pope, sent for a different reason (cf. Letter 69 n. 7), attended this synod. There the *Tome* was at last signed. Cf. P. Mouterde, 'Frag. d'actes d'un synode tenu à Constantinople en 450,' *Mélanges de l'Université St. Joseph, Beyrouth*, XV (1930) 35-50.

true High Priest does not atone for us, using the nature proper to us, and the true blood of the spotless Lamb does not cleanse us, then a true priesthood and true sacrifices do not exist in any other way in God's Church, which is the Body of Christ. Although He is seated at the right hand of the Father, He performs the sacrament of atonement in the same flesh which He assumed from the Virgin. As the Apostle says: 'It is Christ Jesus who died; yes, and rose again, and he who is at the right hand of God, who also intercedes for us.'[4] Indeed, no blame can be attached to our kindness when we take back those who make satisfaction, those for whom we grieved when they were deceived. The favor of being associated with us is not to be harshly denied, nor should it be bestowed at random. For, just as it is fully consistent with fatherly devotion to bestow the Lord's charity on the oppressed, so also is it just to lay the full blame on those who started the disturbance.

As for calling out the names of Dioscorus, Juvenal, and Eustathius at the holy altar,[5] the proper course for your Charity to adhere to is the one which our envoys stationed in your city said should be followed. It is a course which will not be inconsistent with the honor due to the memory of holy Flavian and one which will not cause the minds of the Christian people to be unfavorable to you. It is absolutely unjust and incongruous that those who distressed the guiltless and Catholic by persecuting them should have their names indiscriminately coupled with those of the saints. It is they

---

4 Rom. 8.34.
5 Bishops of Alexandria, Jerusalem, and Berytus, the chief troublemakers at the Robber Council (cf. Pope Gelasius' *Gesta de nomine Acacii*, CSEL 35, pp. 442.6). The early Church kept lists (called *diptychs*) of living or dead laymen and clerics of note, which were read out at services. Leo I does not say here what this 'proper course' was, but presumably the reading of these names was stopped.

who condemn themselves by their depravity when they do not give up a heresy which is condemned. It is but proper that they be punished for their disloyalty or else be put to bother to obtain pardon.

Our brother and fellow bishop Julian[6] and those clerics who by faithful service adhered to Flavian of holy memory—these we also want to adhere to your Charity. They may thus realize that Flavian (who we know lives with our God through the merits of his faith) is present with them in your person. This, also, we want your Charity to know: Our brother and fellow bishop Eusebius, who for the faith's sake endured many dangers and trials, is living with us for the present and now remains associated with us.[7] We want his church protected through your solicitude so that, while he is absent, nothing may be lost there and no one may presume to prejudice his position in any way. See to this until he himself comes to you bearing a letter from us. And in order that a greater affection toward you may be engendered from us and from all the Christian people, we want this letter which we are writing to your Charity to be brought to the notice of all, so that those who serve our God may rejoice over your reconciliation with the Apostolic See. Concerning other problems and persons, however, your Charity will be instructed more fully in a letter which you will receive through our envoys.[8] May God keep you safe, dearest brother.

Issued on the thirteenth of April in the consulship of the most illustrious Adelfius.

---

6 Cf. Letter 81 n. 2.
7 Cf. Letter 79 n. 6.
8 The Easterners said in paragraph 1 to carry Letters 78-81 were hardly the Pope's envoys. In Nos. 78-79 Leo uses the epistolary perfect tense; at the end of Nos. 80-82 he changes to the future—meaning that his envoys will be sent later, that is, on June 9 (cf. Letter 83 n. 3). Possibly, the 'instructions' noted at the end of Nos. 78-79 were merely temporary.

81. Bishop Leo, to his dearly beloved brother, Julian (April 13, 451).[1]

Through our sons, the clerics of Constantinople, I have received your Fraternity's letter expressing your greetings. In it you point out that you have been distressed by great troubles. That is quite natural, since there has been no lack of that concern and worry which wear out the mind which adheres to truth in the midst of bold adversaries of the Catholic faith. And as you put it, your intention was to use the opportunity brought on by necessity to recall yourself to us and your fatherland.[2] I had, in fact, hoped this would occur so that I might learn from your own lips all the wiles of the heretics. But we thank God that both your safety and the cause of the Church reaped the advantage of your being free, dearest brother, to stay for a while with men whose beliefs we have learned to be acceptable to us, as the letter of our brother Anatolius attests and the actions taken in his city in the presence of the envoys point out.[3] Hence, by the clerics mentioned above who are returning I am sending you my greetings in exchange, and I firmly exhort you to remain constantly diligent against the snares of falsehood. Your own mind and our suasion support you in doing this. There have been signs of better attitudes on the part of many; I mean that they are sorry they were deceived and are asking to share the favor of our society after having condemned their perfidy together with its authors. Hence, we quite willingly

---

1 The texts here are Silva-Tarouca, 15 xxv; Schwartz, II.4, p. 40.
2 Leo I sent many letters to Julian, Bishop of Cos. It appears from this reference that the bishop was once a Roman, or at least from Italy.
3 Cf. Letter 80 n. 3.

accede to this, intending to restore to them this association which they desire, once they have fulfilled their promises. We have learned, however, that certain individuals are persisting in their obstinacy. It is but proper that these be quite strictly suppressed if they cannot be cured by kindness. To this end we will send our envoys after the venerable feast-day,[4] men to carry out what we have decided after they consult with you. May God keep you safe, dearest brother.

Issued on the thirteenth of April in the consulship of the most illustrious Adelfius.

[*82* (Schwartz, II.4, p. 41). Pope Leo to the new emperor, Marcian, April 22, 451: compliments for his desire for peace in the Church; the synod proposed is to treat only the views of Dioscorus and Eutyches; he is sending envoys.]

---

4 Presumably Pentecost, since Easter (April 8, in 451) was already five days past.

LETTERS   153

83. Bishop Leo, to his most glorious and clement son, Marcian, Augustus (June 9, 451).[1]

Your letter, which I was honored to receive, and my fellow bishops returning from Constantinople have given me much confidence to write to your Clemency. They reveal, not only through statements but through the very results of what you have already undertaken, that in you there thrives a God-given bulwark for the defense of the Catholic faith. Not only the position of the Church, of course, but also the vigor of your government, is thereby fortified; hence, you may deservedly ask for the protection of Him whose truth you cherish, O most glorious [Augustus]. The following items are due to your ability, are the fruit of your piety: my brother Anatolius has shown his integrity more quickly, and the revived supporter of an already condemned heresy did not receive a place in Christ's Church; the Catholic bishops, whom the persecution of heretics was recently unable to corrupt, were recalled from unjust exile; and the one who condemned Flavian of blessed memory recognized his impiety when the bishop's remains were brought back with fitting honor.[2] I trust that you will also accumulate tokens of other victories, so that, just as the church of Constantinople rejoices in recovering the liberty of the apostolic faith, all the provinces of your realm may glory in being cleansed from the contagious contact of a diabolical teaching. So, as I indicated in previous letters,[3] I am sending my brothers, Lucensius[4] the bishop and Basil

---
1 The texts here are Silva-Tarouca, 15 xxvi; Schwartz, II.4, pp. 42-43.
2 Cf. Letter 79 n. 5.
3 That is, Letters 80-82.
4 The Pope was not hasty in sending envoys to the council proposed by Marcian. The name of the episcopal envoy is variously written Lucenses and Lucentius; the Greek minutes of the Council of Chalcedon

the priest, who are capable of being responsible in my place. We commend them to your Piety's favor in all the affairs which are to be dealt with. I learned from my brother Anatolius' letter and the report of our envoys that many of those who were constrained by the faction of Dioscorus at Ephesus to yield regrettable consent to the detestable decisions are now asking pardon for their inconstancy and seeking to rejoin our Catholic society by making satisfactory amendment. Hence, the conversion of such men was not to be put off, for they are known to have fallen into these errors in which they did not have free judgment, not through their own thinking, but through the urging of a wicked and presumptuous man.

So, in order to prevent too long a delay from wearying those who are desirous of making amends and to prevent a careless lack of strictness from readmitting some men rashly and without a test, the regulations of the Apostolic See have enjoined that no infection of this pestilence be allowed in and no remedies for restoring health be rejected; the Bishop of Constantinople is to be associated with the Apostolic See in its deliberations. This zeal in correcting all that was wrongly done will, with the Lord's assistance, get speedy results if your Piety will deign to join his efforts for the restoration of peace in the Church. If you so rule that you deserve to have the kingdom of God within you, no falsehood will corrupt the Catholic faith, no heresy will disturb it; and no one will be permitted to desert the teaching of the Gospels and at the same time glory in possessing the priestly dignity. Now, we ourselves, as your Clemency remembers, also asked for a

(Schwartz, II.1, p. 65 n. 9 and p. 56 n. 4) spell the name Loukinsios; in II.1, p. 31 n. 19, it is Loukensios. Cf. Silva-Tarouca, *Nuovi Studi*, p. 122, where he is said to have been 'Bishop of Ascoli.'

council. But the necessities of the present time under no circumstances permit the bishops of all the provinces to congregate, for those provinces from which bishops ought particularly to be summoned, being disturbed by war,[5] do not permit them to leave their churches. Hence, your Clemency should order it put off to a more opportune time when, through the mercy of God, a more dependable security has been restored. Those whom I am sending will be able to talk with your Piety more in detail about this and other matters.

Issued on the ninth of June, in the consulship of the most illustrious Adelfius.

[84. (Silva-Tarouca, 15 xxvii; Schwartz, II.4, pp. 43-44). Letter from the Pope, June 9, 451, to Pulcheria, with much the same content as in Letter 83; he asks her to replace Eutyches with a Catholic abbot.]

---

5 The Roman patrician Aetius was having difficulty at this time checking Attila the Hun. The Pope felt that a council was then inopportune. Since Pulcheria and Marcian were already restoring Catholic dogma, he probably wanted no council at all. When the delegates of this letter failed to convince the rulers, Leo complied by sending the envoys mentioned in Letters 89-93.

85. Bishop Leo, to his dearly beloved brother, Anatolius (June 9, 451).[1]

Although I hope that your Charity is devoted to every good work, still, in order to render your zeal more efficacious, it was necessary and proper to send our brothers, Lucensius the bishop and Basil the priest, as we promised.[2] Your Charity is to be associated with them so that nothing may be done indecisively or sluggishly in those matters which pertain to the well-being of the universal Church. For, while those whom we instructed to carry out our arrangements are staying with you, those affairs can be treated with all moderation; that is, neither the claim of kindness nor the claim of justice will be slighted, but in everything God's judgment will be thought about without regard to persons. So that both these can be retained in the proper manner, let the preservation of the integrity of the Catholic faith be the first consideration. And since the way which leads to life is everywhere narrow and arduous,[3] let there be no deviation from this path either to the left or to the right. And since the faith of the Gospels and the Apostles defeats all errors (on the one side it hurls down Nestorius, on another it crushes Eutyches and his associates), remember that this is the rule to be observed in regard to those who attended that council which really cannot have or merit the name of council, one in which Dioscorus displayed his malice and Juvenal his ignorance. Any of those who, as we have learned from your Charity's report, are now distressed that they could

---
1 The texts here are Silva-Tarouca, 15 xxviii; Schwartz, II.4, pp. 44-45.
2 Cf. Letters 80, at note 8, and 83 n. 4.
3 Cf. Matt. 7.14.

have been forced to agree to a most nefarious decision, when they were overcome by fear and terror, and are now desirous of being restored to Catholic society are to be granted peace with the brethren once they make reparation. But they must first anathematize Eutyches with his teachings and his associates, in professions that condemn without being ambiguous.

In this case, however, there were those who sinned more greviously and claimed for themselves a superior position in the same unfortunate council so as to overwhelm with their arrogant prejudgments the simplicity of their more lowly brethren. As to these, if, perchance, they repent and if, ceasing to defend what they did, they are induced to condemn their error, if the satisfaction they make is such as to appear unquestionable, then let their case be reserved to the more deliberate counsels of the Apostolic See. Thus, after everything has been weighed and examined, an opinion may be had as to what ought to be decided about their actions themselves. And as we wrote you previously[4], no name of anyone in that group is to be read out at the altar in the church where God wished you to preside until a review of the situation shows what ought to be decided about them.

As to the advisory letter sent to us by your Charity's clergy, it was not necessary for us to put in a letter what seemed best, since it sufficed to entrust all the answers to the envoys, through whose words you will be quite carefully instructed about everything. And so, dearest brother, strive faithfully and vigorously to accomplish what is fitting for God's Church, co-operating with those brothers whom we have chosen as suitable agents in so important a problem. You should do this especially since the very nature of the case and the hope of getting divine assistance exhort you

---

4 Cf. Letter 80, at note 5.

and because the faith of our most clement rulers is so holy and their devotedness so religious that in them we have proof not only of Christian but even of priestly dispositions. Naturally, because of that piety through which they glory in being servants of God they will deign to accept all your suggestions which will be of profit to the Catholic faith, so that through their efforts, also, Christian peace can be restored and impious heresy eliminated. If there has to be additional deliberation about some men, send us a report in haste so that, having considered the aspects of the problems, we in our solicitude may decide what course should be followed. May God keep you safe, dearest brother.

Issued on the ninth of June in the consulship of the most illustrious Adelfius.

[86 (Silva-Tarouca, 15 xxix; Schwartz, II.4, p. 42). Leo I to Julian, Bishop of Cos, June 9, 451, commending papal envoys to his care.]

[87 (Schwartz, II.4, p. 45). Leo I to Anatolius of Constantinople, June 19, 451, about the priests Basil and John, who, when accused of heresy, came to Rome to defend themselves.]

88. Bishop Leo, to his dearly beloved brother, Paschasinus (June 24, 451).[1]

I have no doubt that your Fraternity has been made fully aware of the whole origin of scandals about the Incarnation of our Lord Jesus Christ which were stirred up in the Eastern Churches. Still, in order to avoid the possibility that anything could by chance remain unknown to your solicitude, I am sending you for careful consideration and review the very thorough letter of ours which we sent to Flavian of holy memory on this subject and one which the universal Church accepts.[2] Understanding thus how completely the impiety of this entire heresy has been destroyed with the help of God, you also, because of your love for God, may be imbued with the same spirit. And you may realize that those men are absolutely to be despised who dared to say that in our Lord, the only-begotten Son of God, who in Himself undertook to restore salvation to men, there are not two natures (that is, one of divine perfection and one of perfect humanity), following in this the impiety and folly of Eutyches. They are to be despised for thinking that they can deceive our alertness by professing to believe in one incarnate nature of the Word;[3] whereas, of course, there is one nature of the Word of God, in the divinity of the Father and the Son and the

---
1 The texts here are Silva-Tarouca, 15 xxx; Schwartz, II.4, pp. 46-47.
2 That is, the *Tome*. The date of this letter is close to that of Letter 89, yet there is no mention in it that Paschasinus is to be his chief legate at the Council of Chalcedon. Possibly the invitation was carried orally by Boniface (cf. Letter 89 n. 3), and the two proceeded by sea to Constantinople from Sicily.
3 On 'one incarnate nature of God the Word,' cf. A. Rehrmann, *Die Christologie des heil. Cyrillus von Alexandrien* (Hildesheim 1902) 333.

Holy Spirit; but, according to our belief, our nature was also united to that unchangeable substance by the taking on of the reality of our flesh. We could not speak of an Incarnation if the flesh were not taken on by the Word. This 'taking on' is a union so great and of such a nature that there must be no belief in a separation between the divinity and the animated flesh, either when the blessed Virgin gave birth or even in the act of conception. For divinity and humanity came together into a unity of person, both in the conception and in the child-bearing of the Virgin.

The impiety, then, which was already condemned and destroyed by the Fathers in previous heretics must be abhorred in Eutyches. This quite foolish man should have profited from that by avoiding what he was not capable of understanding, at least in view of what happened to his predecessors. This would have prevented his nullifying the peerless pledge of our salvation by denying the reality of human flesh in Christ our Lord. For, if there is no real and perfect human nature in Him, there is no taking on of our nature, and all that we believe and teach is, according to his impiety, mere deceit and lies. But, since the truth does not lie and divinity cannot suffer, both natures remain in God the Word in one Person; and the Church in speaking of its Saviour professes that He is incapable of suffering in His divinity but can suffer in the flesh. As the Apostle says: 'For though he was crucified through weakness, yet he lives through the power of God.'[4]

In order that your Charity may be more fully informed on all matters, I am sending to your Charity some writings of our holy Fathers on the mystery of the Lord's Incarnation, so that you may have a clear understanding of what they

---
4 2 Cor. 13.4.

thought and preached to the churches. Our envoys also presented these writings at Constantinople, together with my letter.[5] And you should know that the entire church of Constantinople, with all its monasteries and many bishops, has expressed agreement therewith; and by adding their signatures they have anathematized Nestorius and Eutyches, together with their teachings.[6] You should also know that I have recently received a letter from the Bishop of Constantinople, reporting that the Bishop of Antioch has expressed agreement with my letter and subscribed to a like condemnation of Nestorius and Eutyches, after having sent official notes to all the bishops of his province.[7]

There is that other matter which we feel should also be entrusted to your care since you have experience in reckoning dates for the Feast of Easter. You should carefully study and investigate in your area what we find set down in the tables of Theophilus and which causes us considerable concern; you should co-operate with those in a position to have skill in such reckoning and calendars.[8] Whereas the coming Easter, God being propitious, is to be observed on March 23 and in the following year on April 12 and in the third year on April 4, Theophilus of holy memory has set down April 24 to be observed in the fourth year. We find that this is completely at odds with the Church's customary date, for in our Easter calendar cycles (which you deign to know well) the

---
5 Quite likely, these excerpts from the Fathers were first taken to the East by Abundius (cf. Letter 69). Leo continued to add to the collection. For the text, cf. Schwartz, II.1, pp. 20-25; II.4, pp. 119-131; Silva-Tarouca, 9, pp. 34-43; the translation is below, after Letter 165.
6 On this local synod, cf. Letter 80 n. 3.
7 Domnus of Antioch had been deposed by the Robber Council; it is likely that the bishop here mentioned was Maximus (cf. Letter 104 n. 8).
8 Silva-Tarouca omits as an interpolation *qualiter . . . tenendus*, in Migne.

date assigned for celebrating Easter in that year is April 17.[9] And so, in order to free us from all doubt in these matters, we beg you in your solicitude to discuss this quite carefully with all who have experience, so that in future we may avoid errors of this sort. May God keep you safe, dearest brother.

Issued on the twenty-fourth of June in the consulship of the most illustrious Adelfius.

89. Bishop Leo, to his most glorious and clement son, Marcian, Augustus (June 26[?], 451).[1]

It was our belief that your Clemency could yield to our wishes by ordering that the council of bishops be put off to a more opportune time, as required by present difficulties. A really universal council could thus be held by summoning the bishops from all the provinces. But, since in your love for the Catholic faith you wished the meeting to be held at once, in order not to obstruct your devoted decision, I am sending my brother and fellow bishop Paschasinus,[2] summoned from that province which is apparently more secure, who can be present as my representative. To be associated with him are my brother and fellow priest Boniface and those whom we sent previously. They are also to add my

---

9 On the problem of dates for celebrating Easter, cf. Letter 138 n. 1.

1 The texts here are Silva-Tarouca, 15 xxxɪb; Schwartz, II.4, p. 47.
2 Marcian sent out invitations for a council (to meet on September 1) on May 23, 451; Leo sent envoys (Letter 83 n. 4) to arrange a delay. A refusal came back before June 24; Leo sent Boniface to Italy to meet Paschasinus as the principal legate, and the two probably continued by sea. Letter 90, with about the same content, was probably sent to the emperor by a different route.

brother, Bishop Julian, to their number.³ We believe that, with the Lord's assistance, these men will act with such complete moderation that all dissension will be repressed and whatever has come to be involved in dispute and confusion will be restored to the unity of peace and the faith. And no vestige of the Nestorian or Eutychian impiety will remain in the hearts of any bishops. For the Catholic faith, most glorious [Augustus], which we have learned from the blessed Apostles through the holy Fathers under the guidance of the Spirit of God and which we teach, does not allow either of these heresies to creep in. If, then, there are any sicknesses, if there are any wounds, which can be cured by a genuine amendment, it is our hope that a state of real health may be restored. This health, of course, will be unwavering and will not be likely to infect any who are credulous only when it does not seek to hide itself under any excuses. True confession is the only way to gain the remission of sin. But because certain of our brothers (we cannot say this without sorrow) were not strong enough to remain firm in Catholic dogma against the whirlpools of falsehood, it is fitting that the brother mentioned above and our fellow bishop preside over the synod in my place.⁴ I am sure that those to whom we have entrusted this task will work in this same council without hatred or favoritism, so that, once heretical impiety and only that has been cut out, truth and charity will reign in God's churches.

Issued on the twenty-sixth of June in the consulship of the most illustrious Adelfius.

---

3 In all: Lucensius and Basil (who had stayed in the East or quickly returned there), Paschasinus and Boniface, and Julian of Cos. Cf. Letter 109 n. 9.
4 Paschasinus, the legate, not a nominee of the emperor, as was Dioscorus in 449.

[*90* (Silva-Tarouca, 15 xxxi; Schwartz, II.4, p. 48). Another letter to Marcian, June 26, 451, agreeing to the holding of a council and asking that the faith be not discussed as doubtful. He again mentions the envoys.]

[*91* (Silva-Tarouca, 15 xxxii; Schwartz, II.4, p. 49). Leo I to Bishop Anatolius, June 26, 451, to announce his five envoys to the council.]

[*92* (Silva-Tarouca, 15 xxxiii; Schwartz, II.4, p. 49). He announces (June 26, 451) the envoys to Julian, Bishop of Cos, those to be associated with him.]

93. *Bishop Leo, to his dearly beloved brothers assembled at the holy synod of Nicaea, greetings in the Lord (June 26, 451).*[1]

Through love for our dearly beloved colleagues I had hoped for a firm stand by all the Lord's priests in a united devotion to the Catholic faith. I hoped that none was being corrupted by favors from or fear of the secular powers, so as to depart from the path of truth. However, there often are numerous occurrences which can bring about repentance, and the mercy of God overcomes the faults of the erring; hence, punishment is thus put off so that there can be room for amendment. For that reason we should follow the most clement emperor's advice, wholly dictated by religious devotion. He has advised that your holy Fraternities come together in order to destroy the snares of the Devil and restore peace to the Church. He wanted the rights and dignity of the most blessed Peter preserved, so that, in his letter to us on this matter, he invited us to be present at the venerable council. Neither the necessities of the times nor any precedent could allow us to do this.[2] Nevertheless, your Holinesses may consider that I am presiding at the council in these brothers (that is, Paschasinus and Lucensius the bishops, Boniface and Basil the priests) who have been sent by the Apostolic See, and that you are not then deprived of my presence. I am now present in the person of my vicars; and for a long time

---
1 The texts here are Silva-Tarouca, 15 xxxiv; Schwartz, II.4, pp. 51-52 (Greek: II.1, pp. 31-32). The council first met at Nicaea on September 1, but because of disturbances there it was moved by the emperor to Chalcedon, where he could watch and attend. The first session there was on October 8. Cf. Schwartz, II.2 (2), p. 4, for his letter.
2 Cf. Letters 37 n. 3 and 31.

I have not failed in my preaching of the Catholic faith, so that you, who cannot be ignorant of what we believe according to ancient tradition, cannot be in doubt as to our wishes.

Therefore, dearest brothers, casting aside completely the rashness of disputing, let the vain infidelity of those who err in opposition to the faith inspired by God come to an end, and let nobody be permitted to defend what nobody is permitted to believe. For in the letter which we sent to Bishop Flavian of holy memory, in line with the authority of the Gospel, the voices of the Prophets and the teaching of the Apostles, a most complete and clear statement has been made as to what the pious and genuine profession is concerning the mystery of the Incarnation of our Lord Jesus Christ.[3]

Since we are aware that the status of many churches has been disturbed by unprincipled rivalries and that very many bishops, because they did not accept heresy, were expelled from their sees and carried off into exile and that others were substituted for them while they still lived, let the medicine of justice be first applied to these wounds. And let no one do without what belongs to him so that another may enjoy what does not belong to him. When, as we desire, all abandon their error, none should lose his episcopal dignity, but those who have labored for the faith should have their own jurisdiction with all their privileges restored to them, as is proper.[4] But what was especially decreed against Nestorius should be retained, those decisions of the former Council of Ephesus, over which Bishop Cyril of holy memory presided at that time. Otherwise, the heresy condemned at that time

---

3 Letter 28.
4 The new bishops remain bishops, but sees are to be restored to those expelled by the Robber Council, if still alive (Domnus of Antioch was excepted; cf. Letter 104 n. 8).

may now feel itself in some way exalted on the grounds that Eutyches is being chastened by a just condemnation. The purity of faith and doctrine, which we preach in the same spirit as did our holy Fathers, condemns as well as prosecutes both the Nestorian and the Eutychian perversity, together with their authors. Farewell, dearest brothers.[5]

Issued on the twenty-sixth of June in the consulship of the most illustrious Adelfius.

[*94* (Silva-Tarouca, 15 xxxv; Schwartz, II.4, pp. 49-50). Leo I to Emperor Marcian, July 20, 451, with about the same content as in Letter 93.]

---
5 'In the Lord' after 'farewell' in the Greek version.

95. Bishop Leo, to his most glorious and clement daughter, Pulcheria, Augusta (July 20, 451).[1]

In every way I recognize the devoted solicitude of your Clemency, which you unceasingly display for the Catholic faith. And I thank God that I see you possessed of so great a care for the universal Church that I may with confidence suggest to you a course which I feel is in harmony with both justice and kindness. What has been done up to now without fault through your Piety's zeal and the mercy of God may thereby be brought more quickly to an end worth rejoicing over. Your Clemency has ordered the holding of a council at Nicaea,[2] although your Benevolence may recall that I asked that it be held in Italy so that all the bishops in our region might assemble, when summoned, if the safety of the times permitted. Nevertheless, I have accepted your order without disdain to the extent that I named two of my fellow bishops and two fellow priests who are capable of taking my place.[3] They were given an appropriate letter to the venerable council so that the assembled brothers might know the procedure[4] which must be followed at this judicial meeting in order that no rashness may hinder the dogmas of our faith or canon law or the remedies suggested by kindness.

As I have very often written since the start of this case, I wanted the following moderation observed in the midst of discordant opinions and carnal jealousies: namely, that the

---
1 The texts here are Silva-Tarouca, 15 xxxvi; Schwartz, II.4, pp. 50-51
2 Cf. Letter 93 n. 1.
3 But cf. Letter 89 n. 3: three bishops.
4 That is, a council could not publish anything binding until the Pope first approved it. Cf. Schwartz, I.1 (3), p. 58, for Pope Celestine's order; CSEL 35, p. 236, lines 5-10, Pope Vigilius' demand.

remedy of pardon should be given to those who truly return to unity and peace, in order to allow nothing at all to be torn from the integrity of the faith, nothing to be added to it. For the works of the Devil are then more forcefully destroyed when the hearts of men are recalled to the love of God and their neighbor. But it would be a task to explain how contrary to these warnings and entreaties of mine men have acted. And there is no need to include in the writing of a letter what they were able to perpetrate at that robbery[5] at Ephesus; it was not a council. There the leaders of the synod spared neither the brothers who resisted nor those who yielded to them. For, in order to harm the Catholic faith and to strengthen their accursed heresy, they deprived some brothers of their privileged office; others they infected with co-operation in heresy. Indeed, they raged more against those whom they removed from the ranks of the innocent by their persuasion than against those whom they made into blessed confessors by their persecution.

Nevertheless, since such men by their iniquity harmed themselves most and since medication must be applied more carefully to more serious wounds, in none of my letters did I ever decree that pardon should be denied even to such, if they repented. And although we detest heresy as most unrelentingly hostile to the Christian religion, still, if there is no doubt about their conversion and they purge themselves by a suitable satisfaction, we do not regard them as being outside the pale of the ineffable mercy of God. Rather, we groan with those who groan, weep with those who weep, and we employ the justice of warning in such a way as not to lose the remedy of charity. As your Piety knows, this is

---

5 The name Robber Council remained a label for this Council of Ephesus in 449; cf. CSEL 35, p. 379, line 18; p. 390, line 22.

not merely a verbal promise; it is also displayed in deeds. For all those who were induced or forced to agree with the presiding officers were granted complete forgiveness for their fault and the favor of apostolic peace if they rescinded their original decision and condemned what they had written.[6]

If, therefore, your Clemency deigns to reflect upon this assertion of mine, you will have proof that all I have done was with the sole aim of bringing about the destruction of the heresy without the loss of anyone's soul; and that to this end I have modified somewhat my customary attitude in regard to the authors of these most violent disturbances. I hoped that their tardiness could thus be aroused by some sort of compunction to ask for forgiveness. Although, after that decision, as blasphemous as it was unjust, their position among the Catholic brethren is not as honorable as it was before, they still retain their sees and they are in possession of their episcopal dignity. And they have the prospect of either gaining the peace of the entire Church by making real and necessary satisfaction or (may it not be so!), if they persist in their heresy, of being judged as their profession of belief deserves.

Issued on the twentieth of July in the consulship of the most illustrious Adelfius.

[96. Leo I to Ravennius, Bishop of Arles, July (?), 451, asking him to observe Easter on March 23 in the year 452. Cf. Letter 88.]

---

6 Cf. the prescriptions of Pope Liberius for those who repent, in CSEL 65, p. 157, lines 10-22.

LETTERS 171

[97. From Eusebius, Bishop of Milan, reporting that the bishops at his synod signed the *Tome*.]

[98. From the bishops at the Council of Chalcedon, to Leo I. The Pope is congratulated for maintaining Catholic truth. Dioscorus' misdeeds are reviewed. Eutyches has been deposed, having refused three demands that he attend. They ask the Pope to ratify their canon 28, granting second place (and the right to consecrate Eastern metropolitans) to the Bishop of Constantinople—in the interests of good government (not as flattery to the emperor's city) and as a ratification of the same claim made by a local council in the time of Theodosius the Great. The letter admits that the Pope's envoys opposed the canon. Cf. Letter 104 n. 5.]

[99. From Ravennius, Bishop of Arles, to announce that the bishops of Gaul have accepted the *Tome* as the right explanation of the Incarnation.]

[*100-101* (Silva-Tarouca, 23 xvii). From Emperor Marcian and from Bishop Anatolius of Constantinople; they go over much of the content of Letter 96. The Council of Chalcedon accepts the *Tome*. Anatolius is bitter against the Pope's envoys.]

102. Bishop Leo, to our dearly beloved brothers the bishops presiding throughout Gaul: Ravennius, Rusticus, Venerius, Constantian, Maximus, Armazorius, Florus, Savinus, Valerian, Constantius, Nectarius, Maximus, Asclepius, Maximus, Ursus, Igenuus, Justus, Valerius, Superventor, Chrysaphius, Fonteius, Petronius, Ydatius, Etherius, Eulalius, Eutychius, Fraternus, Victurus, Eugenius, Hilary, Verus, Amandus, Gerontius, Proculian, Julian, Elladius, Armentarius, Honoratus, Aparcius, Anemius, Dynamius, Maximinus, Ynantius, and Palladius (January 27, 452).[1]

We had indeed hoped to receive a letter from your Fraternities at the time you promised it in order that the expression of your views might also have been sent along with our brothers setting out for the East—the men we sent to the holy synod in our place for the defense of the Catholic faith. Although numerous obstacles caused you to be unexpectedly tardy, we were grateful to receive your letter through our brother and fellow bishop Ingenuus,[2] however late and long expected it was. And in reviewing it with joy, we obtained proof (as we expected to) that heavenly doctrine thrives among you through the instruction of the Holy Spirit. The astuteness of the ancient foe, through those whom it found to be followers of its falsehood, tried to wear down this heavenly doctrine in the Eastern churches. But the Catholic faith, which is immutable in any of its aspects, is always strengthened and made more illustrious by the very exertions

---
1 The texts here are Silva-Tarouca, 20 XLIIII; Schwartz, II.4, pp. 53-54. Compare this list with that of the Gallic bishops given at the end of Letter 99; cf. Cabrol, *DACL* IX 1343-1554.
2 The Metropolitan of Embrun, the official messenger from Gaul.

of its adversaries. It is the grace of God that effects this so that, if, perhaps, there were any who were less instructed or were less concerned about avoiding these insidious shafts of the enemy, they would become stronger against the lies of the impious after having received the armor of truth. Since, then, as the case demanded, you faithfully and obediently increased the confidence which, in the Lord, we hold in your regard, we are filled with great exultation.

And we know that it was with reason that we intimated to our brothers and fellow bishops in the East that all of us had a single and undivided profession concerning the Incarnation of our Lord Jesus Christ, in harmony with evangelical and apostolic tradition. We intimated that, concerning the reality of this greatest and salvation-bringing mystery, no disputes of heretics could bring us to accept anything different from what we have learned from the teachings of the holy Fathers and the authority of the immutable Creed and which we teach, now that Eutyches in the present and Nestorius before him have been condemned by the universal Church. If anyone chooses to adhere to their intolerable blasphemies, he will cut himself off from the body of Christian unity. No longer is anyone permitted to take refuge in the excuse of lack of knowledge due to ignorance or in difficulty of understanding. For it was to stop that very excuse that the assembled council of nearly 600 of our brothers and fellow bishops[3] did not allow any skill in reasoning or any eloquence in speaking even to breathe against the divinely established faith. Through the efforts of our brothers and vicars (whose complete devotedness stood out in every action), aided by God's grace, it was fully

---

3 *et merito* seems out of place before *roboratis;* Schwartz conjectures *iuste et merito abominando,* which can hardly be right.

and clearly apparent not only to Christ's priests, but even to the emperors and Christian rulers and to all ranks of the clergy and people, that this was the truly apostolic and Catholic faith flowing from the fount of divine solicitude. It was the faith which we preach as we received it and which we defend in union now with all the world. Those teachings which the former heretic as well as his successor (who told a different lie, it is true, but was his equal in impiety) dared to introduce have now been exterminated in the whole world.

Now, Nestorius was not tolerated for asserting that the blessed Mary was the Mother of the man only, a man later taken over by the divinity of the Word, that is, with two persons, distinct and separate, so that the same one who was the Son of God was not Himself the Son of Man, and there was not one Christ in two natures; but one was eternal from the Father, the other was temporal from the Mother. Yet, the authority of the Gospel teaches that the Word was made flesh in such a way that (as it expresses it to us) there were not two Christs and not two sons, but the reality of God and man in the one Lord Jesus Christ. Thus, the special character of both natures (that is, of the Saviour and the saved) cannot be confused nor can the person be doubled. Hence, just as Nestorius was worthy of condemnation for his teaching, so Eutyches (who followed an already condemned heresy), blaspheming by a different sort of profanity, was cut off from union with Catholic solidarity. For he tried to convince certain uneducated and quite simple people that the Word of God was made flesh in this way: He did not assume real flesh from His Mother, and that body of His was not of the same type as ours, but He had one nature made up of His divinity and the flesh. Eutyches thus said that the one Jesus Christ our Lord was a fictitious sort of man and a God who could suffer. Neither piety nor a reasoned account of the mystery accepts this; that is, that God could suffer in His own nature or that truth lied in the taking on of human nature.

The holy council has now with devoted unanimity agreed with the letter written by our humble self, a letter rightly[4] strengthened by the authority of my master, the most blessed Apostle Peter. It has cut off from God's Church these outrageous fictions which are the views of the Devil. It has cut off this abominable disgrace and likewise condemned Dioscorus of Alexandria for his impiety, to keep that church from suffering undeserved captivity under the domination of a heretic. I mean that church which, when the Gospel was first being written, was established by blessed Mark, the disciple of the most blessed Apostle Peter and in every way, naturally, in harmony with the teachings of his master; that church which later, in times closer to our own age, had as its most praiseworthy leaders Athanasius, Theophilus, and most recently, Cyril. Know, then, that all the endeavors of the Devil, by which he attempted to disrupt God's Church, have been brought to naught through the great mercy of God.

Therefore, dearly beloved, having given adequate thanks to God, your Charities should pray with us that as soon as possible we may rejoice in the safe return of those brothers whom we are anxiously waiting to see,[5] and that then we can send you fuller information about all that has taken place with God's assistance. We do not want to delay our

---
4 That is, the Council of Chalcedon, over which Paschasinus presided.
5 Presumably Paschasinus and the other envoys at Chalcedon; if so, then Leo must have received the good news of the council from some other source.

brother Ingenuus with this waiting, since he ought to return to you more speedily for this very reason: that the cause of our common joys may no longer remain unknown to you. We also want this information brought to our brothers the bishops of Spain through your Charities' solicitude,[6] so that the result which the Lord has brought about can be known to everyone. Farewell, dearly beloved brothers.

Issued on the twenty-seventh of January in the consulship of the most illustrious Herculanus.

[*103* (Schwartz, II.4, pp. 155-156). Leo I to the bishops of Gaul (February (?), 452, with a copy of the condemnation of Eutyches and Dioscorus, after the legates' return.]

---

6 As on other occasions, Spain received its news through France; cf. Silva-Tarouca, *Nuovi Studi*, p. 104.

104. Bishop Leo, to his most glorious and clement son, Marcian, Augustus (May 22, 452).[1]

The joys of the entire Catholic Church were multiplied by a great gift of God's mercy when a most pernicious heresy was rooted out through your Clemency's holy and renowned zeal. And our efforts reached the goal aimed at in a shorter time because they were assisted by the faith and power of the God-serving secular rulers. For, although, in the midst of any dissensions whatever, the liberty of the Gospel was defensible in the power of the Holy Spirit acting through the services of the Apostolic See, the grace of God was made the more apparent by granting to the world that, in the course of the triumph of truth, only those perished who started the corruption of the faith, and the Church was restored to its unimpaired state. That war which the enemy of our peace stirred up was ended by the right hand of the Lord fighting so successfully that in Christ's triumph there resulted a single victory for all priests, and only the darkness of heresy with its supporters was cast out by the brilliant light of truth. Just as by the very belief in the Lord's resurrection considerable assurance was given for the bolstering of the infant faith (since some Apostles had doubts about the reality of the Lord Jesus Christ's body), and just as all those in doubt had their uncertainty removed by examining, visually and by touch, the print of the nails and the wound made by the lance, so also now by the refutation of some men's infidelity the hearts of the hesitant have been strengthened, and what caused blindness to some is now profitable to all men for

---
[1] The texts here are Silva-Tarouca, 20 xxxvii; Schwartz, II.4, pp. 55-57 (Greek: II.1[2], pp. 58-60).

their enlightenment. Your Clemency deservedly and justly takes satisfaction in this endeavor. With faithful and special care you have seen to it that the snares of the Devil did not harm the Eastern churches, but that more efficacious sacrifices were everywhere offered to appease God when, through the man Christ Jesus, the Mediator between God and men, the profession of faith made by the people, the clergy, and the rulers was the same.

However, now that these matters (over which so great a gathering of bishops was held) have been brought to a good and desirable end, I am amazed and saddened that the re-established peace of the universal Church is again disquieted by the spirit of self-seeking. My brother Anatolius seems of necessity to have taken his own interests into account when, by salutary amendment, he deserted the heresy of those who consecrated him and changed over to agreement with the Catholic faith.[2] Even so, he ought to have persevered in reform so as not to jeopardize by any depraved cupidity the position which he knows he obtained through your kindness. Although his start was shaky because of those who undertook to consecrate him, we took note of your faith and active interest in the case and strove to be more kind in his regard than just. Our aim was to mitigate, by applying remedies, all the confusion instigated by the intervention of the Devil. These measures should have made him modest rather than immoderate. Even had he been legitimately and regularly consecrated for outstanding merits and by the best selection, still, no amount of support can be in his favor so long as he is in opposition to the canons of the

---
2 Since Anatolius had done little to show his Catholicity while Theodosius II lived, his amendment at this time seemed dictated by 'necessity.'

Fathers, the precepts of the Holy Spirit, and precedents set in antiquity. I am speaking to a Christian, a truly devoted and truly Catholic ruler: Bishop Anatolius greatly detracts from his own merit if he desires to grow in importance through illegal gains.

As is our wish, let the city of Constantinople have its glory and under the protecting hand of God, may it long enjoy your Clemency's rule. Nevertheless, things secular and things religious do not have the same basis;[3] nothing erected is going to be stable apart from that rock which the Lord placed in the foundation. He who hankers after what is not his due loses what is his own. Let it suffice for the man mentioned to have obtained the bishopric of so great a city through your Piety's assistance and my favoring consent.[4] Let him not disdain the emperor's city though he cannot make it into the Apostolic See, and let him not hope in any way to aggrandize himself through injuries done to others. The privileges of the churches established by canons of the holy Fathers and fixed by decrees of the venerable Council of Nicaea cannot be eliminated by any perverse act, cannot be changed by any innovation.[5] With Christ's help I must

---

3 That is, Rome can be first in spiritual matters, Constantinople first in secular matters; the emperor's presence should not raise the see's rank.
4 He really obtained the see through Theodosius' consent. It may mean that, with the return to Catholic teaching in the new regime, Pope and emperor might have ejected him, but did not. Anatolius gets all the blame for the proposed canon 28 of the Council of Chalcedon (cf. Letter 106 n. 10).
5 Canon 6 of the Council of Nicaea (Mansi, II 679); but the version used by Leo, as given by Turner, *Monumenta* I(1), p. 148, made Alexandria the second see, Antioch the third. The bishops at this time were trying to flatter the emperor by making Constantinople second in name also. It had often been that in practice, since its bishops often presided even when those of the other two were present. As usual, Leo addresses the emperor as being on his side, opposed to the culprit, Anatolius; actually, the emperor and Pulcheria were much in favor of the canon, as were most Eastern bishops, including Leo's staunch friend, Julian of Cos (cf. Letter 100 and 107).

render unwavering service in faithfully carrying out this task. The task has been entrusted to me, and it is marked down to my discredit if canonical arrangements, set up under the guidance of the Spirit of God by the holy Fathers at the Council of Nicaea for the governing of the entire Church, are violated with my connivance (may it not be so!) and if the will of one brother has more weight with me than the common welfare of the Lord's entire household.

Hence, knowing that your glorious Clemency is zealous for harmony in the Church and that you agree most devotedly to these ideas, which are in line with peaceful unity, I pray and with constant entreaties I beg your Piety to refuse all consent to these unprincipled attempts, which are opposed to Christian unity and peace. And I ask you to put a salutary check on my brother Anatolius' covetousness, which will harm him if persisted in. Otherwise, he will want to become greater than his predecessors, desiring things that are adverse to your Glory and to the times. Let him be free to shine forth with as many excellences as he can, but he will not share in these in any other way than by wanting to be adorned with charity rather than be puffed up with ambition. Indeed, he ought never to have taken the notion of this unprincipled desire into the secret recesses of his heart; but when those brothers and fellow bishops of mine, who were present as my representatives, withstood him, he might have given up his unlawful aim at least because of their opposition.[6] Both your official report and his letter[7] show that the envoys of the Apostolic See, as was proper, resisted him with contradiction that was fully justified, so that his presumption was the more inexcusable in that, when reprimanded, it was not

---

6 Cf. Schwartz, II.1 (2), pp. 94-99; the Roman envoys all opposed canon 28.
7 Cf. Letters 100 and 101.

LETTERS 181

checked. It is becoming to your Glory's faith that, just as heresy has been destroyed by God acting through you, so also all self-seeking may be crushed. For that reason you should do what is consistent with Christian and royal righteousness so that the bishop mentioned may obey the Fathers, plan for peace, and not think that his actions were licit when he presumed to consecrate a bishop for the church at Antioch, without any precedent to go by and in opposition to canon law.[8] It is from a longing to restore the faith and from a zeal for peace that we have refrained from setting aside this act. Let him, therefore, stop violating ecclesiastical procedures and turn away from unlawful excesses so as not to cut himself off from the universal Church in attempting what is opposed to peace. I prefer to love him acting without fault rather than to have him continue in this presumption, which can separate him from everyone else. Now, my brother and fellow bishop Lucianus,[9] who together with my son

---

8 Domnus was the vacillating Bishop of Antioch. Although favoring Flavian at the Council of Ephesus, he had voted in favor of Dioscorus, yet that council rewarded him in reverse by removing him from his see. Anatolius had then consecrated Maximus in·his place (Letter 88 n. 7); the latter retained the see at the Council of Chalcedon, but there agreed to pay a pension to the ejected Domnus (cf. Schwartz, II.2[2], p. 20). For Anatolius to consecrate thus out of his jurisdiction was against apostolic canon 34; c. 13 of Nicaea; c. 13 of Antioch I (Mansi, I 35; II 681, 1324).

9 Disagreement must be made with Silva-Tarouca's rejection of Lucianus in the manuscripts for Lucensius here, and in Letter 106, at note 16, and Letter 107, at note 2. It is true that Lucensius and Boniface hurried back to Rome after the synod, to argue against canon 28, but the Eastern bishops would hardly have entrusted their cause to them. They sent Lucianus and Basil the deacon from their own numbers—the two who 'did their duty in arguing for the canon, even though it was the wrong cause that kept the Pope from assenting.' Of the two bishops named Lucianus who were at the council, the most likely one was Bishop of Byza, substituting for the high-ranking Bishop Cyriac of Heracleia in Thrace (Schwartz, II.1[2], p. 141). There is added evidence for 'four' returning to the Pope, not two (Letter 101).

Basil the deacon brought me your Clemency's letter, has fulfilled with all devotedness the role of ambassador which he undertook. It must not be thought that he was delinquent in the affair; it was, rather, the case itself which failed him.

Issued on the twenty-second of May in the consulship of the most illustrious Herculanus.

[*105* (Silva-Tarouca, 20 xxxviii; Schwartz, II.4, pp. 57-59). Leo I to Pulcheria, May 22, 452, with much the same content as in Letters 104 and 106.]

106. Bishop Leo, to his dearly beloved brother, Bishop Anatolius (May 22, 452).[1]

As we hoped, the light of the Gospel of truth has been made manifest through God's mercy, and the dark night of a most pernicious heresy has been driven from the universal Church. Hence, we cannot but express our joy in the Lord that the task assigned to us has reached the desired end (as it is also expressed in the words of your letter).[2] Thus, according to the teaching of the Apostle, we may all say the same thing and there may be no dissensions among us, but we may be perfectly united in one mind and one judgment.[3] We con-

---

1 The texts here are Silva-Tarouca, 20 xxxviiii; Schwartz, II.4, pp. 59-62 (Greek: II.1[2], pp. 56-58).
2 Letter 101.
3 Cf. 1 Cor. 1.10.

gratulate your Charity for sharing in devotion to this undertaking. That is, your zeal was useful to those needing correction and you freed yourself from all co-operation with those in error. When your predecessor, Flavian of blessed memory, was rejected for his defense of Catholic truth, there was reason to believe that those who consecrated you had apparently consecrated a man like themselves, contrary to the provisions of the holy canons.[4] But the mercy of God, directing and strengthening you, helped you to make good use of a bad start and to prove that you were promoted by God's kindness, not by the judgment of men. Indeed, this situation is acceptable if only you do not lose this God-given grace by another offense. It is but right that a man who is Catholic, and especially a bishop of the Lord, should, besides not being implicated in any heresy, not be corrupted by any greed. Holy Scripture truly says: 'Go not after thy lusts, but turn away from thy own will.'[5] Hence, we must resist the many allurements, the many vanities of this world, so as to preserve true continence in all its fullness. The first slip therefrom is pride, the beginning of transgression and the origin of sin. For, a mind avid for power does not know how to stay away from what is forbidden or to rejoice in what is allowed; meanwhile, excesses are multiplied in an inordinate and unprincipled series of unpunished transgressions, and there is an increase of those faults which were tolerated merely out of eagerness to restore the faith and out of love for harmony.

Naturally, after such an origin to your being a bishop, one not without fault, after your consecration of the Bishop of Antioch (which you claimed as your right in opposition to canon law), I am grieved that your Charity has also erred

---

4 Cf. Letter 69 n. 3.
5 Eccle. 18.30

in the following matter. You have tried to infringe on the most sacred provisions of the Nicene canons, as though the present time (in which the see of Alexandria has lost the privilege of second place and the church of Antioch its right to third place)[6] gave you an opportunity to substitute your jurisdiction in those places and thus deprive all metropolitan bishops of the honor due to them. You would surpass these excesses, unheard of and never before attempted, to the point of turning into an occasion of self-seeking the holy council assembled through the zeal of the most Christian emperor solely for the elimination of heresy and the strengthening of the Catholic faith.[7] And you would force the council to a nodding co-operation with you on the assumption that there can be no refusal of illicit requests made by a multitude and that it is possible for anyone to rescind in any particular that arrangement of the Nicene canons, actually ordained through the Holy Spirit. Let no councils flatter themselves over having greater numbers present. And let no bishops, however numerous they may be, dare to compare or to prefer themselves to those 318 bishops. For the Council of Nicaea was blessed by God with so great a privilege that, whether ecclesiastical decisions are rendered by fewer or more, anything decided contrary to what those bishops decreed is completely without authority.

Quite unprincipled, then, quite perverted are these decisions, which are found to be contrary to the most sacred

---

6 Alexandria was temporarily out of favor because of its Eutychian bishop, Dioscorus; Domnus of Antioch also had failed to support Flavian, and his successor (Maximus) did not indicate his Catholicity until June, 451.

7 It was Leo himself (Letter 93) who wanted nothing discussed except the wrong done at the Robber Council. The fact is that the Council of Chalcedon passed twenty-seven varied canons that the Pope later approved.

canons. This haughty pride tends to the disruption of the entire Church, for its aim was so to misuse the council as to induce the brothers by corruption or compel them by intimidation to yield to it, although they were assembled only for the work of the faith and had completed the solution of that problem which was to be dealt with. Consequently, our brothers, sent by the Apostolic See, who were presiding at the council in my place, properly and constantly resisted the illegal move; frankly objecting in order to prevent a presumptuous innovation, without principle, from rising up against the Nicene canons. There can be no question as to their opposition, since in your letter you yourself complain about them, saying that they were intent on obstructing your efforts.[8] By writing this you, in fact, highly commend them to me, whereas you accuse yourself in your striving for what is illicit. For you were unwilling to obey them, seeking in vain for what is not allowed and, to your harm, yearning for things objectionable, which will never be able to gain any consent from us. May it not be on my conscience, then, that I supported with my energy so corrupt an ambition, and that it was not crushed rather through my effort and that of all men who are not high-minded but are in agreement with what is lowly.

Those holy and venerable Fathers who at Nicaea condemned the sacrilegious Arius with his impiety and established regulations in the canons of the Church that will last to the end of the world, these men are still living with us and in the entire world through their canons. And if by presumption anything is anywhere decided contrary to their decisions, it is voided without delay. Thus, the general regulations set up to be useful for all time may not suffer any change, and

---

8 Cf Letter 104, at note 7.

what was ordained for the common good may not be adapted to suit private interests; and with the preserving of those limits which the Fathers established no one may branch out into a jurisdiction not his own, but each one may spend himself in the fullness of charity, to the extent that he is able, within his own legitimate boundaries. The Bishop of Constantinople can reap the sufficiently rich fruits of this [apostolate] if he exerts himself in the virtue of humility instead of being inflated with the spirit of ambition.

Brother, 'be not high-minded, but fear';[9] stop bothering the most pious hearing of our Christian rulers with unprincipled petitions. I am sure that you will please them more by modesty than by pride. The fact, as you claim, that certain bishops drew up and signed a petition sixty years ago is absolutely no support for your viewpoint. Nor was the petition ever brought to the attention of the Apostolic See by your predecessors.[10] This petition, which tottered at its start and later collapsed, you wanted to prop up with support that is now tardy and ineffectual by extracting a specious consent from our brothers, one which, to their harm, they gave you after their reverential deference had been worked on to the point of fatigue. Remember the threat which the Lord makes

---

9 Rom. 11.20.
10 The East-West rivalry was one of long standing, though there was no attempt to assume Rome's first position. An Eastern council in the time of Theodosius the Great had also made Constantinople second, but the decree was never sent to or approved by the Pope. It is odd that Leo I and his legates were so opposed to this nondoctrinal matter simply because the old arrangement was made at the Council of Nicaea. In practice, there were numerous instances in which the Bishop of Constantinople presided when the two who outranked him were present. But, as had been agreed, no canon was published without Leo's approval, and the Easterners made a pretence of discarding canon 28. The battle with succeeding Popes continued until Innocent III, at the Fourth Council of the Lateran in 1215, granted second place to Constantinople. Cf. Hefele, *op. cit.* II 815-857, and below, Letters 132 and 135.

against him who scandalizes one of the little ones,[11] and
wisely realize what sort of judgment from God he will undergo
who has not feared to scandalize so many churches, so many
priests. Indeed, I admit that I am so bound by love for all
the brothers that, when any of them seeks what is not for
his good, I cannot at all yield to him. And you can plainly
see that I oppose your Charity with a benevolent intention so
that by saner counsel you may refrain from disturbing the
universal Church. The rights of the provincial bishops are
not to be snatched from them, nor are the metropolitan
bishops to be robbed of the privileges assigned to them in
antiquity. Let the see of Alexandria not lose any of the dignity
it earned through St. Mark the Evangelist, the disciple of
blessed Peter.[12] And let not the splendor of so great a church
be obscured by darkness from other men now that Dioscorus
is in disgrace by persisting in his impious heresy. The church
of Antioch also should continue in the rank decided on by
the Fathers and, having been put in third place, it should
never be lowered. It was in that church, where the blessed
Apostle Peter preached, that the name 'Christian' first began
to be used.[13] Now, the sees and those who preside over them
are two different things; and each individual's honor is
his own integrity. Since this integrity does not lose the glories
proper to it in whatever place it may be, how much more
glorious it can be when set in the splendor of the city of Constantinople if, through your observance, the canons of the
Fathers have a defender and if many priests have an example
of right conduct.

---

11 Cf Matt. 18.6.
12 Cf. Letter 9 n. 3.
13 Cf. Acts 11.26; and a discussion of Leo's source in Turner, *Monumenta* I (1) 157-158; 246-247 n. 4.

In writing this to you, brother, I exhort you in the Lord and warn you so that, putting aside the desire of ambition, you may, instead, grow fervent in the spirit of charity and adorn yourself profitably with its excellences, according to the teaching of the Apostle. For 'charity is patient and kind; [charity] does not envy, is not pretentious, is not puffed up, is not ambitions, is not self-seeking.'[14] Consequently, if charity does not seek its own, how greatly does he sin who seeks what is another's? I want you to refrain completely from what belongs to others and to be mindful of that statement which says: 'Hold fast what thou hast, that no one receive thy crown.'[15] If you seek after what is forbidden, you will, by your own effort and decision, deprive yourself of the peace of the universal Church. Our brother and fellow bishop Lucianus[16] and our son Basil the deacon, as much as they were able, zealously advocated the cause which you enjoined on them, but justice did not allow their efforts to be successful. May God keep you safe, dearest brother.

Issued on the twenty-second of May in the consulship of the most illustrious Herculanus.

---

14 Cf. 1 Cor. 13.4,5.
15 Apoc. 3.11.
16 Letter 104 n. 9.

LETTERS   189

*107. Bishop Leo to his dearly beloved brother, Bishop Julian
(May 22, 452).*

On numerous occasions your Charity has had proof of the constancy and fixity of purpose with which I guard the provisions of the Nicene canons, since I consider all ecclesiastical regulations to be disrupted when any item of that sacrosanct arrangement of the Fathers is violated. I am amazed that you could have sent such a letter[1] through our brother and fellow bishop Lucianus.[2] In it you think that special favor should be granted you. You thereby become seriously involved on behalf of a novel disorder if I agree to this illegitimate request. With however much affection I am attached to you, you will in no way succeed in inducing me by persuasion or bringing me by entreaty to ruin the welfare of the Church. If our brother and fellow bishop Anatolius is wisely aware of the divine privileges he has received and of my agreeing to favor him, he will be satisfied with having succeeding in getting the highest bishop to give thanks to God over his episcopacy. Such men as love him especially ought to bolster him with advice, so that he does not seek what is absolutely impossible and does not harm himself by striving for such things, since there is no influence he can bring to bear on me to cause me to yield to his wishes at the expense of trodding on arrangements made by the Fathers. Hence, in answering your letter, I warn you, out of the affection I hold for you, to consider as more important

---
1 Julian's letter has not survived. The texts here are Silva-Tarouca, 20 XL; Schwartz, II.4, p. 62.
2 The legate Lucianus simply brought the council's request that Constantinople be ranked second in importance after Rome; cf. Letters 104 nn. 5 and 9; 106 n. 10.

the welfare of the universal Church rather than desire to ask this favor for another, you, a man fortified by a most salutary and true consecration. For the favor sought is such as may not be granted by me or gained by you without both of us incurring guilt. May God keep you safe, dearest brother.

Issued on the twenty-second of May, in the consulship of the most illustrious Herculanus.

108. Bishop Leo, to Theodore, Bishop of Forum Julii (June 11, 452).

This is the order in which your solicitude ought to have manifested itself. You should first of all have conferred with your metropolitan on the matter which apparently required investigation. And if what your Charity did not know was also unknown to him, you both should have asked to be instructed. For, in problems which pertain to the general observance of all the Lord's priests, no inquiry should be made without the primates. However, in order that some sort of instruction may be given you, who in doubt consult me, I shall not keep silent about the Church's regulation concerning the status of penitents.

The manifold mercy of God assists human beings who have fallen, so that the hope of eternal life is restored not only through the grace of baptism but also through the medicine of penance. Thus, those who have corrupted the gift received in baptism, condemning themselves by their own decision, may obtain the forgiveness of their crimes. Safeguards were so ordained for the divine goodness that God's indulgence cannot be obtained except through the prayers of priests. The Mediator between God and men, the man Christ Jesus, gave this power to those whom He put in charge of His Church, namely, to grant a course of penance to those who confess and to admit to the reception of the sacraments through the door of absolution those who have been purged by salutary reparation. The Saviour Himself, of course, constantly takes part in this work and is never absent from those affairs which He has entrusted to His ministers to carry out. As He says: 'Behold, I am with you all days, even unto the consummation of the world.'[1] Thus, if anything is carried out through our services in due order and with a praiseworthy result, we do not doubt that it was given us by the Holy Spirit.

Suppose that one of those for whom we entreat the Lord fails to receive the gift of pardon here in the world, being cut off by any obstacle whatever, and (having a mortal status) finishes his life on earth before he has access to the remedy prescribed. After he has put off the flesh, he will then be unable to obtain what he did not receive while still remaining in the body. Nor are we required to weigh the merits and actions of those who have died thus. The Lord our God, whose judgments cannot be comprehended, has reserved for His own justice that which the priestly ministry has been unable to carry out. He wants His power to be so feared that this fright may be useful to all, and everyone may be afraid of what happens to certain tepid and negligent persons. It is very profitable and necessary that the guilt of sinners

---

[1] Matt. 28.20.

be removed before the final day through the prayers of priests.

But satisfaction must not be ruled out or absolution denied to those who in time of necessity or in the moment of pressing danger beg for the protection of penance followed by absolution. For we cannot put limitations on the mercy of God or fix limits to times. With Him there is no delaying of pardon when the conversion is genuine, as the Spirit of God says through the Prophet: 'If being converted you lament, you will be saved'[2]; and elsewhere: 'Tell me your sins first in order that you may be justified'[3]; and again: 'Because with the Lord there is mercy; and with him plentiful redemption.'[4] Consequently, we must not be niggardly in dispensing the gifts of God or disregard the tears and groans of those accusing themselves, since, in our opinion, the very desire for penance was conceived through the inspiration of God, as the Apostle says: 'Lest perchance God give them repentance . . . so that they may recover themselves from the snare of the Devil, at whose pleasure they are held captive.'[5]

Hence, it is fitting that each individual Christian pass judgment on his own conscience, and not defer his conversion to God from day to day and mark out a time at the end of his life for making satisfaction. It is dangerous for human weakness and ignorance thus to confine itself to a condition in which it restricts itself to the uncertainty of a few hours. And when it can earn pardon by a fuller satisfaction, it is dangerous for it to choose the narrow limits of that period

---

2 Cf. Isa. 31.15
3 Isa. 43.26.
4 Ps. 129.7.
5 Cf. 2 Tim. 2.25,26.

when there will hardly be time either for the confession of the penitent or the absolution of the priest. But, as I said, even such must be assisted in their need so that neither the act of repentance nor the grace of membership in the Church is denied them if they ask for it, even through signs showing an unchanged intention in case they have lost the use of their voice. But let us suppose that through some violence of the disease they have grown worse, to the point of not being able to indicate, when the priest is present, the request which they made previously. Then the word of those who are standing about must be of service to them, so that they may at the same time gain the fruit of repentance and of absolution. In regard to the individuals who have sinned against God by departing from the faith, the procedure set forth in the canons of the Fathers is to be preserved.[6]

Now, you will see to it, brother, that these answers which I am giving to your Charity's question come to the attention of your metropolitan. Otherwise, something may be done contrary to these answers on the pretext of ignorance. In this way, if, perhaps, there are some brothers who previously felt that there was something doubtful in these matters, the metropolitan may instruct them about all that I have written to you.

Issued on the eleventh of June in the consulship of the most illustrious Herculanus.

---

6 Cf. Arles c. 22 (Mansi, II 473).

109. Bishop Leo, to his dearly beloved brother, Bishop Julian (November 25, 452).[1]

The deeds which your Fraternity mentions as being perpetrated by crowds of false monks are serious and to be lamented with no small grief.[2] It is the impious Eutyches who, through the madness of his deceivers, wages war against the evangelical and apostolic teachings, a war which is bound to involve him and his associates in ruin. Through God's patience the coming of the ruin is delayed in order to make clear how much the enemies of Christ's cross are serving the Devil. Heretical depravity now comes out from behind the old veil of pretense and can no longer restrain itself within the limits of its hypocrisy. And all the poison which it had kept covered for a long time has now been poured out upon the disciples of truth, not only by the use of the pen but even in manual violence, in order forcibly to extort consent from men either of untutored simplicity or of panic-stricken faith. But the sons of light ought not to fear the sons of darkness in such a way that the healthy yield to those who are mad, or think that any respect should be paid to men of that sort. If those men prefer to perish rather than repent, we must see to it that they do not cause more extensive harm by being left unpunished and that they do not grow strong to the ruin

---

1 The texts here are Silva-Tarouca, 20 XLIII; Schwartz, II.4, pp. 137-138.
2 Theodosius, a wild monk, came from Chalcedon to Jerusalem ahead of Bishop Juvenal. Irked by Juvenal's return to Catholic teaching, he seized the see and, with the support of Eudocia (widow of Theodosius II) who lived in the city, held it for twenty months. He circulated a garbled account of Leo's *Tome*. After a reign of terror throughout Palestine, Emperor Marcian's forces finally caught him when he was fleeing. The council had not ended the heresy. Cf. Letters 115 and 116.

of many while they are being tolerated over a long period.

I realize what charity and what favor are due to our sons, the holy and true monks, who do not abandon the moderate course of their profession and follow out in their lives the intention they had when they took vows. The proud and unsettled ones who boast of contempt for and injuries done to priests must not be considered the slaves of Christ but the soldiers of Antichrist. And they must be brought low, especially in their leaders, who stir up an ignorant mob in order to defend their perversity. The most clement emperor loves the Catholic faith with the complete affection of a devoted heart and, according to reports everywhere, he is greatly offended by this boldness on the part of rebellious heretics. Therefore, the matter should be taken up with his Clemency so that the instigators of these seditions may be separated from the mentally sick congregations, and not only Eutyches and Dioscorus, but also all who zealously assist the mad depravity, may be put in those places where they can have no intercourse with their associates in blasphemy. It is possible, dearest brother, that some simple souls will be cured by this process of healing and will more easily be brought back to full health of mind once they are freer from the instigations of unwholesome teachers.

Lest the necessary instruction be lacking or unavailable for strengthening the minds of the pious or refuting the heretics, I am sending the letter of Bishop Athanasius of holy memory, the one which he wrote to Bishop Epictetus and which Cyril of holy memory used as evidence against Nestorius at the Council of Ephesus.[3] In it he has explained the Incarnation of the Word so clearly and carefully that he already beat down both Nestorius and Eutyches in the

---

3 Cf. Schwartz, I.5, pp. 321-334; *PL* 56.664-673.

person of the heretics of his own age. Let the followers of
Eutyches and Dioscorus, who claim that our teaching departs
from the doctrine and thinking of the Fathers, dare to accuse
this man of such great authority of either ignorance or
depravity.[4] It ought to be helpful in strengthening the views
of all the Lord's priests that the heretics, already uncovered
and condemned in their sources, have now begun to spread
around the tenets of their heresy more openly. Otherwise,
if their views were cloaked in silence, it might seem doubtful
whether the threefold error of Apollinaris and the insane
opinion of the Manichaeans were really rising anew in
these men.[5] Since they do not try to hide themselves now
but boldly attack Christ's churches, should we not take
care to eliminate the force of all their undertakings? But, as
I said, the moderation of restraint must be preserved so
that the incorrigibles may be separated from the more docile.
For, 'evil companionships corrupt good morals,'[6] and the
wise man will be more astute, once the contagion has been
taken to task,[7] so that some vessels may be snatched away
from the Devil when association with the reprobates has
been broken off. We must not be so offended by the
revilings and empty talk of certain men as to have no
concern for correcting them.

Bishop Juvenal[8] (the wrongs he has done are lamentable)
quite rashly coupled himself with the blasphemies of the
heretics and, while embracing Eutyches and Dioscorus,
pushed many ignorant people downhill by his example,

---

4 Cf. Letter 28, n. 21. Easterners would be less likely to disapprove
 of Athanasius' exegesis than they would the *Tome.* Cf. Letter 117,
 at note 8.
5 Cf. Letter 35, at note 5.
6 1 Cor. 15.33.
7 Cf. Prov. 21.11.
8 Cf., above, note 2; Letters 80 n. 5, and 85.

although later on, through saner advice, he corrected himself. Those, however, who were more avid in drinking the poison of heresy have become the adversaries of him whose pupils they previously were; thus he himself has suffered from the food he gave to others. It is to be hoped that they will imitate the same course of amendment that he chose, if they change their views because of the very testimony of the holy places in the midst of which they dwell.[9] There can be no doubt about what sort of man has usurped the place of a living bishop, to judge from the very nature of what he has done.[10] Nor should there be any doubt that he is perverse since he was loved by the opponents of the faith. In the meantime, may your Fraternity deign to continue this task of devoted solicitude and keep me informed by more frequent letters as to how matters are faring. May God keep you safe, dearest brother.

Issued on the twenty-fifth of November in the consulship of the most illustrious Herculanus.

[*110*. From the emperors to Leo I: they ask him to send a letter confirming the work of the Council of Chalcedon; otherwise, people will still follow Eutyches.]

---

9 That is, the Holy Land ought to affect their views; it was no place to be a heretic.
10 Theodosius even had himself consecrated bishop, to replace Juvenal.

[*111-113* (Schwartz, II.4, pp. 62-67). These letters from Leo I, March 10, 453 (to Marcian, to Pulcheria, to Bishop Julian of Cos) are said to be spurious by Silva-Tarouca, *Nuovi Studi,* p. 183. The Pope claims that Anatolius has wrongly removed Aetius from the office of archdeacon and substituted Andreas, a heretic. Leo has received a report from Julian as the basis for his complaint.]

[*114* (Silva-Tarouca, 20 xli; Schwartz, II.4, pp. 70-71; in Greek: II.1[2], pp. 61-62). Leo I agrees, March 21, 453, to the work done at the Council of Chalcedon, but refuses to accept canon 28 giving second place to Constantinople.]

[*115* (Silva-Tarouca, 20 xlv; Schwartz, II.4, pp. 67-68; in Greek: II.1[2], pp. 62-63). Leo I to Emperor Marcian, March 21, 453, to thank him for repressing heresy, Anatolius' ambition, and the Palestinian monks. He sends approval of the decrees of the Council of Chalcedon through Julian of Cos.]

[*116* (Silva-Tarouca, 20 xlvii; Schwartz, II.4, pp. 69-70). Leo I to Pulcheria, March 21, 453, with about the same content as in Letter 115. She had already died, on February 18.]

117. Bishop Leo, to his dearly beloved brother, Bishop Julian (March 21, 453).[1]

The content of your letter shows how vigilantly and how devotedly your Fraternity watches over the Catholic faith. My solicitude is greatly relieved by the information in it, since it is supported by the devoted concern of the most religious emperor, a concern which (as is clearly apparent) God has prepared for the strengthening of the universal Church. Hence, so long as the Christian rulers act with holy zeal for the faith, the Lord's priests may confidently pray for their realm. I have willingly complied, therefore, with what the most clement emperor thought necessary by sending a letter[2] to all the brothers who were present at the Council of Chalcedon to show thereby that the decisions taken by our holy brothers concerning the tenets of the faith were pleasing to me. My doing so was naturally on account of those who want the decisions of the council to appear weak and dubious, as an occasion for cloaking their own perfidy, on the grounds that the decisions were not ratified by any assenting opinion of mine; whereas, in fact, after the return of the brothers whom I sent as my representatives, I did dispatch a letter to the Bishop of Constantinople.[3] And so, if he had been willing to publish it, men could have learned thereby with what joy I approved what the council had decided concerning the faith. But, since the same letter contained an answer such as his self-seeking had earned, he wanted my views about the decrees made by our brothers

1 The texts here are Silva-Tarouca, 20 XLVII; Schwartz, II.4, pp. 69-70.
2 Letter 114.
3 Letter 106.

to remain unknown in order not to disclose in the process what I had written in defense of the inviolable authority of the Nicene canons.[4] Hence, your Charity should strive to advise the most pious emperor by frequent suggestions to order the forwarding of the letter of the Apostolic See to the bishops of individual provinces, after adding to it his own comments. This is to prevent any enemy of the truth from presuming to excuse himself in the future on the pretext that I did not commit myself.

I admit my great gratification over the edict of the most Christian emperor in which he set forth what certain monks deserve because of their ignorant foolishness, and over the response of the most pious Augusta,[5] in which she took to task the heads of the monasteries. I am well aware that this fervor of faith is bestowed on them by divine inspiration so that all their excellence may appear to be not only one of high royal rank but also one of priestly holiness. I am now asking, and have already asked, them to have a more intimate confidence in your Fraternity. I trust that in their good will they will graciously deign to accept what is of necessity suggested to them.

The most clement emperor has deigned to instruct me in secret through our son Paul about admonishing our most clement daughter Eudocia, Augusta.[6] I have, therefore, done as he wished in order to have her learn from my letter how profitable it would be for her if she favored the Catholic faith. And I have had her admonished on this matter by

---
4 Cf. Letter 104 n. 5.
5 These letters of Marcian and Pulcheria are in Mansi, VII 512-518.
6 The widow of Theodosius II, retired at Jerusalem, who may have favored the Eutychians from the beginning. Leo's letter to her is below (No. 123).

a letter from the most clement prince, her son.⁷ I do not doubt that she also will work with pious zeal so that the authors of the sedition may realize the true significance of what they profess and, if they do not understand the preaching of their teachers, they may at any rate fear the power of those who take vengeance. I am naturally desirous of knowing right away by a letter from your Charity just what result this show of concern on our part effects and whether their ignorant rebellion is at last subsiding. If they think there is anything uncertain about our teaching, at least let them not deny the writings of those Alexandrian bishops of holy memory, Athanasius, Theophilus, and Cyril.⁸ The tenets of our faith are so in harmony with theirs that the man who says he agrees with them will in no way be at odds with us.

We sympathize with our son Aetius the priest in his unhappiness. And since another man, previously judged deserving of rebuke, has been substituted in his office, injury to those who are Catholic is undoubtedly involved in this change.⁹ But, for now, he must bear this with patience in order that we may not appear to go beyond the limits of our customary moderation. For, at the present time it can suffice for the priest mentioned that he is protected by the favor of our most clement rulers. I have commended him to them recently in my letter,¹⁰ so that his favor in their most religious minds is, I am sure, bound to be on the rise.

This, also, we want you to know. Bishop Anatolius, after being rebuked by us, so persists in the rashness of his presumption that he has called on the bishops of Illyria to

---

7 Very likely, her son-in-law, Valentinian III.
8 Excerpts from writings of these bishops are given after Letter 165.
9 Cf. Letters 112, 132, and 135. For Aetius and Andreas, cf. Letter 127 n. 6.
10 In Letters 111 and 112 (if these two letters are authentic).

subscribe to his views. We learned this from the bishop who was sent to us from Thessalonica to announce the consecration there.[11] We did not want to write to Anatolius (although he himself was seeking to make this a necessity), since, as we perceived, he was unwilling to be corrected.

I have made two copies of my letter to the council;[12] to the end of one of these I have attached a copy of the letter I sent to Bishop Anatolius, and the other one does not have a copy attached. I thus leave it to your judgment to give to the most clement emperor the one which you think proper; you yourself keep the other one. May God keep you safe, dearest brother.

Issued on the twenty-first of March in the consulship of the most illustrious Opilio.

[*118* (Schwartz, II.4, pp. 71-72). Leo notes, April 2, 453, his own labors in the cause of the faith; asks Julian of Cos to arouse the emperor against the heretical Palestinian monks. Considered spurious by Silva-Tarouca, *Nuovi Studi,* p. 183.]

---

11 Euxitheus succeeded the vicar of Thessalonica, Anastasius; cf. Letter 150.
12 Cf. Silva-Tarouca, *Nuovi Studi,* p. 85. Leo sends two copies of Letter 114, and attaches a copy of Letter 106 to one of them.

LETTERS   203

119. Bishop Leo, to his dearly beloved brother, Bishop Maximus (July 11, 453).[1]

How much your Charity is pleased by the most sacred unity of our common faith and the calm harmony of peace within the Church is shown by the content of your letter, which our sons Marinian the priest and Olympius the deacon brought to me. They are the more pleasing to us in that through them we exchange ideas in conversation. In this way the grace which causes rejoicing throughout the entire world over the manifesting of the light of Catholic truth may more and more become known. Yet, as the report of the messengers indicates, certain men are still attached to their darkness; this causes us great sorrow. And although the splendor of day has risen on all sides, they even now take delight in the darkness of their blindness. Thus, having lost the faith, they have remained Christians by a mere empty title, not being intelligent enough to discern one error from another and to distinguish the blasphemy of Nestorius from the impiety of Eutyches. Hence, no falsehood of theirs can appear to be excusable on the grounds that they themselves are opposed to each other in their corruptions. For although the disciples of Eutyches detest Nestorius, and the followers of Nestorius condemn Eutyches; nevertheless, in the opinion of Catholics, both factions are condemned. And the two heresies together are cut off from the body of the Church, since neither falsehood can be in harmony with us. And

---
1 The texts here are Silva-Tarouca, 20 XLII; Schwartz, II.4, pp. 72-75. Anatolius had gone out of his jurisdiction to consecrate Maximus as Bishop of Antioch after the Robber Council had deposed Domnus; cf. Letter 104 n. 8 and Letter 106.

it is not important through which sacrilege they are out of line with the truth of the Lord's Incarnation, since neither the authority of the Gospels nor a reasoned account of the mystery accepts their most depraved views.

And so, dearest brother, it is fitting that your Charity be aware with all your heart of which church's government the Lord wished you to be in charge, and that you be mindful of that doctrine which the chief of the Apostles, the most blessed Peter, established by his uniform teaching throughout the entire world, but particularly by his teaching in the cities of Antioch and Rome.[2] In that way you will realize that Peter, being pre-eminent in the place of residence where he was glorified,[3] insists on the institutions which he handed down, exactly as he received them from that very Truth which he professed. And you should not at all allow any breaking away from the Gospel by unprincipled heretics in the Eastern churches, especially in those which the Nicene canons of the most holy Fathers assigned to the see of Antioch.[4] Nor should you allow anyone to support the teachings of either Nestorius or Eutyches, since, as I said, the rock of the Catholic Church, whose name the Lord gave to the blessed Apostle Peter,[5] accepts no leftovers from either impiety. It clearly and openly condemns Nestorius, who, by separating the nature of the Word from that of the flesh in the blessed Virgin's conceiving and by dividing the one Christ into two, would have it that the divinity and the humanity were different persons; whereas He is absolutely one and

---

2 Cf. Leo, *Sermo* 72.5 (*PL* 54.425).
3 Peter had been Bishop of Antioch, but was pre-eminent in Rome, where he was martyred (glorified); however, there was no question about Rome's first position.
4 Cf. Letter 104 n. 5; the Pope used one of the many versions of canon 6 of Nicaea (Turner, *Monumenta* I, p. 197, col. 2).
5 Cf. Letter 28 n. 40.

the same person who was born from the Father outside of time in respect to the eternal Godhead and born from His Mother in time as regards His real flesh. It likewise condemns Eutyches, who, by doing away with the reality of human flesh in the Lord Jesus Christ, asserted that the Word Himself was transformed into the flesh. In that way, being born, eating, growing, suffering, dying and being buried, and rising on the third day were works of His divinity alone, a divinity which did not assume the reality, but only the semblance, of our servile form.[6]

Hence, it is necessary that you exercise the greatest vigilance in preventing this heretical depravity from daring to assert any claims for itself, since you ought to resist these men with your episcopal authority and instruct us more often by your reports as to what is being done about the progress of the churches. It is fitting that you share in this concern of the Apostolic See and rely on the privileges of the third-place see as confidence in acting, privileges which may in no way be slighted by anyone's self-seeking. I have so great a reverence for the Nicene canons that I have not allowed and will not allow decrees made by the holy Fathers to be violated by any innovation.[7] Although, at times, bishops are of different merits, the rights of the sees remain; factious men can perhaps bring some confusion into these sees, but they cannot lessen the dignity of the sees. Hence, when your Charity believes that something should be done on behalf of the privileges of the church of Antioch, make haste to explain it in a letter of your own so that we can give a final and proper answer to your inquiry.

---
6 *Ibid.* nn. 24-45.
7 On the defense of third place for Antioch, cf. Letters 104 n. 5 and 126 n. 2.

For the present, however, it is sufficient that I make a general pronouncement to cover all cases: If anyone in any council has attempted anything or appears for a time to have exacted anything by force in opposition to the provisions of the Nicene canons, nothing can be done that is prejudicial to those unchangeable decrees. And no matter how many agree on an arrangement, it will be easier to do away with it than for the canonical regulations mentioned to be violated in any particular. Self-seeking, of course, does not pass by opportunities for stealing an advantage. And whenever a general council of bishops meets because of problems that do arise, it is difficult to restrain the cupidity of unprincipled men from striving to gain something beyond their due. That also happened at the Council of Ephesus (which overthrew the impious Nestorius with his doctrine), when Bishop Juvenal thought he could succeed in getting the primacy over the province of Palestine and could bolster his insolent attempt by writing a lying letter.[8] Cyril of holy memory, Bishop of Alexandria, was rightly dismayed at this and in his letter informed me of what was being attempted by the greed of the bishop mentioned,[9] and with solicitous entreaty he urgently insisted that no consent be given for this unlawful attempt. Now, be it known to you that, after a search in our archives, we found the original of that letter of Cyril of holy memory, of which you sent us a copy. This, however, is the important point in my decision: If through the connivance of certain bishops (no matter how much more numerous

---

8 Cf. Letter 126 n. 2.
9 The most likely explanation: in 431, Leo was archdeacon to Pope Celestine, and Cyril wrote to him (a decade before he became Pope) instead of to Celestine. If so, the letter has not survived.

they may be)¹⁰ anything were decided that is found to be at variance with the arrangements made by those 318 Fathers, it would be nullified out of consideration for justice. It is impossible to keep the tranquility of peace in any other way than by preserving intact respect for the canons.

In fact, if those brothers whom I sent to represent me at the holy council are shown to have done what was out of keeping with the cause of the faith, it will have absolutely no validity.¹¹ For they were dispatched by the Apostolic See only for this purpose: that by the cutting out of heresy they might be the defenders of the Catholic faith. Whatever is brought in for the examination of the bishops that is in addition to the special problems for which the meetings of the council are held can be passed on by them with some justification, but only if nothing was decided about it by the holy Fathers at Nicaea. It will never be possible to get the consent of the Apostolic See for anything not in harmony with their arrangements and decrees. With how much concern we actually hold to this course you will discover from the copy of that letter which we sent to the Bishop of Constantinople to restrain his cupidity.¹² You will have this letter brought to the attention of all our brothers and fellow bishops so that they may know that peace in the Church must be preserved through harmony which is pleasing to God.

There is also another matter about which it is necessary for your Charity to be cautious. Apart from those who are

---
10 Cf. Letters 104 and 106.
11 Even the Pope's legate, Julian of Cos, supported canon 28 giving higher rank to Constantinople (Letter 107). Where the Nicene canons were discarded, Leo would not back up even his own envoys, of whom Julian was one.
12 Letter 106.

priests of the Lord, no one may dare to claim for himself the right to teach and preach, whether he be monk or layman, one who boasts a reputation for some learning. For, although it is desirable that all the Church's sons be learned in what is right and holy, no one outside the priestly order is to be allowed to assume for himself the rank of preacher. For it is necessary that all things be in order in God's Church; that is, in the one body of Christ the superior members are to carry out their office, and the inferior members are not to resist the superior ones. May God keep you safe, dearest brother.

Issued on the eleventh of June in the consulship of the most illustrious Opilio.

[*120* Schwartz, II.4, pp. 78-81; also given by Silva-Tarouca, 20, pp. 169-175). Leo I to Theodoret, Bishop of Cyrrhus, June 11, 453, on heresy in the East and on who may preach in church. Silva-Tarouca *(Nuovi Studi,* p. 183) considers the letter spurious.]

[*121-122* (Silva Tarouca, 20 xlviii-xlix; Schwartz, II.4, pp. 75-76). Leo I to Emperor Marcian and to Julian, Bishop of Cos, June 15, 453, asking them to inquire into the proper date for Easter in 455.]

LETTERS 209

[*123* (Silva-Tarouca, 20, L; Schwartz, II.4, p. 77). Leo I to Eudocia, widow of Theodosius II, June 15, 453, asking her to help bring the heretical Palestinian monks back to Catholic doctrine as defined by the Council of Chalcedon; he does not even hint that she has supported the heresy.]

[*124* (Schwartz, II.4, pp. 159-163). From the Pope to the heretical Palestinian monks, *c.* June 15, 453. He upbraids them for circulating a falsified version of his *Tome* and exhorts them to return to Catholic belief. There is considerable theology in the letter, but the ideas all appear again in Letter 165.]

[*125* (Schwartz, II.4, p. 78). Leo chides Julian, Bishop of Cos, June 25, 453, for not writing; the Pope wants information about the status of the faith in the East.]

126. Bishop Leo, to his most glorious and clement son, Marcian, Augustus (January 9, 454).[1]

It is with joy over two letters from your Clemency that I write back thanking you as you deserve. I rejoice over the mercy of God, who, in your Providence's virtues, has set up a most glorious bulwark for the profit of the Roman state and the peace of the Catholic Church. Hence, I trust that both these most salutary concerns of your Piety will be so assisted by God that complete peace may be granted to the Christian religion and to your government. The fact, then, that God's people in the provinces of Palestine were recalled to the unity of the faith and that, as you deign to mention, their hearts have been turned to evangelical and apostolic doctrine, after the endeavors of the erring were repressed; and the fact that my brother and fellow bishop Juvenal was finally allowed to return to his episcopal see, with the people no longer resisting but even desiring his return[2]—this is the work of your faith, this is the fruit of your devotedness. In order to increase it, united prayers are multiplied throughout all Christ's churches. Thus, if there still remains some gloom in Egypt where the

---
1 The texts here are Silva-Tarouca, 20 LI; Schwartz, II.4, pp. 81-82.
2 Juvenal was Bishop of Jerusalem for a long time. At the first Council of Ephesus he was Catholic, but schemed to become not only a metropolitan but a patriarch (at the expense of the Bishop of Antioch). At the Robber Council he voted with Dioscorus against Flavian. At Chalcedon he returned to Catholicism, but when he went back to Jerusalem the heretical elements refused to let him rule, and Marcian restored him by force; that the people 'desired his return' is a bit sanguine. At Chalcedon he was granted some Palestinian provinces and metropolitan status; and while Leo promised Maximus of Antioch (Letter 119, at note 7) that the arrangement made at the Council of Nicea would be retained, nothing was done to curb Juvenal. He seems to have tried to restore Catholic teaching until his death, about 458. Cf., also, Silva-Tarouca, *Nuovi Studi,* pp. 170-171.

rays of truth have not yet penetrated, it may receive the remedy of illumination through the prayers of the whole world and may no longer be burdened with the infection of the accursed Dioscorus, and the Lord's sheep may not love with imprudent affection the person of a bishop in whom they have experienced a man most barbarous in character and a destroyer of the faith. Hence, may your Clemency persevere in your holy and admirable zeal, so that, if anything sick or disturbed is discovered in any place, it may be restored to health and peace. It is fitting that you should so rule over human affairs that you may rejoice to be of service to the divine mysteries.

Issued on the ninth of January after the consulship of the most illustrious Opilio.[3]

127. Bishop Leo, to his dearly beloved brother, Bishop Julian (January 9, 454).[1]

We have often had proof through the clearest evidence of the faith of the most Christian emperor. And I thank our God that in His fatherly concern He has deigned to grant such a ruler in human affairs, one who would use the greatest vigilance in watching over the problems of the faith and the State, ever resisting the endeavors of heretics and allowing no license to any of their insanity against the Catholic faith.

---

[3] A reconstrution by Silva-Tarouca, *Nuovi Studi*, p. 136, for this and a few following letters, since Leo did not then know the names of the two Eastern consuls.

---

[1] The texts here are Silva-Tarouca, 20 LII; Schwartz, II.4, pp. 82-83.

We owe it to his benevolence, after God, that the Bishop of Jerusalem was restored,² and by his august authority he recalled to health the monks whom the perfidy of heretical error had laid hold of. Hence, as soon as I received your letter containing such news, I hastened (not only on the same day but almost at the same hour) to send you an answer so as to give you information on all mattters about which you had written. I am gratified that my brother Proterius, Bishop of Alexandria,³ sent us a letter filled with evidence concerning his faith and indicated more clearly what his tenets are. I must show him favor worthy of the sincerity of his faith so that he may in no way destroy the honor of his church, but may possess the privileges of his see, following the example of the Fathers in antiquity in accord with the unchanged provisions of the canons.

We can have no doubt about the feast of Easter for the present year. But we have made inquiries about the coming year because Theophilus, Bishop of Alexandria, thought that the day to be assigned was April 24, a day which has never been so celebrated since the time of the Lord's Resurrection. Hence, it was right that this be looked into with more care so as to remove every occasion of error. As we read in our annals, the day quite clearly assigned and celebrated by our Fathers was April 17.⁴ And in order that no discrepancy may arise among us or among those in the East on this point, your Charity should deign to take vigorous action with the most Christian emperor about this matter, in our name; although the most clement emperor himself has

---

2 Cf. Letter 126 n. 2 and Letter 139.
3 Cf. Letter 129 n. 1.
4 The date of Easter was frequently a problem for the Pope; cf. Letters 88, 131, 133, 134, and 138 n. 1.

deigned to inform us in his letter that he has charged those in Egypt with investigating this point most carefully.

In your letter you mentioned that the letter I sent to the Council of Chalcedon was in fact read to the bishops and clergy present, but only up to that section where it is apparent that my views corroborated the actions taken concerning the faith.[5] I was, therefore, astonished that the rest of what followed was not likewise brought to the attention of those listening to the reading. All of them should have been especially informed that we had taken to task unprincipled self-seeking and novel usurpations so that the practice of antiquity, which is set forth in the canons, may be preserved inviolate, as we have always written. Now, as to Aetius the priest, whom you mention as having been dismissed,[6] we are gratified that through the holding of a trial he has been acquitted on all points. Know, too, that I am sending a letter to the most Christian emperor, thanking him for having deigned to inform me of his concern as much for the cause of the faith as for the security of the State. He also sent another letter to us,[7] interceding for Bishop Anatolius. He asked us to show a favorable attitude toward Anatolius, since he promises that the man will amend and will in every respect satisfactorily discharge duties pertaining to the observances of the faith. May God keep you safe, dearest brother.

Issued on the ninth of January after the consulship of the most illustrious Opilio.

---

5 That is, in Letter 114 they read only the first paragraph, did not go on to read about his disapproval of Anatolius and canon 28 of Chalcedon.
6 Mentioned also in Letters 111, 117, 132, 135, and 136. Anatolius removed his archdeacon Aetius, put in Andreas, a man with Eutychian leanings. Aetius was later restored under pressure from the Pope and Emperor Marcian.
7 The two letters mentioned at the start of Letter 126 have not survived. Leo's answer to the two are Letters 126 and 128.

[*128* (Silva Tarouca, 20 LVII; Schwartz, II.4, p. 86). Leo I to Emperor Marcian, May 29, 454, promising favor to Bishop Anatolius if he holds to the canons.]

129. Bishop Leo, to his dearly beloved brother, Bishop Proterius (March 10, 454).[1]

Your Charity's letter, dutifully carried to me by our brother and fellow bishop Nestorius, has brought me joy. It was right that a letter be sent to the Apostolic See by the head of the Alexandrian church, such as would prove that the Egyptians had learned at the start from the teaching of the most blessed Apostle Peter through blessed Mark, his disciple, that belief which the Romans held, as is well known: namely, that outside the Lord Jesus Christ 'there is no other name under heaven given to men by which we must be saved.'[2] But all men do not have the faith,[3] and that insidious tempter inflicts no wounds on the hearts of men with more joy than when he infects unwary minds with those errors that are in conflict with evangelical truth. Hence, we must exert ourselves with the aid of Holy Spirit's

---

1 The texts here are Silva-Tarouca, 20 LV; Schwartz, II.4, pp. 84-86. For St. Proterius, Bishop of Alexandria after Dioscorus, cf. Smith-Wace, *Dictionary of Christian Biography* IV 497-499; 1030-1032. The heretics in the city never accepted Proterius; at the death of Marcian they rose under Timothy Aerulus (the cat), killed Proterius and, burning his body, scattered the ashes to the winds. Aerulus made himself bishop then, in 457. The new emperor, Leo, consulted the Pope, St. Simon Stylites, and others, but did not have his general in Alexandria remove the heretic until 460. The Egyptian trouble saddened the Pope's last three years.
2 Acts 4.12.
3 Cf. 2 Thess. 3.2.

vast knowledge so that the minds of Christians cannot be corrupted through the falsehoods of the Devil. It is particularly necessary for the heads of churches to guard against this danger and to divert lies that are colored with something of the semblance of truth from the minds of simple people. Narrow and arduous is the way that leads to life.[4] And the trickery lies hidden not so much in what they do in action as in distinctions in meanings, when the force of statements is corrupted by a very small addition or change, and a statement that was effective for salvation, by a subtle corruption, sometimes inclines toward death.[5] The Apostle says: 'There must be factions, so that the approved may be made manifest among you.'[6] Hence, it tends to the profit of the whole Church (as often as the impiety of contrary opinions shows itself) if things that are harmful are not disguised and if what cannot be brought back to salvation does not harm the unimpaired state of others. Therefore, those who with foolish obstinacy have preferred to lie in their guilt, rather than rise to the proffered remedy, must impute their ruin and their blindness to themselves. Your Fraternity is right in being displeased at their obstinacy, and you are to be praised for embracing that doctrine which has flowed down to us from the blessed Apostles and holy Fathers.

Indeed, there is no new teaching in my letter about the Incarnation of our Lord Jesus Christ, the one which I sent in response to the report against Eutyches by Flavian of holy memory. In nothing did I depart from that system of faith which was clearly supported by our predecessors and yours. If Dioscorus had been willing to follow and imitate them,

---
4 Cf. Matt. 7.14.
5 By a falsified translation of the *Tome* into Greek, aiming to show that the Pope was a Nestorian; cf. Letters 124, 130, and 131.
6 Cf. 1 Cor. 11.19.

he would be abiding in the body of Christ. He has matter for instruction in the works of Athanasius of blessed memory, and in the discourses of Theophilus and Cyril[7] he has material for laudably contradicting a teaching already condemned rather than choose to be associated with the Eutychian impiety. This, therefore, dearest brother, is my admonition, given out of solicitude for the common faith: Since the enemies of Christ's cross lay traps for all our words and syllables, we should not give them even a slight opportunity for falsely saying that we are in agreement with the teaching of Nestorius. In your diligence you should exhort the people and the clergy and all our brothers to make progress in the faith, in such a way as to show that you are teaching nothing new but are instilling into the hearts of all what the Fathers of venerated memory were in accord in teaching, and with which our letter is on all points in agreement. This must be shown not only by your saying it but by the very reading out of our predecessors' statements, so that God's people may know that the doctrine being instilled in them at the present time is that which the Fathers received from their predecessors and handed down to posterity. Hence, after the statements of the bishops mentioned have first been read, let my letter also be read afterwards, so that the ears of the faithful may have proof that we preach nothing other than what we received from our predecessors. And since they have minds with less experience in discerning these matters, let them at least learn from the writings of the Fathers how ancient this evil is, which we have now condemned both in Nestorius and in Eutyches, who were ashamed to preach the Gospel of Christ according to His teaching.

---

7 Cf. Letter 117, at note 8.

In every way, therefore, may the standard of antiquity be adhered to in regard to the tenets of the faith and the observance of discipline, and may your Charity exercise the constancy of a provident ruler. In that way it will be of profit to the church of Alexandria that I solicitously obstructed the unprincipled ambition of certain men by preserving your right to long-standing privileges, and that I wanted the dignity of all metropolitans to remain undiminished. This you will learn from the tenor of the letters I sent: to the holy council,[8] and to the most Christian emperor,[9] as well as to the Bishop of Constantinople.[10] And you will clearly see that this is my special concern: that there be no deviation from the faith in the Lord's churches and that no one's privileges be infringed on through anyone's evil conduct. Since this is the situation, your Fraternity should adhere to the customs of your predecessors. And by proper authority you should hold in restraint your provincial bishops, those who by ancient regulation have been subject to the see of Alexandria, in order that they may not rebel against ecclesiastical custom. But either at prescribed times or when it is required for handling some problem, let them not delay meeting with your Charity. And if anything which will be of profit for the service of the Church is to be handled by conferring in common, let the brothers come together and decide the matter in unison. There is no cause that should draw them away from obeying you in this, for we have found out that your Fraternity's faith and character are such that we do not permit you to lose any of the authority exercised by your predecessors, or to be slighted with impunity. May God keep you safe, dearest brother.

Issued on the tenth of March after the consulship of the most illustrious Opilio.

---

8 Letter 114.
9 Letter 104.
10 Letter 106.

130. Bishop Leo, to his most glorious and clement son, Marcian, Augustus (March 10, 454).[1]

My brother and fellow bishop Nestorius has brought me your letter. In it you have again displayed the purity of Christian faith with which your Clemency shines forth. You have shown most deserved favor to my brother Proterius, Bishop of Alexandria, and thus he has become on all counts more acceptable to me. When your Piety deigns to give a testimonial to anyone, the man would unquestionably have to be approved of even if he remained silent. But he is favored besides by being known through his own writings, and his own profession of faith makes patent his integrity as a preacher of Catholic doctrine. Hence, I welcome the love of my Catholic brother with the fullest affection. I thank God that, after removing the man who sought to contradict Christ's Gospel and to dissent from the thinking of the holy Fathers, He has provided such a bishop for the Alexandrian church as will be in harmony with his predecessors both in faith and in life. When with his whole heart he professes to accept that letter against Eutyches which I sent to Flavian of blessed memory, what does he show himself to be if not a disciple of the Apostles, since the doctrine of truth abides in his light. And that which is one and divine cannot be at variance.

Hence, I have replied to the brother mentioned as was proper and have admonished him to persevere in his holy zeal. He will doubtless be more constant if he is also aided by your Clemency's exhortations and if he is in no way deterred by the ignorant dissension of certain men whose

---

[1] The texts here are Silva-Tarouca, 20 LIV; Schwartz, II.4, pp. 83-84.

stupidity, stimulated by a few heretics, makes them harmful. Consequently, that which men cannot acquire through their own endeavor should be suggested in their hearing at opportune times. And to keep them from thinking that the bishop mentioned is introducing what is new and building up his own position, let them reread the writings of the venerable Fathers who were in charge of the same church. Let them realize what blessed Athanasius, what Theophilus, what Cyril, what even other Eastern teachers thought about the Lord's Incarnation. And may they not be deceived by errors sprung up anew, errors already laid low by the power of the word of the Gospel. For, almost all heresies which have existed at different times have departed from the Gospel in their misunderstanding of the mystery of the bodily birth, the passion, and the resurrection of Christ. We could labor less in repelling heretics if these lies, eradicated of old, no longer disturbed untutored minds. But, as I said, the best method of teaching in the present instance is to let the words of the Fathers be made known to the ears of the people and clergy of Alexandria. And if there are some who have no use for what we have written, let them at least yield to those who agree with us in apostolic teaching. In so doing I take great pleasure in the devotedness of my fellow bishop. I also rejoice in his being of one mind with us, since brotherly peace is not preserved except by having a single profession of faith.

According to report, the clever malice of certain heretics has falsified the letter which I sent to Flavian of blessed memory with the aim of confusing the simplicity of our flock; that is, by changing certain words or syllables in my letter they claim that I accept the heresy of Nestorius.[2] Hence,

---

2 Cf. the letter of the Alexandrian legates in CSEL 35.469; above, Letter 129 n. 5.

I beg your venerable Clemency to order a careful and exact translation of this same letter made into Greek; it can be made by my brother, Bishop Julian, or by those whom your Piety chooses as suited to this task. I entreat you to have it carried by a worthy messenger and handed to the judges of Alexandria, who are to have it read to the clergy and people of the same city, together with the teachings of the bishops mentioned above and with which my letter is in agreement. Thus they may learn that they should no longer be deceived by the trickery of false men and they may be proved to be sincere followers of the Apostolic See. Neither Eutyches nor Nestorius is in good standing with this See, since the universal Church has condemned them as well as other heretics.

Issued on the tenth of March after the consulship of the most illustrious Opilio.

131. Bishop Leo, to his dearly beloved brother, Bishop Julian (March 10, 454).[1]

From a letter received from our brother and fellow bishop Proterius, in charge of Alexandria, I have learned beyond doubt that he is zealous for Catholic doctrine and resists heretics with a right heart. Hence, we can rightly hope that he will be of service to the church over which he presides, both by the example of his acts and by his teaching of the faith. But the Eutychian factions are stirring up no small trouble for him. They are said to have corrupted the letter I sent to Flavian of blessed memory by an erroneous transla-

---

1 The texts here are Silva-Tarouca, 20 LVI; Schwartz, II.4, p. 87.

tion and then passed it around to certain simple-minded or untrained persons; the result is that certain passages seem to agree with the heresy of Nestorius. Consequently, in order that this cancer may not boast of having contaminated the faithful, I enjoin the following task upon your Fraternity. Kindly translate this same letter of mine from Latin into Greek, being careful in translating; it is a letter in every way consonant with apostolic teaching, as is proved by passages in harmony with it taken from our predecessors. Then, as I have asked, let the most glorious and faithful emperor send it, impressed with his own seal, to the Alexandrian judges. Let it be read to the Christian people in church, together with the teachings of the holy men who have themselves been in charge of that church.[2] In that way those who are reported to waver because of ignorance, once they have learned the truth, may in future not be easily drawn into error by depraved influences. Lest your Fraternity be left uninformed of anything, the copies joined to this letter will show what sort of letters I am sending to the most clement emperor and to the Bishop of Alexandria himself.[3]

Concerning the coming Easter, as I have often written already, be solicitous and seasonably inform the most clement emperor in my name that he should let me know what reply he got (for the days are close at hand) so that we can know what day we ought to set down in the calendar[4] and the doubts of all in this matter can be settled with certainty. May God keep you safe, dearest brother.

Issued on the tenth of March after the consulship of the most illustrious Opilio.

---

2 Cf. Letter 117, at note 8.
3 Letters 129 and 130.
4 Cf. Letter 127, at note 4.

[*132* (Silva-Tarouca, 23 XXI). Bishop Anatolius to Leo I, May 29, 454. He complains that letters go to others, not to him. He has complied with all the Pope's demands; Aetius, for instance, is restored to office. He humbles himself, disclaiming all ambition; it was not his fault that the Pope's approval of the canons of Chalcedon failed to receive publicity. Cf. *PL* 54.1083, note h.]

[*133.* From Proterius of Alexandria to Pope Leo. The date of Easter assigned in Roman calendars is held to be wrong. Proofs are offered for keeping the Eastern date, April 24.]

[*134* (Schwartz, II.4, pp. 87-88). Leo I to Marcian Augustus, April 15, 454: he will favor Anatolius when the man repents; he wants Eutyches exiled farther away; he again asks for the correct date of Easter for the year 455.]

[*135* (Silva-Tarouca, 23 XXII; Schwartz, II.4, pp. 88-89). Leo I to Anatolius, May 29, 454: his answer to Letter 132. The Pope would prefer a frank admission of faults committed, rather than blame put on others.]

136. Bishop Leo, to his most glorious and clement son, Marcian, Augustus (May 29, 454).[1]

I have with due reverence received the manifold favor of your Clemency's letter and rejoiced to learn what dutiful solicitude you have for the Christian religion, as has been customary with you. For you are desirous of strengthening that harmony among the Lord's priests which is suited to the universal Church and the worship of God. That commendable peace is, in fact, also the true charity about which the blessed Apostle preaches most fully, saying, 'Charity from a pure heart and a good conscience and faith unfeigned.'[2] Hence, complying with and willingly consenting to your Piety's holy suggestion, I am answering the letter of my brother and fellow bishop Anatolius with a return letter, as I should.[3] He could have attributed my not writing to his own silence, since he kept neglecting to answer that letter of mine in which I had warned him with fraternal charity to cease incurring blame by his self-seeking.[4] But, while I did not write to him, in my solicitude I did not cease to make suggestions to your Clemency that would be of profit for the peace of the universal Church. Your Clemency accepted what I had to say so willingly that you always deigned to reply and you dealt with these matters, so that what has been corrected must be attributed to your Glory. For Anatolius has already sent us the sort

---
1 The texts here are Silva-Tarouca, 20 LVI; Schwartz, II.4, p. 87.
2 1 Tim. 1.5.
3 Letter 135.
4 Letter 106, on May 22, 452. For about two years the Pope did not write to him. Julian, Bishop of Cos, seems to have moved to the court at Constantinople from March, 453, until some time in 457, to act as representative (*apocrisiarius*) of the Pope. Anatolius, at any rate, was bypassed.

of letter in which he claimed that the blameworthy fault of self-seeking should be imputed to others rather than to himself.

Therefore, venerable Augustus, let the bishop mentioned realize how much more he should grow in humility than in self-exaltation. Being mindful of the limits decreed by the Fathers, let him in future preserve the integrity of the canons set up for the peace of the universal Church by observing them as he should. Let him also be unceasingly on guard for the defense of the Catholic faith, set up a diligent watch for the protection of the Lord's flock, rely in everything upon your Piety's most devoted assistance; and if any of the enemy's trickery lies hidden anywhere, cloaked in the title of Catholic teaching, let him at once hunt it out for handing over to your Glory. For, how will you suffer this error to breathe under the rays of your faith, you who have also ejected sacrilegious error from faraway provinces and have recalled the darkened hearts of the people of Palestine to the light of truth? For we believe that, with God assisting you in every way, all the remnants of the depraved teaching will be extinguished in a short time, even throughout Egypt. In your kindness you are planning for those from whom you have removed the license to follow an accursed heresy.

And so, I rejoice that what was disturbed has been settled, now that the memory of blessed Flavian is honored, to the consolation of his disciples; Andreas is removed from the office of archdeacon;[5] men finally cease from injustice toward the holy Fathers and refrain from violating the canons. In consequence, your reign is tranquil because Christ reigns; it is strong because Christ defends it. Hence, since in everything I take delight in complying with your Clemency's wishes, I welcome with all my heart the love of my brother Anatolius.

---

5 Cf. Letter 127 n. 6.

Let him show himself lovable and trustworthy, and not disassociate himself in future by any deviation from that love which I promise him. Let him with sincere affection join to himself those whom we have proved to be defenders of the faith. He has your Piety's example to follow in all matters, especially since he is aided by your Clemency's benign assistance. I beg you to listen kindly (as you do) to the suggestions of my brother and fellow bishop Julian, whom I commend to your Piety. If you deal worthily with him, whom I have desired to be there in the interests of Catholic doctrine, this will also be of profit to my brother Anatolius.

I also make the following request, which is most salutary for the church of Constantinople. The monk Carosus, a man quite unlearned and perverted, who (as I have learned) corrupts the hearts of many, should no longer continue to spread his poison because your Piety is indulgent. Otherwise, the glory of your faith and the authority of the council will be violated through a mean and unprincipled defender of a condemned heresy in the region where practically every endeavor of heretics has been voided through your Clemency's holy zeal.

Issued on the twenty-ninth of May after the consulship of the most illustrious Opilio.

[*137* (Schwartz, II.4, p. 89). Leo I to Marcian, May 29, 454: thanks to the emperor for inquiring about the date of Easter; Church stewards should be tried in ecclesiastical courts. Silva-Tarouca, *Nuovi Studi,* p. 183, considers it spurious.]

138. Leo, Bishop of Rome, to all our dearly beloved brothers, the Catholic bishops established in Gaul and Spain (July 28, 454).

Since it is proper that the bishops have a unified practice in carrying out prescribed regulations, we must be particularly and above all cautious that no fault occur in keeping the Easter festival on different dates, through ignorance or presumption. The season for the most sacred solemnity has dates so arranged that the salutary mystery may properly be celebrated at one time earlier, at another later. Hence, the solicitude of the Apostolic See is ever on the watch to prevent any uncertainty from disturbing devotion in the Church. On certain lists of the Fathers we find that the day assigned for the coming feast of the Lord's Passover is set by some as April 17, by others as the 24th of the same month.[1] Hence, this divergence bothered us so much that I explained my worry over this matter to the most clement Emperor Marcian, that at his order the problem might be carefully discussed in his area by those who are skilled in this sort of reckoning, and an inquiry made as to the day on which the venerable solemnity can be more correctly celebrated. He has replied that the day decided on is April 24. Because, therefore, I have preferred, in the cause of unity and peace, to yield to this decision made in the East rather than be at odds in the observing of so great a festival, your Fraternities should know that the Lord's Resurrection is to be celebrated by all on April 24. You must

---

1 The Pope accepts the date fixed by an earlier Bishop of Alexandria, Theophilus, but only in order to have uniformity. On the discrepancy in Easter dates, cf. B. Krusch, *Studien zür Christlich-mittelalterlichen Chronologie* (Leipzig 1880) 129-138; also, Letter 127 n. 4.

pass on this same information to the other brothers, so that, as we are joined together by one faith in a union of divine peace, we may observe the feast with one solemnity. May God keep you safe, dearest brothers.

Issued on the twenty-eighth of July after the consulship of Opilio.

139. Bishop Leo, to his dearly beloved brother, Bishop Juvenal (February 4, 454).[1]

When I received your Charity's letter, brought to me by our sons Andrew the priest and Peter the deacon, I indeed rejoiced over the fact that you were permitted to return to your episcopal see. But there poured into my mind all the causes which, through certain excesses, got you into trouble. And I grieved that you yourself were the source of your troubles and that you lost constancy in resisting heretics on the grounds that, in their opinion, you are not at liberty to dare contradiction of men who, as you admitted, were once acceptable to you as heretics.[2] For, what was the condemnation of Flavian of blessed memory, what was the acceptance of the most impious Eutyches, if not the denial of our Lord Jesus Christ according to the flesh? He Himself in His great mercy rendered void this denial when the Council of Chalcedon with its holy authority destroyed

---
1 The texts here are Silva-Tarouca, 20 LIII; Schwartz, II.4, pp. 91-93 (Greek: II.1[1], pp. 63-65).
2 Cf. Letter 126 n. 2; Juvenal had in timidity voted against Flavian at the Robber Council.

that detestable decision of the Council of Ephesus—but in such a way as not to keep any of the fallen from the remedy of amendment. Hence, because you chose to repent rather than be obstinate at a time when indulgence was being shown, I rejoice that you sought heavenly medicine so that you can at last defend the faith when it is attacked by heretics. Although no priest is allowed to be ignorant of what he preaches, any Christian at all living in Jerusalem has less excuse than all others who are ignorant. He is taught to understand the truth of the Gospels not only by the words in books but also by the testimony of the places themselves. And that which elsewhere cannot be disbelieved cannot there remain unseen. Why should the intellect be in trouble when sight itself is the teacher? Why are things read and heard doubted in a place where all the mysteries of man's salvation bear down on one's sight and touch? It is as though the Lord were using a bodily voice and saying to all individuals still in doubt: 'Why are you disturbed, and why do doubts arise in your hearts? See my hands and feet, that it is I myself. Feel me and see; for a spirit does not have flesh and bones, as you see I have.'[3]

Therefore, dearest brother, make use of the most invincible proofs for the Catholic faith and defend the teaching of the Evangelists with the testimony of the holy places in which you live. With you is Bethlehem, where the salvation-bringing offspring of a virgin of the house of David began to shine forth, a child wrapped in swaddling clothes, for whom the manger of an inn served as a bed in the midst of poverty. With you the Saviour in His infancy was announced by angels, adored by the Magi, and sought for by Herod in the midst of the killing of many infants. You have with you the

---
[3] Luke 24.38,39.

place where He grew into a boy, matured as a young man, and where His truly human nature became a perfect man through the growth of His body—not without food for His hunger, not without tears of pity, not without fear when frightened.[4] He is one and the same person who, in His aspect as God, performed great miracles of power, and who in the aspect of a slave endured the savagery of His passion. Here the cross itself speaks to you without ceasing; here there cries out the stone over the sepulchre in which the Lord lay in His human aspect and from which in His divine power He arose. And when, in order to venerate the place of the Ascension, you approach the Mount of Olives, does not that angelic saying resound in your ears, the one made to those who were astounded at the Lord's ascent from the earth: 'Men of Galilee, why do you stand looking up to heaven? This Jesus who has been taken up from you into heaven, will come in the same way as you have seen him going up to heaven.'[5]

The true cross, then, confirms the true birth of Christ, since He who is crucified in our flesh is Himself born in our flesh—which, admitting of no sin, could not have been mortal had it not been of our species. In order to restore life to all, He took up the cause of all; by paying it for all He rendered void the force of the old bond,[6] which He alone among all did not owe. Thus, just as all were made sinners through the guilt of one man, so also all might become guiltless through the guiltlessness of one, with justification flowing upon all men from Him who took on man's nature. By no consideration is He lacking in the reality of our body, about whom the

---

4 Cf. Letter 28 nn. 23-29.
5 Acts 1.11.
6 Cf. Letter 165.

Evangelist says at the start of his teaching: 'The book of the origin of Jesus Christ, the son of David, the son of Abraham';[7] the teaching being in accord with that of the blessed Apostle Paul, when he says: 'who have the fathers, and from whom is the Christ according to the flesh, who is over all things, God blessed forever';[8] and he also says to Timothy: 'Remember that Jesus Christ arose from the dead and was descended from David.'[9]

By how many authorities of the Old and New Testament this truth is expressed you evidently know, considering how long you have been a priest, since the faith of the Fathers and the letter which I sent to Flavian of holy memory (both of which you yourself have mentioned), now that the universal council has added its support, are sufficient proof.[10] Hence, it is necessary that your Charity see to it that nobody murmurs against the ineffable mystery of our redemption and our hope. But if there are still some who are in darkness through ignorance or are out of harmony through perversity, let them be instructed by the authority of those whose doctrine in God's Church has been apostolic and unequivocal. In that way they may realize that we believe what those men believed about the Incarnation of the Word of God, and they may not by their obstinacy put themselves outside the body of Christ, in which we died and were resurrected with Him. For, neither the reverence of our faith nor a reasoned account of the mystery admits that the Deity in His essence was capable of suffering or that Truth lied in

---
7 Matt. 1.1.
8 Rom. 9.5.
9 2 Tim. 2.8.
10 It is true that Letter 28 is based largely on Scripture. The Council of Chalcedon approved of it; cf. Letter 102.

the taking on of our nature. May God keep you safe, dearest brother.

Issued on the fourth of February[11] after the consulship of the most illustrious Opilio.

[*140* (Schwartz, II.4, pp. 93-94). Leo I to Julian of Cos, December 6, 454: amendment in the East should be easier now that Dioscorus is dead; the Pope requests further information on the Church at Alexandria.]

[*141* (Schwartz, II.4, pp. 94-95). A second epistle to Julian, March 11, 455, about the amendment of Carosus; he also requests information on a certain John, sent to Egypt in the interests of the faith, and about Maximus, Bishop of Antioch, accused of some malfeasance in office. Considered spurious by Silva-Tarouca, *Nuovi Studi,* p. 183.]

[*142* (Silva-Tarouca, 20 LVIII; Schwartz, 11.4, p. 95). Leo I to Emperor Marcian, March 13, 455, concerning the monks Carosus and Dorotheus; and about the West's acceptance of the Eastern date for Easter.]

---

11 The date in Migne is September 4; the correction is by Silva-Tarouca; cf. Letter 126 n. 3, for the name of the consul.

143. Bishop Leo, to his dearly beloved brother, Bishop Anatolius (March 13, 455).[1]

It is with pleasure that I learn of your Charity's concern for the works of charity (and I exhort you to perform these more frequently), for it is of profit to the entire Church when we know what is being done. As part of this solicitude, your Charity should be on the watch, as you unquestionably know, since you are aware that some of the leftovers of unprincipled men have remained in your area. We want you to be constantly active in suppressing or, rather, in abolishing them in so far as God assists you to do so. Otherwise, that which took a long time to be destroyed may revive again (may it not be so!) through some sluggishness resulting from a mild policy. May God keep you safe, dearest brother.

Issued on the thirteenth of March in the consulship of Valentinian Augustus (eighth time).

144. Bishop Leo, to his dearly beloved brother, Bishop Julian (June 1, 455).[1]

I thank God that your Charity's zeal has in no way failed me in all matters pertaining to the welfare of the Church and the mystery of the faith. I know that you vigilantly watch over it to prevent the snares of heretics from being able to accomplish anything against evangelical and Apostolic doc-

---

[1] The texts here are Silva-Tarouca, 20 LVIIII; Schwartz, II.4, p. 94.

[1] The texts here are Silva-Tarouca, 20 LX; Schwartz, II.4, p. 138.

trine. Now, as you deign to point out, those disturbances which the Eutychians tried to stir up after the death of the Emperor Marcian of venerable memory[2] have been destroyed through your energy and that of the people whom the Spirit of God aroused together with you, truth itself being active in its own defense. That is because there is truly nothing more fruitful for eternal life for your Fraternity and all Christ's faithful and especially for the Augustus, glorious and (as we have proof) Catholic, than that those matters which the very Author of our hope has established may not be violated by any untoward action on the part of perverse men but may endure in secure peace, to the lasting tranquility of the Church. Whatever, therefore, with the Lord's assistance has been done piously and usefully must be strengthened by persevering labor. Certain rumors are being brought to us about the rash endeavors of the people of Alexandria. We cannot decide more fully about them because we have not yet had the whole story about the actions that are reported to have taken place.[3] But you must strive in the interests of the universal Church to the end that, if the actions which are reported to have been done are true, they cannot be allowed to prejudice the holy Council of Chalcedon. In that way what was defined under the Holy Spirit's instruction for the welfare of the entire world may remain unchanged. May God keep you safe, dearest brother.

Issued on the first of June in the consulship of the most illustrious Constantine and Rufus.

---

[2] Marcian died on January 26, 457. He was succeeded by Leo I, an army tribune put in by the Arian *magister militum per orientem*, Ardabur Aspar Alanus. However, the new emperor seems to have become Catholic, and finally even succeeded in executing Aspar for duplicity in a war against his fellow Arians, the Vandals. Cf. Letter 153, at note 2.

[3] The Eutychians, after Marcian's death, arose under Timothy Aerulus and killed the Catholic bishop, Proterius, on March 28, 457. Cf. Letter 129 n. 1; Letter 164 n. 7; Letter 156 n. 6.

145. Bishop Leo, to his most glorious and clement son, Leo, Augustus (July 10, 457).[1]

I have already performed my duty in congratulating you on your coming to power.[2] I am adding, also, this letter of needed entreaty, in which I ask for the protection (of God's preparing) of your favor for the Catholic faith. For from the report of my brother and fellow bishop Anatolius I have learned that in the Alexandrian Church such deeds have been perpetrated that the entire Christian religion would feel itself attacked and violated if it were not watched over by the complete devotedness of your faith, and if Christian liberty were not returned to the church mentioned (one previously famous for its Catholic bishops), so that, with the stopping of attacks by heretics, the teaching of the Gospel, which was vigorous there before the time of Dioscorus, may be restored in union with the peace of the entire Church. This task, suited to your powers and your glory, will have a speedy outcome and one pleasing to God if you do not allow the decisions taken at the holy Council of Chalcedon concerning the Incarnation of the Lord Jesus Christ to be discarded by any retraction. For at that council, assembled through the Holy Spirit, everything was confirmed by such complete and perfect definitions that nothing can be added to or withdrawn from that arrangement, which was produced through God's direction.

We do not doubt that your Clemency also has complete knowledge about this, since, as we have learned from reports from many persons, you have not permitted the machinations

---
1 The texts here are Silva-Tarouca, 20 LXI; Schwartz, II.4, pp. 95-96.
2 The Pope's first letter of congratulation has not survived.

of heretics, which were trying to revolt against the authority of the council mentioned above, to dare anything of this sort. Hence, since you saw on your own account that they had to be opposed, it would be to your glory to assent to the universal Church on my supplication and to grant for always and without change that no future action can disrupt what has been firmly established in the matter of Christ's Gospel and the truth of apostolic teaching by the one faith and one understanding of all preceding ages. Therefore, as the mercy of God through the counsel of His Spirit has instructed your Piety's mind, first plan for the restoration of peace to the holy church of Alexandria. And order that the Catholic bishops select the type of bishop in whom nothing reprehensible can be found, either in the probity of his acts or in the perfection of his faith. Thus, with everything duly settled, the same preaching of the truth may everywhere be adhered to. May the omnipotent God watch over your realm and your welfare unto length of days, O most glorious and clement Emperor, Augustus.

Issued on the tenth of July in the consulship of the most illustrious Constantine and Rufus.

[*146* (Silva-Tarouca, 20 LXII; Schwartz, II.4, p. 96). Leo I to Anatolius, July 10, 457, covering the points in Letter 145.]

[*147* (Silva-Tarouca, 20 LXIII; Schwartz, II.4, p. 98). Leo I to Julian of Cos, July 10, 457, complaining about not receiving enough letters and eliciting his support for the canons of Chalcedon, the orthodoxy of Emperor Leo, and the selection of a worthy bishop of Alexandria (following the assassination of Bishop Proterius).]

[*148* (Silva-Tarouca, 20 LXIV; Schwartz, II.4, p. 98). Pope Leo I to Emperor Leo, September 1, 457, congratulating him for adhering to Catholic dogma.]

149-150. Bishop Leo, to the bishops: Basil, Juvenal, Euxitheus, Peter, and Luke (September 1, 457).[1]

According to the custom of the Church, I should really have learned of your Charity's consecration[2] by a letter from you or from our brothers, the provincial bishops. Causes were not lacking to impede your taking care of this, and the Emperor Marcian of holy memory in a letter of his informed us of your consecration; we can have no doubt about your

---

1 The texts here are Silva-Tarouca, 20 LXV; Schwartz, II.4, pp. 97-98. It seems that five duplicate (except for perhaps minor changes, such as the opening three sentences addressed solely to Basil) letters were sent to the East; cf. Silva-Tarouca, *Nuovi Studi*, pp. 68-69, and *Textus et Documenta* 15, p. xvii. Very likely, Euxitheus, the vicar of Thessalonica, passed on the copies to Peter of Corinth and Luke of Dyrrhacium; Aetius or Julian of Cos sent the copies on to Basil and Juvenal (cf. Letter 153, at note 4).
2 Basil had evidently succeeded Maximus as Bishop of Antioch.

merits. Hence, while we are warning a number of our brothers about present difficulties, in our letter we also include your Charity, whom we know of.

Now that I have learned what was done at Alexandria through the fury of the Eutychians, deeds which I am sure your Fraternities have learned of, I am sending this letter because of the solicitude which I owe to all God's churches. I thought your Charities should be warned by it to resist criminal endeavors with holy constancy, lest the common faith be found to be timid or lukewarm in any of us. For, through the mercy of God, who does not desert His Church in any tribulation, we have in our most pious emperor a mind so religious and so Catholic that what we believe about him must be the same (of this we had proof) as we held concerning Marcian of august memory. We must so believe since, even up to now, without any action on our part, the most faithful emperor has been so horrified by the crime of assassination that he has granted the heretics no opportunity to act. After the barbarous crime was perpetrated,[3] they thought that it was possible for them to have the canons of the holy Council of Chalcedon rescinded and a new council of bishops summoned to treat matters in another way. Dearest brother,[4] this is rashly opposed to the Christian faith, and the only purpose in requesting it with so much perversity is to overturn the teaching of the Gospel and the mystery of the Lord's Incarnation. Therefore, I beg your Charities not to unhinge your minds in any way

---

3 Cf. Letter 144 n. 3.
4 There are two instances of singular vocatives, but the second (next-to-last sentence) is simply a substitution by Silva-Tarouca. It would seem more likely that in the general letter the plural vocative was used throughout.

from the decisions of the Council of Chalcedon and not to allow arrangements made with divine inspiration to be infringed on by any novelty. I am sure that the most clement emperor and illustrious patrician, together with the entire group of renowned authorities, will not suffer the heretics to do anything to disturb the Church, so long as they see that there is absolutely no hesitation in the minds of the bishops.[5] May you in your diligent concern see to it, then, that this exhortation can come to the attention of all our brothers and fellow bishops, for the entire Christian religion (and this must often be repeated) is disturbed if any of the decisions made at Chalcedon is done away with. May God keep you safe, dearest brother.

Issued on the first of September in the consulship of the most illustrious Constantine and Rufus.

[*151* (Silva-Tarouca, 20, LXVI; Schwartz, II.4, pp. 138-139). Pope Leo to Anatolius, September 1, 457, exhorting him to keep heresy out of his church and to expel the priest Atticus as a Eutychian.]

---

5 This is certainly wishful thinking; the emperor later had the patrician Aspar executed as an Arian and a traitor; cf. Letter 144 n. 2.

152. Bishop Leo, to his dearly beloved brother, Bishop Julian (September 1, 457).[1]

I have a suitable opportunity for sending a letter to your Charity now when our son Gerontius is returning to Constantinople. In this letter we arouse your zeal in the causes of the Church and those which pertain to the faith, so that you may stand firm against the attempts of heretics, trusting that the mercy of God will provide that these criminal endeavors are justly punished even in these times. Your Charity should know that we are sending letters to certain of our brothers and fellow bishops, the metropolitans;[2] your diligence or that of our son Aetius the priest will have to provide that the letters reach each of them immediately. If the bishops remain firm in not departing from the canons of the holy Council of Chalcedon, I am sure that the most clement and Christian emperor will willingly support their views; and that which he has done already of his own accord he will do even more when asked; so that what has been settled and brought to a good end cannot be infringed on by any innovation. I am really amazed that in the letter of mine[3] which pleased the entire world there still appears to be anything obscure to the empty vanity of my calumniators, so that, in their view, there ought to be a clearer explanation of it. I am amazed since the expression of that doctrine is so plain and so solid that it can suffer no change either in ideas or in wording. For, whatever we wrote at that time is proved to have been taken from the teaching of the

---
1 The texts here are Silva-Tarouca, 20 LXVII; Schwartz, II.4, p. 99.
2 Letter 149-150.
3 Letter 28.

Apostles and the Gospels. May God keep you safe, dearest brother.

Issued on the first of September in the consulship of the most illustrious Constantine and Rufus.

153. Bishop Leo, to his dearly beloved son, Aetius the priest (September 1, 457).[1]

We have received your Charity's letter, which attests your diligence in the interests of the Church. We briefly exhort you at this time to work vigilantly, as you have begun, in order that the perversity of heretics may not accomplish anything to disturb the Lord's Church. In our concern, then, we are sending letters (needed for the cause of the faith) to the most clement emperor and to the illustrious patrician Aspar.[2] These will doubtless be able to effect the desired results if you, also, in your concern, are on the watch. It has also pleased us to send a general letter to the metropolitan bishops[3] to strengthen and fortify their minds so that they may know that they must strive with zeal as well as with harmonious unity to defend the Council of Chalcedon. Of these letters, if it meets with your common approval, you will send one to the Bishop of Antioch, the other to the Bishop of Jerusalem; but to the Illyrian bishops we ourselves have already sent similar letters.[4]

---
1 The texts here are Silva-Tarouca, 20 LXVIII; Schwartz, II.4, p. 99. On Aetius, cf. Letter 127 n. 6.
2 Cf. Letter 144 n. 2.
3 Letter 149-150.
4 Cf. Letter 149-150 n. 1.

We must now act without any conflicts as regards the mystery of the Catholic faith, since nothing can be investigated with more care or defined with more truth. We are also sending copies of the letters which the bishops of Gaul and Italy,[5] united in their belief, sent to us, so that you may not be unaware how their faith also is one with ours. Besides, we want your Charity or our son Storacius (if he is still with you) to present both the letter to the most clement emperor and those to other persons who should receive them,[6] which we are sending through our son Gerontius; and we want the letters to be supported by such additional remarks as are suitable. In order that you can know what we have written, we are sending copies; you can thus be instructed about everything. May God keep you safe, dearest son.

Issued on the first of September in the consulship of the most illustrious Constantine and Rufus.

[*154* (Schwartz, II.4, p. 104). Leo I to the bishops of Egypt, October 11, 457, who have been exiled by and suffer the attacks of heretics. Considered suspect by Silva-Tarouca, *Nuovi Studi*, p. 183.]

[*155* (Schwartz, II.4, p. 100). Leo I to Anatolius, October 11, 457, asking him to be vigilant against heretics and sympathizers.]

---

5 Letter 99 from Gaul; Letter 97 from the Italian bishops.
6 Letters 148 and 151.

156. Bishop Leo, to his most glorious and clement son, Leo Augustus (December 1, 457).[1]

I have with reverence received your Clemency's letter, full of vigorous faith and the light of truth. I should like to comply with it, even to the point where your Piety thinks that my presence is necessary,[2] in order that I might attain greater fruit from the sight of your splendor. But I think that what reason has shown to be preferable will please you more. Everywhere you strengthen the peace of the Church with holy and spiritual zeal, and nothing is more suited for the defense of the faith than adherence to what has been faultlessly decided with the ever-present instruction of the Holy Spirit. For those reasons, we ourselves will appear to destroy what has been well decided and, at the whim of heretics' petitions, to infringe on authorities which the universal Church has embraced, and thus seem not to limit attacks on the churches, but to put off the fighting rather than end it, by granting liberty for rebellion. After those blasphemies of the Council of Ephesus, in which the Catholic faith was refuted and the Eutychian perversity was accepted through the criminal action of Dioscorus, nothing more profitable for the preservation of the Christian faith could be ordained than that the holy Council of Chalcedon should abolish the crime of the council mentioned above, and that so great a concern for heavenly doctrine should there be shown that nothing out of harmony with the teaching of the Prophets and the

---
1 The text here is Schwartz, II.4, pp. 101-104.
2 Presumably, Emperor Leo asked for a new council, with the Pope present. But, after getting this answer from the Pope and a similar answer from St. Simon Stylites, he decided to oppose the Alexandrian heretics without having the council.

Apostles might remain in anyone's thinking. This was done, naturally, while preserving that sort of moderation which removed only those who were rebellious and obstinate from union with the Church but did not refuse pardon to anyone who amended. Consequently, what can your Piety decree that is more commendable, more religious, than that in future no one be permitted to attack decrees established not so much through human as through divine decisions? Otherwise, those who dared to have doubts about God's truth may really deserve to lose so great a gift of God.

The universal Church has become rock through the erection of that original rock, and the first of the Apostles, the most blessed Peter, heard the voice of the Lord saying: 'Thou art Peter, and upon this rock I will build my Church.'[3] Hence, who would dare to beat against this impregnable solidarity, except either Antichrist or the Devil? It is he who, persevering unconverted in his malice, seeks to plant lies, using instruments suited to his wrath and falseness, while under the false label of carefulness he feigns to be seeking the truth. His unrestrained fury and blind impiety have deservedly marked out for themselves a reputation to be despised and shunned. Thus, while he rages against the holy church of Alexandria with diabolical intent, we may learn what sort of men desire to have the Council of Chalcedon nullified. It could not possibly have happened that at that Council we held views contrary to the holy Council of Nicaea; this is a lie put out by the heretics, who act as though they are the ones who hold the faith of the Council of Nicaea. It was there that our holy and venerable Fathers, being assembled against Arius, affirmed that the divinity of the Son, not the Lord's flesh, is consubstantial with the Father. At

---
3 Matt. 16.18.

the Council of Chalcedon, however, it was decided, against the impiety of Eutyches, that the Lord Jesus Christ took on the reality of our body from the substance of His Virgin Mother.

It is with a most Christian emperor, then, and one to be numbered with due honor among those who preach Christ, that I use the freedom of the Catholic faith and without fear exhort you to be on the side of the Apostles and Prophets. I would have you condemn and repel with constancy those who have lost the Christian name through their own fault, and not allow impious assassins, who are known to aim at nullifying the faith, to treat of the faith in sacrilegious pretense. Since the Lord has endowed your Clemency with so much insight into His mysteries, you should readily recognize that royal power was conferred on you not only for the rule of the world, but particularly for the protection of the Church, so that by suppressing the nefarious ventures you may defend the good decrees that have been made and restore true peace to places that have been disturbed. You will do this, that is, by expelling those who usurp the rights of others and by restoring the see of the Alexandrian church to the ancient faith, so that, with the wrath of God mitigated by your reforms, He may pardon what has been done rather than lay it to the charge of a city that was previously religious. Set before the eyes of your heart, venerable Emperor, all the Lord's priests living throughout the world, who make entreaty on behalf of that faith in which the whole world is redeemed. In this faith the followers of the apostolic faith who have presided over the Alexandrian church entreat your Piety with even greater urgency not to allow heretics and men deservedly condemned for their perversity to enjoy what they usurped. Whether you regard the impiety of their heresy or note the mad act which they perpetrated, they not only cannot be admitted to the dignity of the priesthood but deserve to be cut off from the Christian name itself. By a sort of contagion (and I ask indulgence of your Piety for saying this) they cloud your Serenity's splendor, since, as sacrilegious assassins, they dare to ask for that which even the guiltless may not obtain, O most glorious Emperor.

Petitions were presented to your Piety, copies of which were joined to your letter.[4] Signatures are attached to those coming from orthodox plaintiffs and, because their cause is righteous, the names of the individuals and the dignity of their office are confidently displayed. But on those which the guile of heretics did not fear to present to a Catholic emperor under the vague label of unspecified 'unanimity' no certain name is put down, lest they disclose not only the fewness of the individuals but also their worth. They think it is useful to them to keep quiet about the number of those on whose worth judgment has been passed, and it is to be expected that men who have deserved condemnation are afraid to admit the place they are from. On the one list, then, is given the Catholic petition; on the other the fictions of heretics are set forth. The one bemoans the overthrow of the Lord's priests and of the entire Christian people and of the monasteries; on the other is displayed a succession of enormous crimes, for the purpose of securing permission to keep discussing what ought not to have been listened to.

Is it not obvious which ones your Piety should support and which ones you should oppose in order to prevent the church

---

[4] Both heretics and Catholics sent petitions to the new emperor; the Pope's analysis of the two petitions is masterly. The emperor was convinced.

of Alexandria, which was always a 'house of prayer,' from being 'a den of thieves'?[5] Indeed, it is obvious that all the light of the heavenly mysteries has been extinguished there, through a most cruel and insane barbarity. The offering of the Sacrifice has been cut off; there is no more blessing with chrism; and all the mysteries have withdrawn themselves from the murderous hands of the impious. Nor can there be any doubt as to the decision which ought to be made about these men, who, after unspeakable sacrileges, after shedding the blood of a most upright bishop and scattering the ashes of his burned body to be made sport of by the winds of heaven,[6] still dare to demand for themselves the rights of an office they usurped and to summon before a council the inviolable faith of apostolic teaching. It would, therefore, be a wonderful thing to have added to your imperial diadem a crown of faith from the hand of the Lord, and for you to triumph over the enemies of the Church. If it is praiseworthy for you to crush enemy nations in warfare, how great a glory will it be for you to free the Alexandrian church from a completely insane tyrant—a church in whose affliction lies injustice to all Christians?

I have concluded that, in order that my letter may offer to your Piety the words as it were of one present, whatever I had in mind to suggest about our common faith must be said in letters yet to follow. In order to keep the pages of this letter from becoming too extensive, I have included in another letter statements which are in harmony with a profession of the Catholic faith. Although what the Apostolic See has taught would suffice, I have added these statements

---
5 Cf. Luke 19.46.
6 Cf. Letter 129 n. 1, and Letter 144 n. 3.

in order that they also may disclose the snares of heretics.[7] In fact, this evil deed should also enkindle your Piety's priestly and apostolic mind to execute a just vengeance, an evil which like a plague clouds the purity of the church of Constantinople, where certain of the clergy are found to be in agreement with the views of heretics and, while living in the very vitals of the orthodox, to assist the heretics by their statements. If my brother Anatolius (since he is too kind in sparing others) is found to be too sluggish in ejecting these men, may you, because of your faith, deign to offer to the Church this remedy, also: Let such men be expelled not only from the clerical order, but even from living in the city. Otherwise, God's holy people may continue to be polluted by contact with perverted men. In my petition I recommend Julian the bishop and Aetius the priest,[8] men who honor your Piety, in order that you may deign to listen calmly to their suggestions for the defense of the Catholic faith. They are truly the sort of men who can be found in all ways useful to your faith.

Issued on the first of December in the consulship of the most illustrious Constantine and Rufus.

[*157-158* (Schwartz, II.4, pp. 104; 109-110). The first letter is from Leo I to Anatolius, December 1, 457, about the troubles in Alexandria and asking him to do something about the local heretics, Atticus and Andreas; the second he sends to the Alexandrian bishops exiled in Constantinople, to console them. Silva-Tarouca (*Nuovi Studi,* p. 183) considers both suspect.]

---

7 Presumably, Letter 165 followed by *Testimonia Patrum,* although they are dated more than eight months later than this Letter 156.
8 Cf. Letter 127 n. 6; on Julian, cf. Letter 136 n. 4.

159. Bishop Leo, to Nicetas, Bishop of Aquileia, greetings (March 21, 458).

On his return to us, my son Adeodatus, a deacon of our See, reminded us of your Charity's request that you receive from us the authoritative answer of the Aposolic See about those matters which are apparently quite difficult to decide. We must take care, considering the necessities of the times, that the wounds inflicted by the attacks of the enemy may be healed particularly by the wise action of religion.

You mention that, through the destruction of war and the extremely heavy assaults of the enemy, certain marriages were broken up in this way: When the husbands were carried off into captivity, their wives were left behind deserted. And because they either thought their husbands were killed or felt that they would never be liberated from slavery, under pressure of loneliness these women married other men. And now that the situation, with the Lord's help, has taken a turn for the better, some of those who were thought dead have returned. Therefore, your Charity is apparently in doubt, and with reason, as to what we ought to ordain about the women who married other husbands. We know that it has been written, 'A women is joined to a man by God';[1] and we have learned still another commandment that 'what God has joined together, let no man put asunder.'[2] Hence, we believe that the bonds of legitimate marriages should necessarily be restored; now that the evils introduced by the enemy have been removed, each one should get back that

1 Prov. 19.14.
2 Matt. 19.6.

which he legally possessed. [And, with all zeal, provision should be made for each one to get back what belongs to him.][3]

Nevertheless, the man who took the place of that husband who was thought to be dead must not be judged guilty nor considered the usurper of another man's rights. That is, many things belonging to those who were led into captivity could pass into the possession of another; yet it is absolutely just that on their return these men have restored to them what was theirs. If this is the proper procedure in the case of slaves and fields or even for houses and personal property, how much more should it be the practice in the matter of renewing marriages? That is, what was thrown out of order by the duress of war is to be restored by the remedy of peace.

Therefore, if men returning after a long captivity have persevered in the love of their wives to the extent of wanting them to return to union with them, that which was introduced through necessity must be eliminated and judged to be without fault;[4] what fidelity asks for must be restored.

But if some women are so taken with love for their second husbands that they prefer to stay with them rather than return to their lawful unions, they are deservedly to be condemned; that is, they are even to be excommunicated from the Church. For in a situation that is excusable they have chosen to taint themselves with crime, showing that because of their incontinence they were pleased with a condition which a just restitution could rectify. Let them, then, return to their proper status by a voluntary renewal of their marriage; in no way may a condition introduced through com-

---
3 This appears to be an interpolation.
4 Is it true that the restoration of marriage depends only on whether the first husband wants it?

pulsion be extended into a source of reproach due to evil desires. For, just as those women who are unwilling to return to their husbands must be condemned, so also those who go back to the love they began with God's approval are rightly to be praised.

We believed that this answer also should be given to your Charity's inquiry concerning those Christians who are said to have been polluted by eating foods used for sacrifices, while they lived with those who captured them. Let them be purged by the satisfaction of doing penance; and this is to be evaluated not so much by length of time as by compunction of heart. Whether terror forced them or hunger urged them to do this, there should be no hesitation in absolving them, since this type of food was taken out of fear or need, not out of reverence for their pagan religion.

Your Charity also thought we ought to be consulted about those who were forced by fear or led by erroneous thinking to repeat their baptism and now realize that they did this in opposition to the sacrament of the Catholic faith. In this case a mild course should be adhered to, in which they are to be taken into the unity of our society, but only through the remedy of penance and the imposition of the bishop's hands. The length of the penance (with moderation being observed) is left to your judgment. That is, it is to be proportionate to the devoted dispositions you see in the penitents; you are likewise to be considerate of old age and take note of the requirements of sickness and of all trials. If anyone is so seriously burdened by these that his safety is despaired of while he is doing penance, it is proper that through priestly solicitude he be assisted by the favor of being admitted to communion.

Those who have been baptized by heretics, not having

been baptized previously, are to be confirmed by the imposition of hands, while only the Holy Spirit is invoked,[5] since they have received the bare form of baptism without the power of sanctification. As you know, we preach that this practice must be observed in all churches, so that, once the washing has been performed, it may not be violated by any repetition, as the Apostle says: 'One Lord, one faith, one baptism.'[6] The washing of baptism, therefore, must not be contaminated by any repetition, but, as we said, only the sanctification of the Holy Spirit is to be invoked. In that way what no one gets from heretics may be received from Catholic bishops. You will provide that this letter of ours, which we are sending at your Fraternity's inquiry, reaches all the brothers and your fellow bishops in the province, so that the authoritative answer given may be useful for everyone's observance.

Issued on the twenty-first of March in the consulship of Majorian, Augustus.

[*160-161* (Schwartz, II.4, pp. 107-108). Pope Leo to the Catholic clergy of Alexandria exiled in Constantinople, March 21, 458, to console them; the second letter is to the clergy of Constantinople: against heresy and the heretics Atticus and Andreas. Both are considered of doubtful integrity by Silva-Tarouca, *Nuovi Studi,* p. 183.]

---

5 Presumably not confirmation, but a bishop's blessing connected with the sacrament of penance. Cf. Letters 166 and 167.
6 Eph. 4.5.

162. Bishop Leo, to his most glorious and clement son, Leo, Augustus (March 21, 458).[1]

My mind exults in the Lord with great joy, and I have good reason for rejoicing when I learn that your Clemency's most excellent faith is in every way increased by the gifts of heavenly grace and when through your increased diligence I experience the devotedness of a priestly mind in you. In your Piety's letter is obviously disclosed what the Holy Spirit is effecting through you for the welfare of the entire Church, and through how many prayers of all the faithful it is to be hoped that your reign will reach out to attain every glory. Aside from your care of temporal affairs, you perseveringly put yourself out in the service of devoted foresight with divine and eternal dispositions. You do this, of course, in order that the Catholic religion, which alone gives life to the human race and alone sanctifies it, may abide in one profession of faith; and dissensions, most glorious Augustus, which arise from the variety of earthly opinions, may be driven from the solidity of that rock on which the City of God is built. These gifts of God will thus finally be divinely conferred on us if we are not found ungrateful for those already granted us and if we do not rather seek what is opposed thereto, as if what we have gained is nothing. To search for what has been made clear, to go back over what has been perfectly established, to tear apart what has been defined—what else is that than to fail to return thanks for what we have received and to stretch out the evil desires of death-bringing greed to the fruit of the forbidden

---

1 The texts here are Silva-Tarouca, 20 LXXII; Schwartz, II.4, pp. 105-107.

tree? Hence, because you deign to have regard for the peace of the universal Church and the defense of the Catholic faith with more solicitous care, you are obviously aware of what is being attempted by the enormous snares set by heretics. That is, they would have a more diligent discussion take place between Eutyches' and Dioscorus' disciples and the man whom the Apostolic See has sent,[2] just as though nothing had been previously settled; and, to the injury of even the most sacred Council of Nicaea, they would remove the force of that which the Catholic bishops of the whole world approve of and rejoice over as established by the holy Council of Chalcedon. That which was confirmed in our times at Chalcedon concerning the Incarnation of the Lord Jesus Christ is the same as was defined by the mystical number of Fathers at Nicaea, to prevent the profession of Catholics from holding that the only-begotten Son of God is in any way unequal to the Father, or that the same Son, when He became the Son of Man, did not have the real nature of our flesh and our soul.

Hence, we must detest and constantly avoid what the trickery of heretics is trying to accomplish, and matters which have been religiously and fully defined must not be brought up again for debate. Otherwise, in the judgment of those who were condemned, we ourselves will appear to have doubts about these definitions, which are in every way consonant with the teaching of the Prophets and Evangelists and Apostles. Hence, if there are some who disagree with these divinely made decisions, let them be abandoned to their opinions and let them depart from union with the

---

[2] Probably an epistolary perfect tense; even so, it is probably that no delegates were sent until September (cf. Letter 164). In paragraph 3, below, Leo speaks of promising to send delegates.

Church, together with that perversity which they have chosen. It cannot possibly be that those who dare to contradict the divine mysteries may share in any society with us. Let them boast in the empty vanity of their eloquence and let them exult over the cleverness of those arguments of theirs that are opposed to the faith. May it please us to obey the injunction of the Apostle, which says: 'See to it that no one deceives you by philosophy and vain deceit, according to human traditions.'[3] According to the same Apostle, 'If I reconstruct the things that I destroyed, I make myself a sinner,'[4] and subject myself to those same punitive sanctions which were established not only on the authority of the Emperor Marcian of blessed memory but also by myself in that I consented thereto. For, as you have justly and accurately said: 'Perfection does not admit of increase nor fullness admit of addition.' I am aware, venerable Emperor, that you, being endowed with the most clear light of truth, are not in doubt about any part of the faith, but you discern the right from the wrong with just and perfect judgment and you separate the acceptable from what is to be repudiated. Therefore, I beg you not to think my humble self worthy of blame for lack of confidence. For, this warning of mine is not only made in the interests of the universal Church but even assists your Glory, by preventing the perversity of heretics from appearing to have increased and the safety of Catholics from appearing to have been disturbed at the time when you are ruling.

I am, therefore, filled with great confidence in your Piety's attitude and I perceive that you have been instructed by the Spirit of God dwelling in you and that no heresy can

---
3 Col 2.8.
4 Gal. 2.18.

make sport of your faith. Even so, I am trying to comply with your order so far as to send some of my brothers to act as my representatives with you and point out what the Apostolic Faith consists of, although, as I said, this is well known to you. They will explain all points of the faith and prove that those who do not follow the decisions of the venerable Council of Nicaea and the canons of the holy Council of Chalcedon must not at all be counted among Catholics. For, it is obvious that the holy ordinances of both councils proceed from the Gospels and the Apostles as their source and that whatever drink does not come from Christ is from the viper's cup. Hence, your Piety should know, venerable Emperor, that the men whom I promise to send will depart from the Apostolic See not to contend with the enemies of the faith and not to fight against any of them. For we do not dare enter into any discussion of matters that were defined in a manner pleasing to God at Nicaea and at Chalcedon, as though these matters which so great an authority established through the Holy Spirit were doubtful or unstable.

We are not refusing the assistance of our ministry for the instruction of our little ones who, after having taken the nourishment of milk, desire to be filled with solid food. But, just as we do not spurn the more simple souls, so also we avoid rebellious heretics, being mindful of the Lord's precept, which says: 'Do not give to dogs what is holy, neither throw your pearls before swine.'[5] It is indeed quite wrong and quite unjust that liberty to discuss should be granted to those men whom the Holy Spirit through the Prophet has in mind when He says: 'The children that are strangers have lied to me.'[6] Even if they were not resisting the Gospel,

---
5 Matt. 7.6.
6 Ps. 17.46.

they would still reveal themselves to be of the number of those about whom it is written: 'They profess to know God, but by their works they disown him.'[7] The blood of the just Abel still cries out against the impious Cain, for Cain, when blamed by the Lord, did not retreat to do penance but blazed forth to commit murder.[8] We wish to leave the punishment of this man to the judgment of the Lord, but we want the plunderer and cruel assassin to be reduced to himself alone and not hold on to what is ours. And may you not allow the lamentable captivity of the Alexandrian church to continue any longer. It is proper that its liberty be restored to it, aided by your faith and justice, so that throughout all the cities of Egypt the dignity of the Fathers and the rights of bishops may be restored. May the omnipotent God watch over your realm and welfare unto length of days, most glorious and clement Emperor, Augustus.

Issued on the twenty-first of March in the consulship of Leo and Majorian, Augusti.

[*163* (Schwartz, II.4, p. xliv). Pope Leo to Anatolius, March 23, 458, asking that Atticus be required to read a public condemnation of Eutyches.]

---
7 Titus 1.16.
8 Cf. Gen. 4.8.

164. Bishop Leo, to his most glorious and clement son, Leo, Augustus (September 1, 458).[1]

Being glad to have it shown to me by many and sure proofs how zealously you plan for the universal Church, I have wasted no time in complying with your Piety's orders as soon as possible. I am sending my brothers and fellow bishops Donatian and Geminian,[2] who, by urging my solicitous entreaties upon you, are to ask you for a settled state of evangelical doctrine and obtain liberty for the faith, in which you yourself are especially pre-eminent, following the instruction of the Holy Spirit. This would result from driving far away the enemies of Christ, who would not go undetected even if they had wanted to conceal their madness, since the disguise of beasts hiding under the skins of sheep is a different thing from the holy simplicity of the Lord's flock, and those who have been exposed by their insane madness can no longer creep in by guile. Realize, therefore, venerable Emperor, for how great a protection of the entire world you have been prepared by Divine Providence, and know what assistance you owe to your Mother, the Church, which is particularly boastful of you as her son. Let not contentions that have died out rise up with renewed drive against the triumphs of your all-powerful hand, especially since the endeavors of heretics, already condemned long ago, have absolutely no permission to do so and since the final result due to dutiful labors is this:

---
1 The texts here are Silva-Tarouca, 20 LXVIIII; Schwartz, II.4, pp. 110-112.
2 The two bishops are mentioned in Letter 170 as having returned, but they are not otherwise known.

that all the faithful of the Church may endure in security on the solid foundation of its unity and that there may be no more reviewing of matters that have been well settled. For to want to argue about decisions made legitimately and by divine inspiration is the mark of a rebellious, not a peaceful, mind, as the Apostle says: 'For to dispute with words is useless except to lead to the ruin of the listeners.'[3]

If the opinions of men are ever at liberty to argue, there will never be lacking those who dare to revolt against truth and to put their confidence in the prattling of worldly wisdom. Faith and Christian wisdom know how much they have to avoid this most harmful vanity. They know it from the very teaching of the Lord Jesus Christ, who, when He was about to call all nations to the light of faith, did not choose those who were to serve in spreading the Gospel from philosophers and orators, but selected those who were to make Him known from the lowly and from fishermen. Otherwise, heavenly doctrine, which was filled with power, might seem to require the help of words. Hence, the Apostle protests and says: 'For Christ did not send me to baptize but to preach the gospel, not with wisdom of words, lest the cross of Christ be made void. For the doctrine of the Cross is foolishness to those who perish, but to those who are saved, that is, to us, it is the power of God. For it is written, "I will destroy the wisdom of the wise, and the prudence of the prudent I will reject." Where is the "wise man"? Where is the scribe? Where is the disputant of this world?'[4] This is the particular boast of rhetorical arguments and of the cleverness in speaking devised by men: if in uncertain matters and those befuddled by various opinions each one can draw the thinking

---
3 Cf. 2 Tim. 2.14.
4 1 Cor. 1:17-20.

of the listeners over to that view which he has picked out to be supported by his own talent and eloquence. Thus it happens that what is defended by greater eloquence is considered to be more correct. The Gospel of Christ, in which the doctrine of truth is manifested by its own light, does not need this skill; it does not seek that which pleases the ears when, for the true faith, it is sufficient to know who the teacher is.

There is nothing which does more to disassociate from the light of the Gospel those who are deceived by their own inventions than their view that the reality of the Lord's Incarnation is not connected with human nature, that is, our nature, as though it were unworthy of God's glory that the majesty of the non-sentient Word should assume the reality of mortal flesh. Yet, in no other way could the salvation of men be restored than by having someone in the form of God deign to take on the form of a slave. Hence, since the holy Council of Chalcedon (which was frequented by all the provinces of the Roman Empire with the consent of the whole world, and whose decisions did not differ from those of the most sacred Council of Nicaea) cut off from the body of Catholic communion all the impiety of the Eutychian teaching, how will there be a return to the peace of the Church for any of the lapsed unless they are purged by making a perfect satisfaction? What license to discuss can be given to these men who have earned condemnation by a deserved and just sentence? That is, they have most truly come under that sentence of the blessed Apostle John in which, at a time when the Church was in its very infancy, he strikes at the enemies of Christ's cross, saying: 'Every spirit that confesses that Jesus Christ has come in the flesh is of God. And every spirit that severs Jesus is not of God, but is of

Antichrist.'[5] We must dutifully and constantly make use of this already existing teaching of the Holy Spirit, most glorious Augustus, lest the authority of divinely inspired decisions be minimized while the arguing of such men is permitted. For, that faith which was strengthened at Chalcedon is preserved in the most enduring peace throughout all the parts of our realm and in all the bounds of the earth, and he is not deserving of the name of Christian who disassociates himself from union with us. It is about him that the Apostle says: 'A factious man avoid after a first and a second admonition, knowing that such a one is perverted and sins, being self-condemned.'[6]

The sin, therefore, which the impious assassin committed in seizing the holy church of Alexandria and in most cruelly murdering the bishop himself cannot be wiped out by pardon from men unless He be prevailed on by prayer who alone is properly able to bind in such matters and who alone is able to loose, through His ineffable mercy.[7] Truly, we are not desirous of revenge, but we cannot in any way be associated with the ministers of the Devil. If we learn that they give up their views, repent of their heresy, and are converted from the weapons of discord to the tears of repentance, then even we can pray for them that they may not perish forever. That is, we may use the example of the Lord's devotedness, who, when nailed to the wood of the cross, prayed for His persecutors, saying: 'Father, forgive them, for they do not know what they are doing.'[8] In order that Christian charity may profitably do this for

---
5 1 John 4.2,3.
6 Titus 3.10,11.
7 He is speaking against Timothy Aerulus; cf. Letter 129 n. 1, and Letter 173 n 2.
8 Luke 23.24.

its enemies, let the impious cease from attacking the ever-religious and ever-devoted Church of God; let them not dare to disturb the minds of simple people with heretical falsehood, so that, in those places where the most untainted faith flourished in all past ages, evangelical and apostolic doctrine may now also be able to thrive. For we, also, imitating Divine Mercy as much as we can, do not desire that anyone be punished with justice but that all may be freed through mercy.

I beg your Clemency to make use of the suggestions of my brothers mentioned above. As I already told you in a previous letter,[9] I am not sending them with a view to arguing with those who are condemned, but merely to entreat you in the interests of the stability of the Catholic faith. May your Piety, because of your faith and from consideration for Divine Majesty, grant this favor in particular: that, once the disputes of heretics have been wholly eliminated, you deign to show merciful concern for those who have unfortunately fallen; and that, once the liberty of the Alexandrian church has been restored to its original state, a bishop be consecrated there who observes the decrees of the Council of Chalcedon and who is in harmony with the teachings of the Gospel, one who is able to pacify a disturbed people. And likewise by your Piety's order let those bishops and clerics be recalled whom the impious murderer expelled from their churches. Let others, also, be restored to their original state, those whom a similar ill-will has made exiles from their own homes, in order that we may rejoice fully and perfectly over the grace of God and the merits of your faith, without any further noise of contentions. If anyone has so lost sight of Christian hope and his own salvation as to pre-

---
9 Letter 162.

sume to violate by any disputation the evangelical and apostolic decisions of the Council of Chalcedon, made in corroboration of the most sacred Council of Nicaea, we condemn him as well as all heretics who have held impious and detestable views concerning the Incarnation of our Lord Jesus Christ. We condemn them by a like and equal anathema; that is, the remedy of penance is not to be denied to those who have reformed by performing the required satisfaction, and the sentence of the council (which is filled with truth) is to remain operative against those who rebel. May the omnipotent God watch over your realm and your welfare unto length of days, most glorious and clement Emperor, Augustus.

Issued on the first of September in the consulship of Leo and Majorian, Augusti.

165. Bishop Leo, to his most glorious and clement son Leo, Augustus (August 17, 458).[1]

Venerable Emperor, I recall my promise[2] that a fuller letter from my humble self would be sent to you in the interests of the faith, about which I know that your Clemency is dutifully solicitous. With God's help, now that I have a sure opportunity, I am fulfilling my promise, so that you may not lack instruction, useful (in my judgment) for your

---
1 The texts here are Silva-Tarouca, 9, pp. 44-58; Schwartz, II.4, pp. 113-119; Greek version, *Abhandlung d. Bayer. Ges. d. Wiss.* 32 (1927), 52-62.
2 Cf. Letter 156 n. 7.

Piety's holy zeal. Although I am aware that your Clemency does not lack instruction from men and that, from the abundance of the Holy Spirit, you have imbibed the purest doctrine, it is my duty to make clear what you know and to preach what you believe, in order that the fire which Christ at His coming cast on the earth,[3] being aroused by the impulse of frequent meditation, may so heat up as to glow, may so burn as to give light. The heresy of Eutyches attempted to overcast the Eastern world with enormous clouds and tried to blind the eyes of the unskilled to that light which, as the Gospel says, 'shines in the darkness, and the darkness grasped it not.'[4] Although the heresy itself collapsed in its own blindness, that which failed in the author is now sprouting anew among his disciples.

Two enemies (the one shortly after the other) attacked the Catholic faith, which is one and true; nothing can be added to or subtracted from it. The first of these to rise was Nestorius; then came Eutyches. They[5] sought to introduce into God's Church two heresies, the one contrary to the other. As a result, both were rightly condemned by the advocates of truth, for the teachings of both men, false in different ways, were utterly foolish and blasphemous. Nestorius believed that the blessed Virgin Mary was the mother of the man only and not of God; that is, in his opinion, the divine Person was different from the human Person. He did not think there was one Christ existing in the Word of God and the flesh, but taught that one was the son of man and the other the Son of God, each separate and distinct

---

3 Cf. Luke 12.49.
4 John 1.5.
5 Most of the rest of this letter was written about five years earlier, as Letter 124, paragraphs 2-7.

from the other. For this he was condemned. The truth is that, while that essence of the unchangeable Word remained (which is timeless and co-eternal with the Father and the Holy Spirit), the Word was made flesh in the womb of the Virgin in such a way that, by an ineffable mystery, through one conception and one birth the same Virgin and Handmaid was also the Mother of the Lord, according to the reality of both natures. Elizabeth also realized this and said, as Luke the Evangelist relates: 'And how have I deserved that the mother of my Lord should come to me?'[6] Eutyches is likewise crushed by the same condemnation. Wallowing about in the impious errors of old heretics, he picked out the third teaching of Apollinaris;[7] that is, in denying the reality of the human flesh and soul, he stated that the whole of our Lord Jesus Christ is of one nature, as if the very divinity of the Word had changed Itself into the flesh and soul. By this view, to be conceived and born, to take food and grow, to be crucified and to die, to be buried and to rise again, and to ascend into heaven and to sit at the right hand of the Father, whence He will come to judge the living and the dead—all these pertained only to His divine nature, which in fact did none of these in Itself apart from the reality of the flesh. For the nature of the only-begotten Son is the nature of the Father, is the nature of the Holy Spirit—at once incapable of suffering, unchangeable, the undivided unity and consubstantial equality of the eternal Trinity. Hence, if any Eutychian departs from the error of Apollinaris in order to avoid having a non-sentient God feel and be mortal, yet dares to proclaim that there is but one nature of the Word Incarnate, that is, the Word and the

---

6 Luke 1.43.
7 Cf. Letter 21 n. 13, and Letters 26 and 109.

flesh, he has obviously veered over into the madness of Valentinus and Mani.⁸ And he believes that the man Christ Jesus, the Mediator between God and men, did all these things by trickery; that is, He had no human body, but to the eyes of the beholders there was an imaginary appearance of a body.

Since the Catholic faith of old detested these impious lies, and the views of the blessed Fathers, in accord throughout the entire world, have already condemned such sacrilegious statements, there is no doubt that we preach and defend the same faith which the holy Council of Nicaea established. It stated: 'We believe in one God, the Father Almighty, the Maker of things visible and invisible, and in our one Lord, Jesus Christ, the Son of God, the Only-begotten of the Father, that is, from the substance of the Father, God from God, light from light, true God from true God, begotten not made, being of one substance with the Father (which they call in Greek *'homoousion'*), by whom all things were made, whether in heaven or on the earth, who for us and for our salvation came down and was made flesh; and being made man, suffered, and arose on the third day; He ascended into heaven and will come to judge the living and the dead; and in the Holy Spirit.'⁹ In this profession of faith is most clearly contained what we also profess and believe concerning the Incarnation of the Lord. To restore salvation to the human race, He did not bring from heaven with Him the real flesh containing our weakness, but He assumed the flesh in the womb of His Virgin Mother.

---

8 Cf. Letter 59, paragraphs 1 and 5.
9 For the version of the Nicene Creed used by St. Leo, cf. Turner, *Monumenta* I 306. In the *Tome*, Leo had relied upon the Apostles Creed. Since the heretics kept claiming to abide by Nicene definitions, Leo proved them wrong there, also. Cf. Letters 54 and 69.

Whoever, then, are so blinded and so estranged from the light as to deny the reality of human flesh in the Word of God from the moment of the Incarnation on, ought to show what right they have for using the title of Christians. They should show by what process of reasoning they are in agreement with the Gospel of truth in their claim that, when the blessed Virgin gave birth, there was produced either flesh without divinity or divinity without the flesh. As it is impossible to deny that, according to the Evangelist's words, 'The Word was made flesh and dwelt among us,'[10] so it is impossible to deny that, according to the teaching of blessed Paul the Apostle, 'God was in Christ, reconciling the world to himself.'[11] What reconciliation could there be in which God might again be made propitious to the human race if the Mediator between God and men did not take upon Himself the cause of all men? How, indeed, might anyone fulfill the reality of a mediator unless he shared in the nature of God, equal to the Father, and also in our servile nature, so that the bonds of death, brought about by the lie of one person, might be loosed by the death of One who alone was in no way subject to death? The outpouring[12] of Christ's blood for sinners was so rich in value that, if all the enslaved believed in their Redeemer, none of them would be held by the chains of the Devil. For, as the Apostle says: 'Where the offense has abounded, grace has abounded yet more.'[13] And since those born under the sentence of original sin have received the power of rebirth unto justification, the gift of freedom became stronger than the debt of slavery.

---

10 John 1.14.
11 Cf. 2 Cor. 5.19.
12 From here to note 19 is taken largely from his *Sermo* 64.6 (*PL* 54.359-361).
13 Rom. 5.20.

Consequently, what hope do they leave themselves in the refuge of this mystery who deny the reality of the human body in our Saviour? Let them say by what sacrifice they have become reconciled; let them say by what blood they have been redeemed. Who is there, as the Apostle says, that 'has delivered himself up for us an offering and a sacrifice to God to ascend in fragrant odor'?[14] Or what sacrifice was ever more holy than that which the true and eternal Priest placed upon the altar of the cross by the immolation of His own flesh? Although the death of many holy people was precious in the sight of the Lord,[15] the redemption of the world was not effected by the killing of any of these guiltless persons. The just received, did not give, crowns; and from the courage of the faithful came examples of patience, not the gifts of justification. Indeed, their individual deaths affected them individually, and none gave his life to pay another's debt. For among the sons of men only one stood out, our Lord Jesus Christ, who was truly the spotless Lamb, in whose person all were crucified, all died, all were buried, all were even raised from the dead. He Himself said about them: 'And I, if I be lifted up from the earth, will draw all things to myself.'[16] Indeed, true faith, justifying the impious and making just men, being drawn to Him who shares in their human nature, receives salvation in Him in whom alone man finds himself without guilt. And it can freely boast, through God's grace, of the power of Him who in the lowliness of our flesh attacked the enemy of the human race and who turned over His victory to those in whose body He triumphed.

It is true, therefore, that there is in one Lord Jesus Christ,

---
14 Eph. 5.2.
15 Cf. Ps. 115.14.
16 John 12.32.

the true Son of God and man, one person of the Word and the flesh, and without separation and division they perform their acts in common. Still, we must understand the character of the acts themselves and must note, by the contemplation of pure faith, to which acts the lowliness of the flesh is elevated, to which acts the height of Divinity bends down; what the flesh does not perform apart from the Word, what the Word apart from the flesh does not effect. Without the power of the Word the Virgin would not conceive and not give birth, and without the reality of the flesh the infant would not lie wrapped in swaddling clothes. Without the power of the Word the Magi would not adore the boy pointed out to them by the guiding star, and without the reality of the flesh there would be no command to transfer the boy into Egypt and remove Him from Herod's persecution. Without the power of the Word the voice of the Father sent from heaven would not say: 'This is my beloved Son, in whom I am well pleased.'[17] And without the reality of flesh John would not exclaim: 'Behold the lamb of God, behold him who takes away the sin of the world.'[18] Without the power of the Word there would be no curing of the infirm, no restoration of life to the dead, and without the reality of flesh there would be no need for Him to eat when hungry, to sleep when tired. Finally, without the power of the Word the Lord would not claim to be equal to the Father, and without the reality of flesh He would not say that the Father was greater than He. For, both are accepted and defended by the Catholic faith, which, according to the profession of the blessed Apostle Peter, believes in one Christ,

---

17 Matt. 3.17.
18 John 1.29.

the Son of the living God, both man and the Word.[19] Hence it is true that, from that beginning when 'the Word was made flesh'[20] in the womb of the Virgin, there never existed any division between the two natures, and, during the entire growth of His body, His acts were at all times the work of one person. Yet, those very acts which were performed by one person are not confused, in our thinking, by any mixing of them; we decide from the character of the acts what is pertinent to each nature.

Consequently, let those hypocrites (who with blinded minds are unwilling to accept the light of truth) say in which nature Christ, the Lord of Majesty, was affixed to the wood of the cross, which lay in the tomb, and which flesh arose on the third day after the stone of the tomb was rolled back; and in which nature, after the Resurrection, He upbraided some of His unbelieving disciples and blamed the hesitation of the doubting when He said: 'Feel me and see; for a spirit does not have flesh and bones, as you see I have';[21] and to the Apostle Thomas: 'Put thy hand into my side, and see my hands and feet; and be not unbelieving, but believing.'[22] So, by this display of His body He already destroyed the lies of heretics. And thus the universal Church, imbued with the teachings of Christ, did not doubt that it should believe what the Apostles undertook to preach. And if in the presence of so great a light of truth heretical obstinacy does not abandon its darkness, let them show from what source they promise themselves hope of eternal life, which no man can

---

19 Cf. Matt. 16.16.
20 John 1.14.
21 Luke 24.39.
22 Cf. John 20.27.

attain without the help of the man Jesus Christ, the Mediator between God and men. As the blessed Apostle Peter says: 'There is no other name under heaven given to men by which they must be saved.'[23] There is no redemption of captive humanity except in the blood of Him 'who gave himself a ransom for all,'[24] and, as the blessed Apostle Paul says: 'Who though he was by nature God, did not consider being equal to God a thing to be clung to, but emptied himself, taking the nature of a slave and being made like unto men. And appearing in the form of man, he humbled himself, becoming obedient to death, even to death on the cross. Therefore God also has exalted him and has bestowed upon him the name that is above every name, so that at the name of Jesus every knee should bend of those in heaven, on earth and under the earth, and every tongue should confess that the Lord Jesus Christ is in the glory of God the Father.'[25]

Although, then, the Lord Jesus Christ is one and there is really one and the same person in Him, composed of true divinity and true humanity, the exaltation with which God exalted Him (as the Teacher of the Gentiles says) and gave to Him a name superior to every other name—this exaltation, as we know, took place in that same nature which needed enrichment by the increase of so great a glorification. Indeed, in His nature as God the Son was equal to the Father; and there was no distinction of essence between the Father and the Only-begotten, no difference in majesty; and through the mystery of the Incarnation the Word did not lose anything which the Father might restore to Him as a gift. But the servile form, through which the non-sentient

---

23 Acts 4.12.
24 1 Tim. 2.6.
25 Phil. 2.6-11.

God fulfilled the mystery of great and fatherly concern, is human lowliness, which was carried up to the glory of divine power. The divinity and humanity were bound together in so great a unity from the very time of conception by the Virgin that divine acts were not done without the man and human acts were not done without God. For that reason, just as the Lord of Majesty is said to have been crucified, so He who from all eternity is equal to the Father is said to have been exalted. For, since the unity of person remains inseparable, He is one and the same—wholly the Son of Man because of the flesh, and wholly the Son of God because of the divinity He has in common with the Father. Hence, whatever Christ received in time He received in His humanity, on which are bestowed the things it did not have. As regards the power of the Godhead, all that the Father has belongs also to the Son without distinction; He Himself, in His nature as God, was also the giver of those same things which He received from the Father, in His nature as a slave. According to His nature as God, He and the Father are one; in His servile nature He did not come to do His own will, but the will of Him who sent Him.[26] According to His divine nature, 'as the Father has life in himself, even so he has given to the Son also to have life in himself.'[27] But in His servile state, His soul is sad even unto death.[28] As the Apostle teaches, He is at once both poor and rich: 'rich' because, as the Evangelist says: 'In the beginning was the Word, and the Word was with God: and the Word was God. He was in the beginning with God. All things were made through him, and without him was made nothing.'

---
26 Cf. John 10.30; 5.30.
27 John 5.26.
28 Cf. Matt. 26.38.

But he was 'poor' because on our account 'the Word was made flesh, and dwelt among us.'[29] But what is His emptying of self, or what is His poverty, if not the taking on of a slave's nature, wherein the majesty of the Word was veiled and the design for man's redemption was carried out?

The bonds of captivity with which we are born could not be loosed unless a man of our species and our nature existed who was not bound by any previous conviction for sin and who by His stainless blood would blot out the decree of death against us.[30] On that account it so happened in the fullness of appointed time (as had been divinely ordained from the beginning) that the promise expressed in so many ways became the actuality so long awaited; and there could be no doubt about what had always been announced by continual testimony. But the impiety of heretics shows that they live in great sacrilege since they deny the reality of human flesh in Christ, under the guise of honoring His divinity; and they think they are religious in their belief in claiming that what brings salvation in our Saviour is not real. Yet, according to the promise repeated throughout all ages, the world was reconciled to God in Christ, but, if in so doing the Word did not deign to become flesh, no flesh could be saved. The whole mystery of the Christian faith, taken the way the heretics want it, is darkened with profound obscurity if the light of truth is thought to have hidden under the false guise of a phantasm. Let no Christian, therefore, feel that he should blush because of the reality of our body in Christ. For, all the Apostles and their disciples and all the illustrious Doctors of the Church who merited to gain the martyr's crown or the confessor's glory shone

---
29 John 1.1-3, 14; cf. 2 Cor. 8.9.
30 Cf. Col. 2.14.

forth in the light of this belief. They everywhere in harmony proclaimed that we must profess but one Person in the Lord Jesus Christ, composed of divinity and flesh. By what species of reasoning, by what part of the divine books, do the impious heretics think they are supported, those who deny the reality of Christ's body? Yet the Law has not ceased to attest to this reality, the Prophets to herald it, the Gospel to teach it, Christ Himself to point it out. Let them search through all the books of Scripture for a means to escape from their darkness, not a way to obscure the true light, and they will find the truth so shining throughout all ages that they will see this great and wonderful mystery believed in from the beginning, one which finally came to pass. Although no part of holy Scripture is silent about it, it is enough to have set forth certain tokens of harmonious truth. By these, diligence may be directed into the most illustrious fullness of the faith and perceive by the pure light of reason that Christians ought not to blush for but ought constantly to glory in the Son of God, who professes without ceasing that He is the Son of Man and a man.

In order to let your Piety know that we are in harmony with the teachings of the venerable Fathers, I thought some of their views should be added to this letter.[31] If you deign to read these, you will find that we preach nothing different from what our holy Fathers everywhere taught, and that no one is at variance with these ideas, except only the impious heretics. Hence, venerable and most glorious Emperor, from these statements, which I have put together as briefly as possible, you realize that our teaching is also in line with the faith inspired in you by God and that we are in no way at odds with evangelical and apostolic doctrine

---

31 These views are translated at the end of this letter; cf. Letter 117 n. 8.

or with the Catholic profession of faith in the Creed. As the blessed Apostle Paul teaches: 'Great is the mystery of godliness: which was manifested in the flesh, was justified in the spirit, appeared to angels, was preached to gentiles, believed in the world, taken up in glory.'[32] Hence, what is more useful for your salvation, what more in accord with your power, than for you to further the peace of the Lord's churches by your government, to defend the gifts of God for all those subject to you, and under no circumstances to allow the ministers of the Devil through his malice to vent their rage to the ruin of anyone. Thus you who are eminent for temporal rule in this generation will merit to reign forever with Christ. May the omnipotent God guard your realm and your welfare unto length of days, O most glorious and clement Emperor, Augustus.

Issued on the seventeenth of August in the consulship of Leo and Majorian, Augusti.

---

32 1 Tim. 3.16.

TESTIMONIA[1]

(1)[2] Indeed, for the sake of the human race the Son of God, born of the Virgin Mary and of the Holy Spirit, planted the seeds of a body for Himself and instituted the birth of His flesh; the Son Himself shared in this operation, with His (that is, God's) power overshadowing it. He did this in order that as a man produced from a virgin He might take to Himself the nature of flesh and that, by means of this assumption of flesh, the body of the entire human race might be sanctified in Him. Thus, just as all might be established in Him through the fact that He willed to become a body, so also He in turn might be restored to all through that part of Him which is invisible. The unseen image of God, therefore, did not refuse the ignominy of a human birth, and He ran the gamut of all the degradations of our nature: conception, birth, crying, and the cradle. In a word, what fitting return can we make to Him for displaying so great a condescension? The one only-begotten God through an ineffable birth from God, having been placed in the womb of the holy Virgin, grew into the shape of a human body. He who contains all things and in whom all things exist is brought forth according to the law of human birth. And infant cries are heard from Him at whose voice the angels and archangels tremble and the sky and earth and all the elements of this universe will be dissolved. He who is invisible and incom-

---
1 The texts here are Silva-Tarouca, 9, pp. 34-43; Schwartz, II.4, pp. 119-131.
2 St. Hilary of Poitiers, *De Trinitate* 2.24-25; cf. Fathers of the Church 25 (New York 1956), translated and annotated by Stephen McKenna, C.SS.R.

prehensible is now wrapped in a cradle, to be seen, heard, and touched by men. If anyone thinks this unworthy of God, he confesses as much that the kindness he is indebted for is a major one as that these happenings are unsuited to the majesty of God. He through whom man was made did not need to be made man, but we need to have God become flesh and dwell in us, that is, that He might live within all flesh by the taking on of one body. His lowliness is our nobility; His shame is our honor. Because He as God existed in the flesh, we in turn have been remade from this flesh unto God.

(2)[3] He is assuredly ignorant of, he does not know, his own life who is ignorant of Christ Jesus as the true God as well as true man. It is an equally dangerous matter to deny either that Christ Jesus is the Spirit of God or that He is the flesh of our body. 'Therefore,' He says, 'everyone who acknowleges me before men, I also will acknowlege him before my Father in heaven. But whoever disowns me before men, I in turn will disown him before my Father in heaven.'[4] This was said by the Word made flesh and taught by the man Jesus Christ, the Lord of Majesty, the Mediator Himself being established in Him for the welfare of the Church. And through that very mystery of the Mediator between God and men the both exist as one, for He is the same being of two natures, formed by the union of the natures in the same person. He so effected this that, while being in both, He lacked neither of them, lest, by chance, He cease to be God by being born a man, and in turn, not be a man by remaining God. And so, this is the true faith

---
[3] Hilary, *op. cit.* 9.3.
[4] Matt. 10.32.

of man's beatitude: to preach God and man, to confess the Word and the flesh; and not to be ignorant of God because He is also man; and not to be ignorant of the flesh because it is the Word.

(3)[5] The only-begotten God born as man from a virgin and, according to the fullness of time, purposing to lift man in Himself unto God, at all times held to this manner of stating His message: He taught that He believed Himself to be the Son of God and advised that He be preached of as the Son of Man—as a man speaking and doing all the things that pertain to God; as God speaking and doing all the things that pertain to man; but in such a way that in that very speech of both natures He never spoke without revealing both man and God.[6]

(4)[7] Do you see that God and the man are proclaimed in this way: death is ascribed to the man, the quickening of the flesh to the true God? . . . Recognize the nature of God in the power of the resurrection; know the workings of a man in His death. Although both actions were performed by His natures, remember, however, that it is Christ Jesus who is both.

(5)[8] These, therefore, were the matters that I had to present briefly in order to have you remember that in the Lord Jesus Christ it is a question of a person having both natures, for He who had the nature of God assumed the nature of a slave.

---
5 Hilary, *op. cit.* 9.5.
6 Other manuscripts give parts of *De Trinitate* 9.5-7.
7 Hilary, *op. cit.* 9.11.
8 *Ibid.* 9.14.

(6)⁹ If the Lord who proceeded from Mary is indeed the Son of God in substance and nature, how, then, did they who are called Christians even dare to doubt that, as regards the flesh, He is from the seed of David and the flesh of holy Mary?

(7)¹⁰ Hence, in that statement which we read, namely, that the Lord of Majesty was crucified, let us think of Him, not as crucified in His majesty, but because the same God, the same man (God through His divinity, man through the taking on of flesh), Jesus Christ, the Lord of Majesty, is said to have been crucified; because sharing in both natures (that is, the human and the divine) He endured the passion in the nature of man, so that, without distinguishing, we may say that it is the Lord of Majesty who suffered, and, as it is written, it is the Son of Man 'who has descended from heaven.'¹¹

(8)¹² Hence, let empty inquiries about words be silent, for as it is written: 'The kingdom of God is not in the persuasion of the word, but in the display of power.'¹³ Let us preserve the distinct character of the divinity and of the flesh. The one Son of God speaks in both because in the same Son are both natures. And if the same one speaks, He does not always speak in one manner. Notice now the glory of God in Him, now the sufferings of man. As God He speaks of what is divine because He is the Word. As man

---

9 Athanasius, *Epistola ad Epictetum* (*PL* 56.666).
10 St. Ambrose, *De fide* 2.58 (*PL* 16.571).
11 John 3.13.
12 Ambrose, *op. cit.* 2.77 (*PL* 16.576).
13 Cf. 1 Cor. 4.20.

He says what is human because He was speaking in the nature that I have.

(9)[14] While we are refuting these men, others spring up who say that the flesh of the Lord and His divinity are of one nature. What infernal powers have vomited forth so great a sacrilege? Even the Arians are more to be endured, the force of whose perfidy is increased through these men; as a result, the Arians claim with greater vehemence that the Father and the Son and the Holy Spirit are not of one substance, on the grounds that those others tried to say that the Lord's divinity and flesh are of one substance.

(10)[15] They frequently mention to me that they hold to the definition of the Council of Nicaea. In that definition our Fathers said that the Word of God, not the flesh, is of one nature with the Father. Indeed, they professed that the Word proceeded from the nature of the Father, whereas the flesh came from the Virgin. How, therefore, is the name of the Council of Nicaea alleged, while new ideas are brought in which our Fathers never believed?[16]

(11)[17] And so, do not doubt that Christ the man is now in the place from which He will come. Likewise cherish in memory and with faith hold to the Christian profession, for He arose from the dead, ascended into heaven, sits at the right hand of the Father. And it is from no other place that He will come to judge the living and the dead. And as

---
14 Ambrose, *De Incarnatione Dom. sacr.* 49 (*PL* 16.831).
15 *Ibid.* 52.
16 Other manuscripts give some of Ambrose, *Epistola* 46.6-7.
17 St. Augustine, Letter 187.10; cf. Fathers of the Church 30 (New York 1955), translated and annotated by Sister Wilfrid Parsons, S.N.D.

that angelic voice testified, He will come 'as He was seen to go into heaven';[18] that is, in the same form and nature of flesh, to which indeed He gave immortality, but whose nature He did not take away.

(12)[19] He now appeared as the Mediator between God and men in such a way that, by joining both natures in the unity of a person, He might make the ordinary sublime by the extraordinary and might temper the extraordinary with the ordinary.

(13)[20] What then, heretic? Since Chirst is God and man, He speaks as a man, and you calumniate God. He commends human nature in Himself; do you dare to distort the divine in Him?

(14)[21] Let us recognize the double nature of Christ: that is, the divine, in which He is equal to the Father; the human, whereby the Father is greater. But the two are together; there are not two Christs, but one. Otherwise, God would be quaternary, not a Trinity. Just as man is one, rational soul and flesh; so Christ is one, God and man; and hence Christ is: God, rational soul, and flesh. We confess Christ in all these, Christ in them individually. Who is it, then, through whom the world was made? Christ Jesus, but in His nature as God. Who is it that was crucified under Pontius Pilate? Christ Jesus, but in the nature of a slave.[22]

---

18 Cf. Acts 1.11.
19 Augustine, Letter 137.9; cf. Fathers of the Church 20 (New York 1953).
20 Augustine, *Tract.* 78.2; cf. PL 35.1836.
21 *Ibid.* 78.3.
22 Other manuscripts give more of the *Tract.*

(15)[23] Let us see why He comes with the cross. Of course, it is in order that those who crucified Him may realize the blindness of their madness; that is why He carries the symbol of their shamelessness. Hence the Prophet says: 'Then will all tribes of the earth mourn,'[24] seeing their accuser and recognizing their sin. And what marvel is it that He comes carrying a cross since He Himself shows the wounds in His body? Then, he says, 'they shall look upon him whom they have pierced.'[25] And just as after the Resurrection He wanted to dispel the doubt of Thomas and showed him the place of the nails and revealed the wound in His side, and said: 'Bring here thy hand . . . and see; for a spirit does not have flesh and bones, as you see I have';[26] so also He will then show His wounds and display the cross in order to make clear that He was the one who had been crucified.

(16)[27] Just as when two men are separated in an argument, a man planted between the litigants breaks up the quarreling and discord, so also Christ did. God was justly angry with us, and we spurned the angry God and we turned away from the clement Lord. And Christ put Himself in the middle and joined together both natures; He Himself endured the punishment which threatened us.

(17)[28] Christ therefore offered to the Father the first fruits of our nature. And the Father marveled at the gift offered, because so great a dignity made the offering, and what was presented was not spoiled by any spot. Indeed, He

---
23 St. John Chrysostom, *Serm. de cruce* 4 (*PG* 49.404).
24 Matt. 24.30
25 John 19.37.
26 Luke 24.39.
27 St. John Chrysostom, *De ascensione* 2 (*PG* 50.445).
28 *Ibid.* 3 (*PG* 50.446).

lifted up the gift with His own hands and made it a sharer in His throne. And what is more, He seated Him at His right hand. Let us realize who He is who heard the words: 'Sit thou at my right hand';[29] what nature it is to which He said: 'Be a sharer in my throne.' It was that nature which heard: 'Dust thou art, and into dust thou shalt return.'[30]

(18)[31] I cannot find the language to use, in what words to express myself. Fragile nature, contemptible nature, and nature shown to be completely inferior overcame all, conquered all, and on this day merited to be found superior to everything. On this day the angels received what they had long desired; on this day the archangels were able to behold what they were desirous of seeing for a long time: they saw our nature on the Lord's throne, ablaze with immortal glory.

(19)[32] He is a witness of this matter who says, 'All have gone astray together; they have become worthless.'[33] And Christ's Prophets, praying for help, said: 'Lord, bow down thy heavens and descend';[34] not that He might change the places in which all things are now located, but that He might take on the flesh of human weakness for our salvation. Paul says the same thing: 'How, being rich, he became poor for our sakes, that by his poverty we might become rich.'[35] And He came to the earth and proceeded as a man from the Virgin's womb, which He sanctified. Confirming by this process the interpretation of His name, Emmanuel, that

---

29 Matt. 22.44.
30 Gen. 3.19.
31 John Chrysostom, *De ascensione* 4 (*PG* 50.448).
32 Theophilus of Alexandria, in Jerome, *Epistola* 98.4 (CSEL 55 188).
33 Rom. 3.12; cf. Ps. 13.3.
34 Ps. 143.5.
35 Cf. 2 Cor. 8.9.

is, 'God with us,' He began in a marvelous way to be what we are and did not cease to be what He was. He assumed our nature in such a way as not to lose what He Himself was. Although John writes, 'The Word was made flesh'[36] (that is, in other words, 'man'), He was not turned into flesh, since He never ceased to be God. And the holy David says to Him: 'Thou art always the self-same.'[37] And the Father bears witness from heaven and says: 'Thou art my beloved Son, in thee I am well pleased.'[38] Thus, having become also a man, He is said, according to our profession, to remain what He was before man was made. Paul preaches the same as we do: 'Jesus Christ is the same, yesterday and today, and forever.'[39] He shows in what he says that Christ did not change His original nature and did not lessen the riches of His divinity because He took on the full likeness of our condition, being made poor on our account.

(20)[40] The one Son of the Father and our Mediator neither lost His equality nor was separated from association with us: the invisible God and visible man hidden in the nature of a slave, and the Lord of glory, acknowleged in the profession of those who believe. The Father did not deprive Him of title to His nature after He was made man, and a poor one, on our behalf. And at the baptism in the Jordan River the Father called Him His only-begotten Son, not by another title: 'Thou art my beloved Son, in whom I am well pleased.'[41] Neither was our likeness changed into the nature

---
36 John 1.14.
37 Ps. 101.28.
38 Luke 3.22.
39 Heb. 13.8.
40 Theophilus, at *loc. cit.* 96.3 (CSEL 55 161).
41 Cf. Matt. 3.17.

of divinity, nor was the divinity changed into the likeness of our nature.

(21)[42] He was called a man, for (although He is by nature God, the Word of God the Father) He shared in flesh and blood,[43] as we do. That is the way He manifested Himself to those on the earth, not losing what He was, but taking on the nature of a man, complete in respect to itself.

(22)[44] He is therefore one: before the Incarnation the true God, and who in His humanity remained what He was and is and will be. The one Lord Jesus Christ, therefore, is not to be divided, into man on the one side, and God on the other. We say that Jesus Christ is one and the same—not being unaware of the differences in the natures, but keeping them distinct from each other.

(23)[45] When, therefore, God came forth from the Virgin in that human nature which He assumed, being made one out of two elements opposed to each other, that is, of flesh and spirit, the one element is taken up to God, the other dispenses the grace of God. . . .[46] He was indeed sent, but as a man, for there were two natures in Him. In fact, it was as a man that He was wearied from travel, He was hungry and thirsted and became sad and wept, according to the regular custom of human bodies.

---

42 St. Cyril, *Schol. de Incarnatione* 4 (*PL* 48.1008).
43 Cf. Heb. 2.14.
44 Cyril, *op. cit.*, 13 (*PL* 48.1017).
45 St. Gregory, *Orationes* 13.15 (CSEL 46 100).
46 The following two sentences from *idem.* 15.1 (CSEL 46 103).

(24)[47] We see certain qualities in Christ so human that they do not appear to differ in any way from the common frailty of mortals, and certain qualities so divine that they are suited to no other nature than to the ineffable nature of God. And on that account man's limited intelligence is in a quandry, benumbed by so great an admiration; it does not know where to turn, what to hold, whither to betake itself. If it thinks Him a man, it notices him returning from the dead with spoils, having overcome the realm of death. For this reason we must contemplate with all fear and reverence how the reality of both natures is shown to exist in one and the same Person in such a way that nothing unworthy or unbecoming may be thought about the divine and ineffable nature, and, again, the deeds performed as a man may not be considered as ridiculed by false representations.

(25)[48] Therefore, the holy and great council said that He who was born by nature from God the Father, the only-begotten Son, true God from true God, light from light, through whom and with whom the Father made all things —this One came down, was made flesh and became man, suffered, arose on the third day, and ascended again into heaven. We must follow these words, we must accede to these doctrines, considering what is meant by 'was made flesh' and 'the Word of God was made man.' We do not say that the nature of God, being changed or converted, was made flesh, nor that it was transformed into the complete man, composed of soul and body. Rather, we say that the Word joined to Himself flesh animated by a rational soul; became man substantially, ineffably, and incomprehensibly;

---
47 Passage not located.
48 St. Cyril, *Ep. 2 ad Nest.* 3 (*PL* 56.772-774; Schwartz, I.5, pp. 338-340.

and was even called the Son of Man, except that He was not deprived of His will. It was not through the mere assumption of a person, but because really different natures came together in one. The one, however, came from two, Christ and the Son, not by putting off or discarding the difference of natures in the act of joining, but because the two natures together made for us one Lord, both Christ and the Son (that is, divinity and humanity) through that mysterious and ineffable conception to form a union. And so, He who was born of the Father before all ages is also said to have been produced in the flesh from a woman. This was not because His divine nature took its start from the holy Virgin, and not because the divinity undertook the work of a second birth on its own account after that birth which He received from His Father (for it is incongruous and stupid to say that He who was from all eternity co-eternal with the Father needed a second birth in order to begin to exist). No, it was because He joined a human nature to Himself and came forth from a woman, and is therefore said to have been born in the flesh, on our account and for our salvation. It was not that He was first born as an ordinary man from the holy Virgin and then the Word began to dwell in Him afterwards; He joined flesh to Himself in the very matrix and womb of the Virgin, and underwent carnal birth, making His own the nativity of His flesh. Thus, we say that He suffered and arose, not because God the Word suffered in His own nature the blows or the imprinting of the nails or the other wounds (for the incorporeal God is incapable of suffering), but because that body which He made His own suffered—that is why He is said to have suffered all these ills for us. Within that body there was an element which suffered; and God was there, who could not suffer. In like manner, also, we understand His death. For by nature He is immortal and incorruptible, the life-giving Word of God. But, because His own body, according to the words of Paul, 'by the grace of God tasted death for all,'[49] for that reason He is said to have suffered death for us. Not that He Himself experienced death so far as pertains to His own nature (since it is foolish either to think or say that) but because, as we said above, His flesh 'tasted death.' So also at the resurrection of His flesh, again we speak of His Resurrection, not because He had fallen into corruption (far from that), but because His body arose. Thus, we confess one Christ and Lord, not, as it were, adoring a man with the Word, in order not to postulate a certain type of separation; but we now adore one and the same Person because His body is not foreign to the Word, with which it even sits beside the Father Himself. And we do not say this as of two sons sitting beside Him, but of one Son having union with flesh. If we are not willing to accept such a substantial joining on the grounds that it is either impossible or too little fitting, then we fall into the error of saying that there are two sons. For we must make a distinction and say that the man by himself was honored only by the title of son, and again, that the Word, which is from God, is the Son of God in name and in fact. But we must not make the distinction by postulating two sons in the one Lord Jesus Christ. It does not help to explain the faith correctly, even though some men express it as a sort of joining of persons, for the Scripture did not say that the Word of God took upon Himself the person of man, but that He was made flesh. That is to show that the Word of God, just as we do, parti-

---

49 Cf. Heb. 2.9.

cipated in flesh and blood[50] and that our body was His very own, and that as a man He came forth from a woman without casting aside or putting off His divinity or that birth which He had from the Father; but even in the assuming of the flesh He remained God as He was. This is the explanation of the correct belief as it is everywhere stated. We have learned that the Fathers held such a view. Hence, they did not hesitate to call the holy Virgin 'Mother of God,' not because the nature of the Word and the Godhead took their origin in the holy Virgin, but because from her was born that sacred body animated with a rational soul; substantially united to which the Word of God is said to have been born in the flesh.

[*166*. Pope Leo to Neo, Bishop of Ravenna, October 24, 458, concerning the baptism of those returning from captivity with heretics.]

---

50 Cf. Heb. 2.14; cf. above, at note 43.

167. Bishop Leo, to Rusticus, Bishop of Narbonne (458-459?).

It is with pleasure that I received your Fraternity's letter which Hermes your archdeacon brought. It was quite extensive, since various problems were grouped in it, but not so burdensome to my patience as a reader as to cause me to pass over any of them, even though I am beset by concerns on every side. We have read, then, what you stated in your entire letter and reviewed what took place at the investigation conducted by the bishops and leading men. We thus found out that the priests Sabinian and Leo lacked confidence in what you were doing and that they had no just complaint left, since of their own accord they withdrew from the discussion that had been started. I leave to your ordaining what procedure and what measure of justice you should hold to in their regard. I suggest, however, that you should apply a Spiritual remedy for the healing of those who are sick. And since Scripture says: 'Be not over just,'[1] you ought to deal somewhat kindly with those who in their zeal for chastity apparently exceeded moderation in dispensing punishment. Otherwise, the Devil, who deceived the adulterers, will exult over the punishers of adultery.

I am amazed that your Charity is so overcome with tribulation from scandals, no matter from what occasion they may arise, that you say you desire to be freed from the labors of your bishopric and prefer to live in silence and leisure rather than continue handling those problems which were entrusted to you. But, as the Lord said: 'Blessed is he that perseveres to the end';[2] from what will this blessed persever-

---
1 Eccle. 7.17.
2 Cf. Matt. 10.22; 24.13.

ance come if not from the virtue of patience? For, according to the teaching of the Apostle: 'All who want to live piously in Christ will suffer persecution.'³ Persecution is to be reckoned not only as that which is done against Christian piety by the sword or fire or by any torments whatever, for the ravages of persecution are also inflicted by differences of character, the perversity of the disobedient and the barbs of slanderous tongues. Since all the members of the Church are constantly buffeted by these afflictions and no section of the faithful is free from trial (so that there are dangers in a life of either leisure or labor), who will guide the ship through the waves of the sea if the helmsman quits? Who will protect the sheep from the snares of wolves if pastoral care is not vigilantly on the watch? Who, finally, will resist robbers and thieves if love of quietude removes from watchful solicitude the sentinel set to keep on the lookout? You must, therefore, remain in the work entrusted to you and in the labor you have undertaken. Justice must be constantly observed, and clemency must be lovingly extended. Sins, not men, must be hated. The arrogant must be corrected, the weak are to be tolerated. And those sins which must be visited with more severe chastisement are to be punished, not out of vindictiveness, but with the intention of causing amendment. And should a more violent tribulation fall upon us, let us not fear as though that adversity had to be resisted with our own strength. For Christ is our counsel and our strength; without Him we can do nothing, through Him we can do all things. While confirming the preachers of the Gospel and the ministers of the sacraments, He said: 'Behold, I am with you all days, even unto the consummation of the world';⁴ and, again,

3 2 Tim. 3.12.
4 Matt. 28.20.

He said: 'These things I have spoken to you that in me you may have peace. In the world you will have affliction. But take courage, I have overcome the world.'[5] Since these promises have been clearly manifested, we must not allow them to be weakened by any scandals. Otherwise, we may seem to be ungrateful for having been chosen by God, whose assistance is as powerful as His promises are true.

Your archdeacon brought to us the matters on which your Charity wanted to consult us, written in a separate letter. If the opportunity of seeing you presented itself, it would be better to conduct an inquiry face to face as to what decision should be made about each problem. When certain investigations appear to get beyond the limits of a moderate zeal, I know that they are more aptly handled by conversation than by writing. For, just as there are certain matters that cannot be changed by any consideration, so there are many that require compromise out of regard for age or as demanded by circumstances. But the following condition is always to be observed: In those matters which are dubious or obscure, know that a course is to be followed which is not found to be contrary to evangelical precepts or opposed to the decrees of the holy Fathers.

No consideration allows making bishops of those who have not been chosen by the clerics, sought for by the people, and consecrated by the provincial bishops with the consent of the metropolitan.[6] Hence, since there often arises the question of an office illegally received, who can doubt that such men are not at all to receive what was obviously not granted to them? However, if any clerics have been ordained by such false bishops in those churches which actually belong to regu-

---
5 John 16.33.
6 Cf. Letter 10 n. 16.

lar bishops and their ordination was effected by the decision and with the consent of those in charge, this may be considered valid on condition that they stay in those same churches. Otherwise, however, their ordination (which was not established as to place or supported by authority) must be considered void.[7]

It is not customary in the Church for men ordained to the dignity of the priesthood or diaconate to receive the remedy of penance by the laying on of hands once they have committed some crime. This procedure has undoubtedly come down from apostolic times, according to that which was written: 'If a priest sins, who will pray for him?'[8] Hence, those who have thus fallen must seek out a private retreat in order to obtain the mercy of God. There, if the satisfaction they make is adequate, it may also be of profit to them.[9]

The same law of chastity exists for the ministers of the altar as for bishops and priests.[10] When they were laymen or readers, they were able to marry and to procreate children. But, when they attained the ranks mentioned, that which was formerly allowed them became illicit. Hence, in order that a spiritual marriage may evolve from a carnal one, the proper course for them is not to put away their wives, but to have them as if they did not have them.[11] Thus, while love remains in those marriages, the marriage functions are to cease.

Not every woman joined to a man is the man's wife, as

---

[7] In answer to the question about a priest or deacon who lies that he is a bishop and then ordains someone as a cleric.
[8] Num. 6.11.
[9] Concerning the cleric who recognizes his sin and seeks public penance: Should he be forgiven by the laying on of hands? Cf. Letter 159 n. 5.
[10] That is, whether men in the lower sacred orders may have wives.
[11] Cf. 1 Cor. 7.29.

not every son is the heir of his father. The bonds of marriage are valid among the free-born and among equals. The Lord decided this very matter long before Roman law began. And so, a wife is one thing, a concubine is another, just as a slave girl is different from a free woman. For that reason, also, in order to clarify the difference between these two persons, the Apostle sets forth testimony from Genesis, where it is said to Abraham: 'Cast out this bondwoman and her son, for the son of the bondwoman shall not be heir with my son Isaac.'[12] Hence, since the marital union has been so constituted from the beginning that, apart from the joining of the sexes, there might be in it a mysterious symbol of Christ and the Church, there is no doubt that a woman has no part in a marriage in which clearly no marriage rite was performed. Therefore, if, in any place, a cleric has given his daughter to a man having a concubine, he must not be considered as having given her to a man as it were already married. But this does not hold in case that other woman has apparently been freed, legitimately dowered, and honored with public nuptial rites.

Those women who were married at the decision of their fathers are free from fault if the women whom their husbands had were not actually married.

Since a married woman is different from a concubine, to eject a slave girl from union and receive a woman of unquestioned free birth is not bigamy but an honorable procedure.

The negligence[13] of such men is culpable, but we must not abandon them completely, so that what they asked for

---
12 Gen. 21.10; cf. Gal. 4.30.
13 What if those who are sick accept a penance and then refuse to fulfill it when they get well?

as a necessity when they were aroused by frequent admonitions, they may carry out with fidelity. No one must be despaired of so long as he exists in this body, because at times that which is put off through distrust of one's age is later performed through more mature counsel.

Their case must be reserved to God's judgment,[14] with whom it rests to put off such men's death until they receive the remedy of restoration to the society of the Church. We, who did not associate with them when they lived, are unable to be associated with them when they are dead.

It is possible that this dissimulation[15] is not the result of contempt for the remedy but of fear that they will fail more grievously. Hence, the penance which has been put off is not to be denied them when they ask for it with greater earnestness. Thus the wounded soul may in some way obtain the medicine of absolution.

It is indeed one thing to demand back a just debt; another, to feel contempt for one's own property out of a love for perfection. But it is fitting that a man who seeks pardon for a transgression should abstain even from what he may have legitimately, as the Apostle says: 'All things are lawful for me, but not all things are expedient.'[16] So, if a penitent has a grievance which, perhaps, he ought to have redressed, he does better to seek a decision from the Church than from a secular court.

The nature of a gain either convicts or excuses a man doing business, for there is a gain which is honest, another which is disgraceful. It is, nevertheless, more profitable to a

---

14 What about those who accept a penance but die before fulfilling it.
15 Concerning those who in great pain ask for a penance, but when the priest arrives and the pain happens to lessen, refuse to accept it.
16 1 Cor. 6.12.

penitent to suffer loss than to get involved in the dangers of trafficking in business, since it is difficult to avoid sin in the business dealings of buyers and sellers.

It is absolutely against the rules of the Church to return to military service in the world after having done penance, since the Apostle says: 'No one serving as God's soldier entangles himself in worldly affairs.'[17] Hence, he who is eager to involve himself in worldly warfare is not free from the snares of the Devil.

If a young man, induced by fear of death or the danger of being captured, has done penance and afterwards, fearing a lapse into youthful incontinence, has chosen to marry in order not to incur the sin of fornication, he has apparently committed only a venial offense, so long as he has had absolutely no relations with any woman other than his wife. In this, however, we are not setting down a regulation but only what we think more tolerable. For, according to the true way of thinking, nothing is more proper to a man who has done penance than continued chastity of mind and body.

The life of a monk, undertaken of his own free will and decision, cannot be given up without sin. For that which a man has vowed to God he must also pay.[18] Hence, he who abandons his single state and throws himself into military service or marriage must be purged by making the satisfaction of a public penance. For, although military service can be free from fault and marriage can be honorable, to have given up the choice of better things is a sin.

If girls were not forced by the order of their parents but undertook the vow and habit of virginity of their own accord,

---

17 2 Tim. 2.4.
18 Cf. Deut. 23.21; Ps. 49.14.

then afterwards choose to marry, they act in the wrong even if their final consecration has not yet taken place.[19] Naturally, they would not be deprived of this blessing were they to remain faithful to their vow.

If no indications exist among kinsfolk and relatives, among the clergy and neighbors to show that baptism has been received, when there is question of this, care must be taken to baptize such people, since, otherwise, they will obviously perish. In their case there are no grounds for suspecting a repetition of the rite since there is no proof that it ever took place.

Those who can remember that they came to the church with their parents can also remember whether they received the sacrament which was given their parents. But, if they cannot even remember this, it is clear that what they do not know they received ought to be conferred on them, since there is no rash presumption present where dutiful care has been exercised.

Those men are aware that they have been baptized, but they profess not to know the faith of those who baptized them. Hence, since in some fashion they have received the form of baptism, they must not be baptized again. But, through the imposition of hands and the invocation of the power of the Holy Spirit (which they were unable to receive from heretics), they are to be joined to Catholic communion.[20]

If they merely partaken of the banqueting and sacrificial food of unbelievers, they can be purged by fasting and the

---

19 Concerning women who stay for a while in religious life without complete consecration, then decide to marry.
20 What should be done about those who come from Africa or Mauritania and do not know in what sect they were baptized? On imposing hands, cf. Letters 159 and 166.

laying on of hands.²¹ That is, by abstaining from what is sacrificed to idols in the future, they can become partakers of the sacraments of Christ. But, if they have adored idols or been contaminated by homicide or fornication, it is not proper for them to be admitted to communion except through public penance.

[*168*. Pope Leo to bishops in Campania, Samnium, and Picenum, March 6, 459; on baptizing at the Easter and Pentecost seasons; written confessions of the faithful are not to be published.]

169. Bishop Leo, to Leo, Augustus (June 17, 460).¹

Were we desirous of praising your Piety's glorious resolve for the defense of the faith as much as the importance of the fact itself demands, we should be found unequal to giving thanks to you, that is, if we were to celebrate the joys of the universal Church merely with the limited powers of our own tongue. For your acts and merits a more fitting reward will be reserved by Him in whose cause you are outstanding for special zeal and are triumphing for having reached the glorious end aimed at. Your Clemency should know, therefore, that all God's churches are rejoicing and exulting in praise of you because the unprincipled assassin

---
21 Cf. Letter 159, paragraph 6 and note 5.

1 The text here is CSEL 35.51.

has been driven off the neck of the Alexandrian church; and God's people, who were weighted down by the nefarious robber, being restored to the ancient liberty of the faith, can now be recalled to the path of salvation by the preaching of faithful priests, now that they see that the whole source of poisons has been cast out in the author himself. Since, therefore, you have now accomplished this with unwavering purpose and extraordinary spirit, you should add this to the work of faith already completed: You ought to come to a decision, one pleasing to God, about a Catholic bishop for that city, a man who has not been infected by any sprinkling of the blasphemy so often condemned. Otherwise, the wound, apparently healed under a covering of scab, may perhaps spread, and the Christian people, who were freed from the perversity of heretics by your forthright actions, may again be subjected to deadly poisons.

But you see, venerable Emperor, and clearly understand that, in the case of the man whose excommunication is in question,[2] it is not enough just to be cautious about the integrity of his faith. Even if this could be purged by some punishments and professions of belief and he could be restored to health under any terms, the criminal and cruel deeds he committed cannot at all be wiped out by any protestations made in plausible words. For, in the case of a bishop of God, and particularly the bishop of so great a church, the sound of the tongue and the utterances of the lips do not suffice; they are of no use if the voice preaches about God, but the mind is tied to its blasphemous beliefs. The Holy Spirit, through the Apostle, speaks about such men, 'having a semblance indeed of piety, but disowning its power';[3] and

---
2 That is, Timothy Aerulus of Alexandria; cf. Letter 129 n. 1.
3 2 Tim. 3.5.

again, elsewhere: 'They profess to know God, but by their works they disown him.'⁴ Since, therefore, the truth of unimpaired faith and the fullness of good works are sought for in every member of the Church, how much more ought both these qualities to stand out in a most exalted bishop, since the one without the other cannot be connected with the body of Christ.

It is not now necessary to relate all the deeds that made Timothy accursed, since the entire world has received full and clear information about all that has been done through him and on his account. If a riotous mob has perpetrated any deed against justice, may all this devolve upon the head of him whose desires were served by the hands of the raging mob. Consequently, if this man is in no way delinquent even in his profession of faith, if he tricks us in no way, it is [still] most fitting that your Glory completely exclude him from what he desires. For it is right that the entire Church rejoice with holy exultation over the bishop of so important a city, in order that the true peace of the Lord may be manifested, not only in the preaching of the faith but also by examples of conduct.

Issued on the seventeenth of June in the consulship of Apollonius (through Philoxenus, agent of affairs).⁵

[*170* (CSEL 35.52). Pope Leo to Gennadius, June 18, 460, who had succeeded Anatolius as Bishop of Constantinople in 458: to warn him not to allow Timothy Aerulus to remain as an exile in Constantinople, to speak to the people, or to return to Alexandria.]

---
4 Titus 1.16.
5 *agens in rebus*: a title for an imperial messenger.

[*171* (CSEL 35.53). Pope Leo to Timothy, the new Bishop of Alexandria, August 18, 460, asking him to watch over the faith and to write often.]

[*172* (CSEL) 35.54). Pope Leo to the priests and deacons of Alexandria, August 18, 460, asking them to promote harmony and to restore heretics to the Catholic faith by means of penance.]

173. Bishop Leo, to Theophilus, John, Athanasius, Abraham, Daniel, Johas, Paphnutius, Musaeus, Panulvius, and Peter, bishops of Egypt (August 18, 460).[1]

I am gratified to learn from your Fraternities' letter, brought to me by our sons Daniel the priest and Timothy the deacon, that the faith of our glorious and venerable emperor, united to the teachings of the Prophets and Evangelists, has attained the holy results of its undertakings, results pleasing to God. That is, after the most cruel usurper of the Alexandrian church was expelled and exiled to a faraway place, a choice was made by the entire city of a bishop worthy of ruling it.[2] You were not drawn to consecrate him by any self-seeking; no sedition forced you, no evil acts aroused you. But, when

---
1 The text here is CSEL 35.55.
2 Aerulus was finally exiled to Gangra and for sixteen years Alexandria was governed by his namesake, Timothy Solofaciolus. Aerulus was then restored to the see under a heretical Eastern ruler, but in 479 Solofaciolus was restored until his death.

the holiness of his merits was publicly set forth, you did not hesitate to set him over all others whom all the people wanted to preside over them. Hence, rejoicing over the return of God's peace to the Christian people, may we commend to you in turn the dignity of your own task. That is, the bishop who has in every way been religiously consecrated should feel that he is assisted by your fraternal agreement, and should rejoice to be assisted by your co-operation in the elimination of the scandals aroused by heretical error. Now that the follower of the Devil has been expelled, he who 'has not stood in the truth'[3] but made evil use of the outward forms of an office and name he usurped, the Alexandrian church has agreed to honor and love a man whom it has proved to be worthy of so important a bishopric, both by the uprightness of his conduct and the integrity of his Catholic faith. To him we offer the affection of our heart filled with mutual charity, exhorting you, dearest brothers, and urging you with confidence to preserve the practices of charity both in preaching the word and in teaching the commandments; for without that no virtues can be of value. Now, what you know was written to our brother and fellow bishop Timothy about recalling those who, erring from the path of truth, acted savagely and without reason, this your Charities should realize is also a matter for your concern. That is, since that pestilent disease spread itself far and wide, the same medicine must be applied to all wounds in all places, in order that the Lord's flock may be restored in all the churches through the zeal of the shepherds, and through concern for charity and doctrine all Christ's sheep may feel that they have one shepherd.

Issued on the eighteenth of August in the consulship of Magnus and Apollonius.

---

3 John 8.44.

INDEX

INDEX

Abraham, 94, 293
Abundius, Bishop, 139
Acholius, Bishops of Thessalonica, 28
Adelfius, consul, 147, 150, 152, 153, 155, 158, 159, 162, 163, 166, 167, 170
Adeodatus, deacon, 248
Aerulus, *see* Timothy
Aetherius, Bishop, 139
Aetius, priest, 155, 198, 201, 213, 215, 222, 236, 240, 247
Aggaeus, Bishop, 54
Albinus, consul, 32
Ambrose, St., 278, 279
Anastasuis, Vicar of Thessalonica, 27, 57, 58, 127, 202, 219
Anatolius, Bishop of Constantinople, 9, 131, 137, 139, 141, 144, 146-148, 151, 153, 154, 156, 158, 164, 171, 178-182, 189, 198, 201, 202, 213, 214, 222-225, 232, 234, 235, 238, 241, 247

Andreas, heretic, 198, 201, 213, 224, 247, 251
Andrew, priest, 227
Antichrist, 102, 142, 195, 243, 247, 256, 260
Anysius, Bishop of Thessalonica, 28
apocrisiarius, 223
Apollinaris, heretic, 84-87, 112, 196, 264, 299
Apollonius, consul, 299, 301
Apostolic See, 25, 28, 31, 38, 42, 45, 47, 53, 59, 77-79, 108, 124, 138, 139, 150, 154, 157, 165, 177, 179, 180, 185, 186, 200, 205, 207, 214, 220, 238, 240, 248, 253, 255
Ardaburis, consul, 77
Arius, heretic, 185, 243, 279
Asclepiades, deacon, 148
Aspar (Ardabur), magister militum, 233, 238, 240
Asturius, consul, 89, 90, 105, 107, 110, 117, 119, 121, 122, 126, 128, 130

Athanasius, St., 83, 86, 175, 195, 196, 201, 216, 219, 278
Atticus, Bishop of Alexandria, 86
Atticus, Bishop of Old Epirus, 59-61
Atticus, heretic, 247, 251
Attila, 8, 155
Augustine, St., 279, 280
Avienus, consul, 133, 135, 136, 143

Bacillus, Bishop, 76
baptism, by heretics, 250, 251, 296; if death is near, 74; of Christ, 70, 98; of doubtful cases, 296; only at Easter and Pentecost, 10, 68-76, 297; repetition of, 250, 251
Barnabas, St., 34
Basil, Bishop, 86, 236
Basil, deacon, 111, 118, 163, 182, 188
Basil (and John), priests, heretics, 158
Bethlehem, 69, 228
bishops, of Antioch, 181, 183, 184, 187, 203-205; of Caesarea Mauritania, 48; of Constantinople, 186, 187, 199; of Egypt, 48, 241, 300; of Gaul, 8, 102, 120, 134, 137, 172, 176, 226, 241; of Illyria, 27, 57, 100, 201, 240; of Italy, 23, 241; of Sicily, 68, 77; of Spain, 7, 176, 226; of Vienne, 37; consecration of, on Sundays only, 10, 31-35, 45; meet twice a year, 11, 64, 76; only in larger cities, 56; resignation of, 289, 290; selection of, 11, 30, 42, 49-57, 62, 63, 291
Boniface, priest, 159, 162, 165, 181

Calepius, consul, 77
Carosus, monk, 225, 231
Carterius, priest, 148
Celedonius, Bishop of Besancon, 40, 41
Celestine, Pope, 26, 206
Ceretius, Bishop, 137
Christians, first so called, 187
Chrysaphius, of Constantinople, 122, 124
clerics, marriage of, see 'marriage'; not from slaves or serfs, 23, 24; not to move from their diocese, 11, 20, 22, 64; promoted through regular grades, 32, 49-53, 78-80
Coelestians (Pelagians), 9, 19, 20
concubinage, 293
Constantine (and Rufus), consuls, 233, 235, 238, 240, 241, 247
Constantinople, attempts to be ranked after Rome, 178-181, 186, 198; local synods held there, 85, 139, 148
Council, of Chalcedon, 76, 153, 159, 168, 171, 173, 175, 181, 184, 197-199, 209, 210, 213,

227, 230, 233, 234, 238-240, 242, 243, 255, 259, 261, 262; of Ephesus I: 83, 86, 138, 145, 206, 210; of Ephesus II (Robber Council): 5, 33, 80, 105, 107, 108, 122-124, 127-129, 131, 145, 146, 149, 154, 156, 161, 166, 169, 184, 203, 209, 210, 227, 228, 242-244; of Nicaea: 83, 85, 86, 90, 126, 129, 132, 133, 137, 138, 140, 179, 180, 184-186, 189, 207, 243, 253, 255, 259, 262, 265, 279, 285; the Pope not present at: 106, 107, 116, 163, 165
courts, ecclesiastical, 225, 294
Cyril, St., Bishop of Alexandria, 5, 36, 85, 104, 136, 138, 159, 166, 175, 195, 201, 206, 219, 284, 285, 288

Daniel, priest, 300
David, Bishop, 55
David, King, 94, 228, 230
Devil, 46, 82, 96, 97, 99, 115, 145, 169, 175, 178, 192, 194, 196, 215, 243, 260, 266, 274, 289, 295, 301
Dioscorus, Bishop of Alexandria, 33, 84, 106, 123, 124, 127, 137, 149, 152, 154, 156, 163, 171, 175, 176, 187, 195, 196, 211, 215, 231, 234, 242, 253
diptychs, 149, 157
Domnus, Bishop of Antioch, 166, 181, 203
Donatian, Bishop, 257

Donatus, Bishop of Salasia, 54
Dorotheus, monk, 231
Dorus, Bishop of Beneventum, 77, 78
Dulcitius, notary, 105, 109

Easter, 11, 23, 34, 35, 72, 76, 148, 161, 162, 170, 208, 212, 221, 222, 225, 226, 231
Emmanuel, abbot, 131
Epicarpus, priest, 79
Epictetus, Bishop, 195
Epiphany, 68, 74
Eudocia, Empress, 194, 200, 209
Eudoxia, wife of Valentinian III, 131
Eusebius, Bishop of Dorylaeum, 82, 85, 87, 90, 124, 146, 150
Eusebius, Bishop of Milan, 171
Eustathius, Bishop of Berytus, 149
Eutyches, heretic, 33, 81-87, 89, 92-95, 101-108, 110, 114, 130, 143, 145, 152, 155-157, 159-161, 167, 171, 173, 174, 194-197, 203-205, 215, 216, 218, 220, 222, 227, 244, 253, 256, 263, 264
Euxitheus, Vicar of Thessalonica, 202, 236
excommunication, of laymen, 46

Faustus, abbot, 131, 133, 141, 142
Felix, Pope, 83
Flavian, St., Bishop of Constantinople: 9, 82, 83, 89-92, 107-

109, 111, 115, 116, 120, 123, 125, 128, 130, 132, 133, 137, 144, 145, 147, 149, 150, 153, 159, 166, 183, 184, 215, 218-220, 224, 227, 230
food, eating of sacrificial, 250, 296

Gallicanism, 39, 40, 140
Geminian, Bishop, 257
Gennadius, Bishop of Constantinople, 299
Genseric, 8
Gerontius, 239, 241
Gregory, St., 83, 86, 284

hands, imposing of, 34, 251, 292, 296
Herculanus, consul, 176, 182, 188, 190, 193, 197, 231, 236
Hermes, archdeacon, 289
Herod, 69, 228, 268
Hilary, St., Bishop of Arles, 9, 39-48, 120, 127-129, 134, 135
Hilary, deacon, 105, 109, 122-124, 127-129
Hilary, St., of Poitiers, 275-277
homoóusion, 265

Incarnation, 7, 91, 93, 103, 107, 113, 114, 119-139, 159, 160, 171, 173, 195, 215, 219, 230, 234, 237, 259, 262, 266, 270, 284
Ingenuus, Bishop, 176
Innocent, Bishop, 25
Innocent I, Pope, 26

interest taking, 11, 25, 26

Januarius, Bishop of Aquileia, 19, 77
Jerusalem, 70, 228
John, priest, 158
John the Baptist, St., 71, 74, 75, 98
John Chrysostom, St., 281, 282
Julian, Bishop of Cos, 9, 110, 111, 127, 146, 150, 151, 158, 163, 164, 198, 202, 207-209, 211, 220, 223, 225, 231, 232, 236, 239, 247
Julius, Bishop of Puteoli, 80, 105, 106, 109
Julius, Pope, 83, 85
Juvenal, Bishop of Jerusalem, 110, 149, 194, 196, 206, 210, 227, 236

Legitimus, Bishop, 25
Leo I, Emperor, 5, 197, 234-237, 242, 252, 256, 257, 262, 274, 297
Leo, priest, 289
Leontius, Bishop, 47
Lucensius, Bishop, 153, 156, 163, 165, 181
Lucianus, Bishop, 181, 188, 189
Luke, Bishop of Dyrrhacium, 236
Lupicinus, Bishop, 57

Magi, 68, 69, 98, 228, 268
Magnus (and Apollonius), consuls, 301

Majorian, Emperor, 5, 251, 256, 262, 274
Mani (Manes), 84, 112, 265
Manichaeans, 9, 32, 196
Marcian, Emperor, 5, 9, 141, 142, 144, 152-155, 162, 164, 167, 171, 177, 194, 198, 200, 208, 210, 213, 214, 218, 223-226, 231, 233, 236, 254
Marinian, priest, 203
Mark St., Bishop of Alexandria, 33, 75, 175, 187, 214
marriage, of clerics, 11, 24, 25, 29, 41, 50, 51, 53, 62, 292
Martin, abbot, 131, 133, 141, 142
Mary, Virgin, 69, 83, 84, 86, 93, 95-98, 100, 111, 114, 132, 139, 149, 160, 179, 189, 194, 204, 228, 244, 263-265, 268, 269, 271, 275, 286, 288
Mass, to be repeated if huge crowds come, 35, 36
Maximus, Bishop of Antioch, 161, 181, 184, 203, 210, 231, 236
Maximus, count, 142
Maximus, ex-Donatist, Bishop,
Maximus (and Paterius), consuls, 26
mediator, between God and men, 113, 115, 178, 191, 265, 266, 270, 276, 280
metropolitans, 8, 30, 31, 39, 44, 47, 62-66, 134, 135, 193, 217, 239, 241

military service, 295

natures, two, in Christ, 83, 91, 95, 96, 103, 104, 159, 160, 165, 174, 204, 269, 271, 277, 280, 281, 284-287
Neo, Bishop of Ravenna, 288
Nestorius, Bishop, 214
Nestorius, heretic, 9, 81, 84, 86, 111, 130, 138, 143, 145, 156, 161, 166, 174, 195, 203, 204, 206, 214, 216, 218-221, 263
Nicene Creed, 10, 93, 265
Nicetas, Bishop of Aquileia, 248
Nicholas, priest, 27

Olympius, deacon, 203
Opilio, consul, 202, 208, 211, 213, 217, 220, 221, 225, 227, 231
Orders, Holy, those fit for, 23, 24
ordinations and consecrations on Sundays only, *see* bishops
Origen, 114

Palestinian monks, 198, 202, 209
Paschasinus, Bishop of Lilybaeum, 23, 76, 159, 162, 163, 165, 175
Patricius, deacon, 148
Patroclus, Bishop of Arles, 42
Paul, priest, 78, 80
Paul, in Jerusalem, 200
Pelagians (Coelestians), 9, 19, 20

penance, 190, 250, 251, 262, 297, 300; of dying heretics, 193; on deathbed, 192; public, not to be performed by clerics, 292; put off, 294
Pentecost, 25, 35, 72, 76, 152
Peter, St., Apostle, 46, 73, 76, 102, 108, 109, 123, 125, 175, 187, 214; the Rock, 37, 100, 109, 204, 243, 252
Peter, Bishop of Corinth, 236
Peter, deacon, 227
Peter Chrysologus, St., 91
Petronianus, wanderer in Gaul, 121
Petronius, priest, 134, 136
Philoxenus, agent, 299
Pilate, 85, 112
Placidia, aunt of Theodosius II, 131
Pope, not present at councils, 175, 242; treatment of civil rulers, 9, 129
Possidonius, priest, 36
Posthumianus (and Zeno), consuls, 80, 81
Potentius, Bishop, 48, 55
preach, right to, 208
primacy of Bishop of Rome, 8, 9, 31, 33, 37, 39, 64-69, 76, 108, 124, 141, 165, 168, 179, 199
Priscillianists, 67
Proclus, Bishop of Constantinople, 86
Projectus, Bishop, 41-43
property, Church, sale of, 77

Prosper of Aquitaine, 7
Proterius, St., Bishop of Alexandria, 212, 214, 218, 220, 222, 233, 236, 246
Protogenes, consul, 89, 90, 105, 107, 110, 117, 119, 121, 122, 126, 128, 130
Pulcheria, wife of Emperor Marcian, 5, 9, 107, 127, 129, 132, 140-144, 155, 168, 179, 182, 198, 200

Ravennius, Bishop of Arles, 39, 120, 121, 134, 136, 170, 171
Regulus, deacon, 134, 136
Renatus, priest, 105, 106, 109
Restitutus, Bishop, 56
Robber Council: see Council of Chalcedon
Rufus, Bishop of Thessalonica, 28
Rusticus, Bishop of Narbonne, 289

Sabinian, priest, 289
Salonius, Bishop, 137
Samaritan woman, 99
Scripture, 10, 92-94, 101, 183, 230, 273, 287, 289; quotations from or references to:
Acts, 33-35, 73, 74, 101, 187, 214, 229, 270, 280
Apocalypse, 188
Colossians, 75, 113, 254, 272
1 Corinthians, 40, 50, 62, 71, 100, 182, 188, 196, 215, 258, 278, 292, 294

2 Corinthians, 147, 160, 266, 272, 282
Deuteronomy, 295
Ecclesiastes, 183, 289
Ephesians, 21, 38, 50, 251, 267
Ezechiel, 23, 25
Galatians, 75, 94, 98, 254, 293
Genesis, 94, 256, 282, 293
Hebrews, 93, 283, 284, 287, 288
Isaias, 94, 95, 192
John, 40, 43, 68, 73-75, 95, 98, 99, 101, 102, 104, 263, 266, 267-269, 271, 272, 278, 281, 283, 291, 301
1 John, 103, 142, 260
Leviticus, 25
Luke, 21, 67, 69, 70, 75, 78, 95, 98, 99, 101, 104, 228, 246, 260, 263, 264, 269, 281, 283
Mark, 35
Matthew, 19, 25, 34, 35, 37, 40, 67, 69-71, 75, 79, 80, 94, 98-100, 108, 133, 156, 187, 191, 215, 230, 243, 248, 255, 268, 269, 271, 276, 281-283, 289, 290
Numbers, 292
1 Peter, 102
Philippians, 22, 38, 59, 65, 96, 110, 113, 118, 130, 270
Proverbs, 95, 196, 248
Psalms, 37, 53, 92, 192, 255, 267, 282, 283, 295
Romans, 65, 66, 75, 94, 149, 186, 230, 266, 282
2 Thessalonians, 214

1 Timothy, 25, 30, 41, 43, 49, 51, 59, 113, 119, 223, 270, 274, 298
2 Timothy, 24, 52, 192, 230, 258, 290, 295
Titus, 25, 256, 260, 299

Segetius, Bishop, 25
Senator, priest, 139
Septimus, Bishop of Altino, 19, 22
Simon Magus, 84, 86
Simon Stylites, St., 214, 242
Siricius, Pope, 24, 28, 76
Solofaciolus, *see* Timothy
stewards, of churches, 225
Storacius, 241

Theodore, Bishop of Forum Julii, 190
Theodoret, Bishop of Cyrrhus, 131, 208
Theodosius II, Emperor, 5, 9, 32, 89, 106, 107, 116, 122, 129, 131, 133, 137, 139-142, 146, 148, 178, 197
Theodosius, wild monk, 194, 197
Theophilus, Bishop of Alexandria, 161, 175, 201, 212, 216, 219, 226, 282, 283
Thessalonica, 202
Timothy, deacon, 300
Timothy Aerulus, Bishop of Alexandria, 214, 233, 246, 260, 298-300

Timothy Solofaciolus, Bishop of Alexandria, 300, 301
Tome (Letter 28), 10, 92, 106, 111, 112, 118, 137, 138, 144, 148, 159, 171, 194, 196, 209, 265; falsification of, 98, 209, 215, 219-221
Turribius, Bishop of Astorga, 67
Tyberianus, Bishop, 54

Valentinian III, Emperor, 5, 32, 48, 131-133, 135, 136, 140, 143, 232

Valentinus, heretic, 84, 86, 87, 112, 265
Veranus, Bishop, 137
vicar, 8, 27-31, 58-66
virgins, violated by barbarians, 54, 56, 233, 263-269, 271, 275, 277, 279, 288
vows, quitting religious, 295

wives, who take second husbands, 248-250

Zeno, consul, 81

www.ingramcontent.com/pod-product-compliance
Lightning Source LLC
Chambersburg PA
CBHW032028290426
44110CB00012B/718